C++ in Plain English

Brian Overland

MIS:PRESS

A Subsidiary of
Henry Holt and Co., Inc.

Printed in the United States of America.

ISBN 1-55828-472-9

10 9 8 7 6 5 4

MIS:Press books are available at special discounts for bulk purchases for sales promotions, premiums, fund-raising, or educational use. Special editions or book excerpts can also be created to specification.

For details contact: Special Sales Director
MIS:Press
a subsidiary of Henry Holt and Company, Inc.
115 West 18th Street
New York, New York 10011

Associate Publisher: *Paul Farrell*
Managing Editor: *Cary Sullivan*
Development Editor: *Debra Williams Cauley*
Copy Edit Manager: *Shari Chappell*
Production Editor: *Stephanie Doyle*
Technical Editor: *Will Iverson*
Copy Editor: *Betsy Hardinger*

Dedication

To my Uncle Reid,
riding a soft, sunny wave
to a far horizon.

Contents

Contents

Chapter 6: Another Look at Constructors ...133

Chapter 7: Class Operations (Operator Overloading).....................153

Chapter 8: Inheritance: C++ and Good Genes 181

Chapter 9: Virtual Functions and Why They're Good 207

Contents

C++ The Language, An Alphabetical Listing

Contents

Acknowledgments

The book you're holding contains many tables, diagrams, and contrasting fonts, all in the name of simplifying some rather abstract concepts. Many people contributed their production and editing talents to make this happen, including Shari Chappell, Betsy Hardinger, Gay Nichols, and Stephanie Doyle. Special thanks go to the series editor, Debra Williams Cauley, who managed the whole process, showing the patience of a saint while dealing with frequently changing deadlines and page counts. Michael Sprague also played an important role, in helping to get the project started.

On the technical side, Will Iverson made some excellent suggestions that have since been incorporated into the book, particularly Chapter 8. In the process of writing, it was extremely encouraging (if occasionally frustrating) to know what was working and what wasn't.

Much of the content of the book was influenced by conversations I had with Rich Knoph, a talented full-time programmer I work with here in the Northwest. Not only have we had many discussions about programming languages over the years, but he pointed me toward some helpful resources on the history, evolution, and fine points of C++.

And thanks to my cat Purrly, who has been understanding during my long writing sessions, when I've had to ignore him.

1

Introduction: What C++ Will Do for You

In the Dark Ages of computers, programmers were slaves to the machine. Developers had to write all their instructions in hexadecimal codes (representing 1's and 0's), the computer's native language. As time went on, newer programming languages gave programmers better ways to express algorithms. Improvements in computer languages meant that programmers could be less concerned with the internal structure of the computer and more focused on the purpose of the program.

Object-oriented programming takes the evolution of software a little further. Although its benefits have perhaps been oversold, the object-oriented approach does improve programmer efficiency. In traditional, pre-object-oriented programming, the most significant structural element is the division between code and data. This division accurately reflects the internal workings of a computer, but it is not a realistic way of representing the world in general.

Object-oriented programming, on the other hand, is analogous to the human brain. This organ is a colossal set of individual brain cells. To borrow computer terminology, each cell is an *object*, having both its own underlying material (data) and programmed behavior (code). It would be nonsense to try to separate these different aspects of a brain cell, asking where its code is and where its data is. It would

1

be greater nonsense still to ask where all the code of the brain is and where all its data is.

This analogy summarizes what object orientation is all about: it replaces the traditional approach with an approach that makes objects the fundamental units. Objects combine state information and behavior, and each object is able to send and respond to stimuli just as cells in the brain do.

Programs written with object-oriented languages don't automatically model reality better than other programs do. A successful program is more the result of careful thought, planning, and diligence than of the choice of language. Still, if you're going to adopt the object-oriented approach (and an increasing amount of system software requires it), there are features of an object-oriented language, such as C++, that are extremely convenient and helpful.

Why C++? C++ probably isn't the most widely used object-oriented language; more people probably use Visual Basic, and, arguably, Visual Basic is object-oriented. But C++ is a close contender. More significantly, C++ is viewed by most programmers as the most comprehensive object-oriented language. One can argue that Smalltalk or Eiffel is a more pure implementation of object orientation, but certainly C++ sets the standard by which other languages are measured. Knowing C++ has become important to a programmer's career, almost as important today as knowing C was a few years ago. (And thus the justification for this book!) Any large, serious development project started today is likely to be written in C++. To development managers, C++ is the wave of the future.

In any case, it's worth asking: why use C++? As with C, the answer has a great deal to do with the need for both power and efficiency.

The Origins of C++

C++ has its origins in, of all things, the Norwegian armed forces. From Norway came a language called Simula, one of the first languages to use classes (a *class* being a program unit containing both data and associated functions). Classes, as you'll learn in this book, are closely linked to the idea of objects, a class being an object type.

Simula was developed to model events. Although the two concepts are not identical, an *event-driven* model of program organization is not very different from an object-oriented model. This is why Visual Basic, Windows, OS/2 Presentation Manager, and many other event-driven architectures are object-oriented or at least object-based. Object orientation is a natural way to implement an event-driven system, because it's based on the concept of independent objects that can respond to messages.

Enter Bjarne Stroustrup, who in 1978 was writing a simulator for distributed computer systems as part of his Ph.D. at the Computing Laboratory at Cambridge University. Stroustrup found Simula's use of classes a perfect way of expressing the interaction of different machines on a network. The problem was that Simula was inefficient for the large-scale systems programming he was doing. He needed the object-oriented features of Simula combined with the power and efficiency of a language like... well, like C.

C++ was born of this marriage. Stroustrup created C++ as a C language with classes and added Simula's stronger sense of data types. "C with classes" went through a few iterations before it became the C++ accepted as standard today. But the language is basically still a realization of Stroustrup's original vision of C married to Simula classes.

Making the Transition from C to C++

You may have heard that C++ is a "better C than C." What people mean by this is that C++ has a superset of the features found in C. They claim that you can compile the same program in C that you can in C++ and that, in addition, C++ provides some nice refinements you can add to your program without going all the way to object orientation.

The first part of the preceding statement is only approximately true. Many C programs can be compiled as C++ programs without change, but an occasional nagging difference crops up in some programs. One of the goals of this book is to point out these differences as clearly as possible.

The important point is that C++ does not *impose* object orientation on you. It may come as a relief to know that if you are a C programmer, you can switch to C++, observe the few additional restrictions that C++ imposes, and keep right on going. You don't have to rewrite anything as an object. As you spend more time with C++, you can gradually introduce more of the C++ extensions.

Classes: Organization by Objects

If you're going to take the time and trouble to bother with C++ in the first place, though, you probably want to pierce to the heart of what C++ is all about: object orientation. Conceptually speaking, an object is simply a data structure that has built-in functions associated with it. (A class, which you'll read about a lot, is a type of object.) It may seem to you at first that C++ introduces quite a few new operators to deal with variations and special cases. Yet the idea of objects itself is elegant and simple.

Traditional program organization represents how things work in computer software and not how things work in life generally. Technically speaking, all the contents of a computer memory constitute data, but a significant portion of what's stored in memory is a special kind of data called *code*. The code comprises instructions to the processor: add two numbers, jump to a new address, and so on. Other memory contents make up *data* as people normally use the term: data that stores information for you.

Code and data are well segregated inside computer memory, because (unlike a human brain) a computer has only one central processor, and this processor treats code and data differently. Large chunks of code have to be organized together into code segments, because the processor executes them sequentially, only occasionally jumping to a new location. Program organization reflects this fact. Typically, code is organized into a hierarchy of *functions*, each function being a collection of instructions executed as a block. Data is organized into records (structures), arrays, and tables.

Despite all this nice structure, the resulting program is a hierarchy of functions alongside a collection of unrelated data structures. The programming language does not enforce any connection between the two groups.

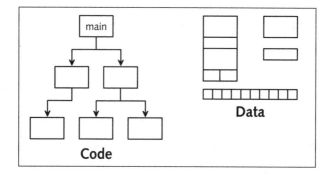

Figure 1.1 Traditional program organization.

Is this segregation of code and data a problem? It's usually fine for simpler programs. But a programmer has to remember which data structures are intended to be used by which functions, or errors arise.

Even the computer's own hardware doesn't fit the traditional model of software, as you'll see if you open your computer. The structure of the computer itself doesn't reflect the code/data distinction! Instead, the board consists of a number of independent chips that are wired to send signals back and forth to each other.

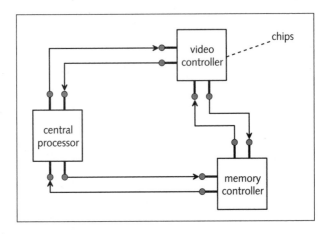

Figure 1.2 Life inside the system box.

In the object-oriented approach, the chips become objects. In C++ terminology, the make and model of a chip (for example, Pentium) is a class; an individual chip is an object. A software emulation of a chip is neither pure code nor pure data. Like a brain cell, a chip has both code (behavior) and data (state information).

If you were to set out to write a program to emulate the internals of computer hardware, you'd find that design and programming would be greatly aided by representing each chip as an object. This is where the object-oriented side of C++ most clearly differs from C: the fundamental unit of program organization becomes not code or data, but the object's class—which is a type containing both code and data.

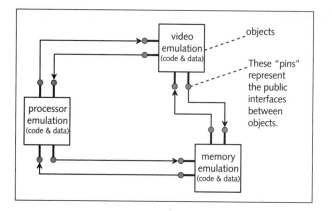

Figure 1.3 Object organization.

Encapsulation: Cure for a Programming Headache

One of the most important ideas in Figure 1.3 is the *black box* concept. Chips communicate with each other only through specific pins; except for these interfaces, each chip is a mystery to all the others. There is no way for one chip to reach in and interfere with the internal workings of another chip. Moreover, people who design computers need know nothing about the internal circuitry of a chip as long as the chip's input and output do precisely what the manufacturer says they do.

The benefits of this black box feature are substantial. The system works because each chip has a functional spec that states exactly how the chip behaves. As long as you can find another chip that adheres to the same specification, you can pop out an old chip and replace it with a new one, and the whole system will continue to work just as it did before. It may be that the internal circuitry of the new chip is completely different—but you don't care. As long as they interact in the same way with the rest of the system, any two chips are interchangeable.

Nowhere is there a greater need for interchangeable parts than in software development. In a typical project, a software team constantly rewrites the internals of every part of the program. To make an analogy, the programmers are continually popping out old chips and replacing them with new ones to fix bugs, improve efficiency, or add new features. With the traditional approach, there is no clean division between different parts of the program. The result is often disaster. A change to any part of a program can potentially affect every other part. The work that programmer A is doing, for example, can reach in and refer to the internals of the part that B is writing. But as soon as B makes any changes, all of A's assumptions become invalid, and errors happen.

To some extent, the features of the C language can be used to mitigate this problem. The connecting links between different modules—the *interfaces*—can be managed at the file level. Specifically, you have programmers A and B stick to working on different files and then be very careful about which data is shared. Certain facilities of C (such as the **extern** and **static** keywords) can be used to control which data and functions in one file are visible to other files.

C++ gives you much finer control over the sharing of data and functions between parts of the program. The unit of data protection is no longer limited to the file level but can be as large or as small a unit as you want: a class. With C++, you can make any functions or data (members) private at the class level. These private members become invisible to the rest of the program; they cannot be accessed. The public members of an object make up its interface. These public members constitute the "pins" that are visible outside an object. The rest of the program can refer to these members, and the assumption is that they will not change. Meanwhile, you can rewrite the internals of a class to your heart's content.

The clean division between interface and internals is called *encapsulation*, which is a fancy name for "protecting the insides of something." C++'s approach to encapsulation not only gives you more control over scope but also makes the public/private distinction explicit in the source code. The language is a great aid to documenting which part of a class is its interface and which part is internal.

 When you're first learning about C++ and object orientation, you may be tempted to use the terms object and class interchangeably. But the distinction is important: a class is a type, and an object is an instance of that type. I'll have a lot more to say about that in Chapter 5, "A Touch of Class."

N O T E

Polymorphism: Decentralized Control

One of the ideals of an object-oriented system is that each object be as independent as possible. I should be able to send a generalized signal to an object and have it respond appropriately. I shouldn't have to know how it carries out the response or even what precise type the object has.

To use another hardware analogy, I should be able to send out a general print command without knowing the make and model of the printer ahead of time. As long as everyone observes the same protocol for communication, my print command should always work. I know in an general way what the command should do: print my document. A dot-matrix printer would respond to the print command in a way quite different from the way a laser printer would respond.

The point is that with object orientation, I want my main function or main loop to know as little as possible. Decisions as to how to carry out a command should reside in the objects themselves. There are times when it is much better for the main function to send only a general signal.

In Chapter 9, "Virtual Functions and Why They're Good," I show a simple example of how this might work. The example uses a series of menu commands. When a user selects a command, the main function sends a message, Do_Command, to the appropriate menu object, which then responds in a completely different way depending on which command it represents.

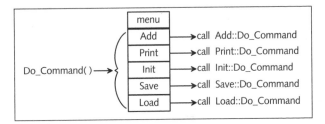

Figure 1.4 A polymorphic menu system.

This approach is superior because the program is never limited to a particular set of commands. All the main function does is to send a Do_Command message to the appropriate menu object, and then the right thing happens. This approach supports future development of new menu commands without the need to rewrite the main function. It also opens up the possibility of dynamically changing menu items. The menu can grow or change at run time, which is impossible with a traditional approach.

Object-oriented theorists refer to this mechanism as *polymorphism* ("many forms," from the Greek). This is a long, ugly word, but all it really means is decentralized control. Different objects can respond to the same message (function call) in different ways. Fewer decisions have to be centralized in the main loop.

This kind of design, by the way, is a critical part of any graphical user interface system, such as the Macintosh or Microsoft Windows. The operating system cannot know ahead of time how all windows might work; otherwise, application development would be extremely limited. Instead, the operating system must rely on the individual windows to respond in their own ways to general messages (such as "Initialize your display").

This same kind of mechanism can be implemented in C by using callback functions. But callback functions are wild and unregulated. To control how objects respond to messages, C++ uses a more structured approach involving inheritance hierarchies and virtual functions. You'll learn more about these terms in Chapters 8 and 9. In practical terms, the important thing to know is that the C++ approach is more reliable, convenient, and self-documenting.

C++ and Strengthened Types

Object orientation is what's most interesting about C++. But perhaps the most fundamental theme in C++ is that it has a much stronger concept of types than C does. Even object orientation can be seen as an extension of the idea of stronger types: C++ strengthens types to the extent that they can contain code as well as data.

C++'s emphasis on types is an aid to safer, more reliable programming, whether or not you use objects. In C, it is easy to accidentally use a variable declared as a four-byte floating-point number in one module and as an eight-byte number in another module. The result is a large error at run time. C++ prevents such errors through *type-safe linkage*, which prevents the linker from equating two symbols having different type information.

Another concept that runs through C++ is *overloading*, which uses type information to distinguish how functions and operators should work. Overloading reflects the importance of types in the language.

Function Overloading

Overloading means reusing a name. In C++, one of the most common examples of this is *function overloading*, which means writing two different versions of the same function. In actual fact, overloaded functions are completely distinct and have separate function definitions as well as separate declarations. But from the programmer's perspective, function overloading is a convenient way of providing multiple variations on the same theme.

For example, you can write two different versions of the GetNum function. One version takes a pointer to an integer, and the other version takes a pointer to a floating-point number. Each version has a separate function definition. C++ uses the type information in the argument list to differentiate the functions. When a call to GetNum appears in source code, C++ looks at the data type of the argument to determine which of these two functions to call.

```
void GetNum(int *pn);
void GetNum(double *pf);
```

Operator Overloading

Operator overloading is similar to function overloading. When C++ encounters an operator (such as +, - , /, or *), it examines the types of the operands to determine how to evaluate them. Implicit in this last statement is the idea that operators can be applied to any type. And this is basically true. In C++, you can apply addition (+), subtraction (-), or any of the other standard operators to a type—provided that the type declaration defines how the operator works. In other words, you can write a function that defines how the addition operator (+) works when applied to your type.

For example, in Chapters 5, 6, and 7, I build a CStr class that uses addition (+) to concatenate strings, just as in Visual Basic.

```
CStr name, first("Bernie"), last("Schwartz");

name = first + last;
```

Operator overloading, in effect, enables you to create types that look like true extensions to the C++ language. These types are as fundamental as **int** (integer) or **long** (long integer).

The Plan of this Book

People in the market for a book on C++ have usually spent some time living with C and want to know what's new, different, and exciting about C++ compared to C. Aside from a few differences (which I make a point of highlighting), almost all C code can be recompiled as C++. You don't have to learn a whole new language; you mainly just need to learn what's new.

If you know C well enough and want to get to the heart of C++, you should start with Chapter 5, "A Touch of Class," in Part II. This part of the book focuses on learning the new features of C++, particularly object orientation, given a background in C. You may want to first skim through Part I, paying close attention to notes identified with the "C/C++" icon.

People who already know C might also want to look at the sections on stream operators in Chapter 4. You don't have to use these operators, but many C++ programmers prefer them over the traditional C input-output functions.

Part I is provided so as not to leave anyone out in the cold. It provides a brief review of features common to C and C++. If you're unfamiliar with C, though, I recommend that you start with the previous book in this series, *C in Plain English*, especially if you don't have much programming experience. These two books have some overlapping material, but they are designed to complement each other. *C in Plain English* devotes more space to the idiosyncrasies of C syntax (although I touch on them in this book as well), and all these quirks carry over into C++.

Part III covers some advanced topics not covered in Parts I and II along with a guide to the C++ language, organized as an A-to-Z reference. This organization lets you look up exotic C++ features as well as get concise, to-the-point descriptions of terms, such as *encapsulation, data abstraction*, and *inheritance*, that are peculiar to C++ and object orientation. You may have heard these terms kicked around for a long time without coming across clear explanations of them—until now.

Throughout the book, I've placed several different kinds of notes, identified by the following icons.

 This icon signifies a technical note that digresses from the main discussion. There are many ands, ifs, and buts in C++, not because the language is arbitrary but because it is so flexible. To be technically correct without being too distracting, the text relegates additional information to notes.

This icon points to information about a common language feature that is supported by both C and C++ but is handled differently. C has some restrictions that C++ does not have, and vice versa. You'll want to pay special attention to these notes if you're porting C code to C++ or if you're a C programmer moving to C++.

 This is a note that recommends an alternative way to do something that might be faster or more convenient. These notes are always in the form of a mild suggestion.

C++: The Future Is Now

Predicting the future is a tricky business. As St. Augustine once observed, the only real moment is the present, and the future is only imagined.

All the same, it is not hard to see that the future of C++ is big. The architecture of new operating systems is inclining more and more toward object orientation. If you want to work with these systems, you'll need to learn to package software as objects—independent units that can respond to messages. And in this area, C++ excels.

Beyond that, C++ corrects some of the sloppiness of C with regard to types, while retaining C's efficiency and direct access to the hardware. C++ is the systems programming language of the future and not just of the moment.

You should be forewarned that C++ is best learned a little a time. A novice is likely to be overwhelmed by the number of strange incantations in the literature (*encapsulation*, *virtual function*, *abstraction*. Don't let the terminology intimidate you. C++ is not an arcane priesthood (despite all the magic words thrown around. Instead, it's an exceptionally broad set of useful tools ranging from low-level operations to elegant object-oriented descriptions of data. If you only have the patience to learn them one at a time, these tools will serve you well.

2

Basic Features of C/C++ Programs

The core features of C and C++ are not significantly harder to learn than those of other languages. Most of C/C++ is almost as basic as, say, the language called Basic. When people have difficulty learning C/C++, it is usually because of pointers—a topic we'll save for the next chapter.

At the same time, C/C++ has unique features you'll need to pay special attention to. There's more to C/C++ than just ending every line with a semicolon. For the most part, C/C++ features do not complicate the language syntax, and in some ways they make it more flexible. With this flexibility comes the power to make more errors, but if you're careful you'll often find that you can do more in fewer lines of code.

C and C++ are two distinct languages, but they share the same basic structure. I'll refer only to C++ from now on, pointing out places where the rules for C are different from those of C++.

Your First C++ Program

The first test of a programming system is to print a simple string. Such a program in C++ is not quite as simple as in Basic, but neither is it very long it:

```
#include <stdio.h>

void main () {
    printf("Can you C++ now?");
}
```

As you type this program, notice several things. First, capitalization counts in C++, in contrast to many languages, such as FORTRAN and Basic, in which you can randomly type every other character as uppercase if you want to. When you enter keywords and identifiers (for example, a variable or function name) C++ expects you to match uppercase and lowercase letters *precisely*, and it gets badly confused if you don't. Another thing to watch for is the punctuation: the semicolon (;) and the braces ({}). You must enter these characters exactly where indicated in the example.

However, there are some things you can be freer about with C++ than you might with other languages. On any given line, you can space things many different ways, and you can even put syntax elements on different lines—C++ doesn't care. As C++ is concerned, the following program is the same as the one shown previously:

```
#include <stdio.h>

void
main ()
{
    printf
        ("Can you C++ now?");
}
```

This version works because C++ uses the semicolon (;) to determine where the **printf** statement ends; it usually ignores the end of the physical line (except in the case of directives and comments). On the one hand, you have to do a little more typing, but, on the other hand, the C++ syntax grants you more freedom than Basic does.

NOTE After entering this program in a source file, you use a compiler or development environment to compile it, which is the process of translating the program into an executable form. I don't discuss specific compilers in this book. For information on how to build a program, see your compiler documentation.

Everything in this section applies equally well to the C language, except for one thing: in C, the void keyword in front of main is optional. In C++, it is required. Here, void means that the function (main) does not have a return statement. More about that later.

You can, of course, print your own string instead of "Can you C++ now?" Here's the general pattern for the program:

```
#include <stdio.h>
void main () {
    printf("enter-your-string-here");
}
```

Enter any text you want in place of *enter-your-string-here*.

Adding Data Declarations

Programs start to become interesting and useful at the point where they can store and manipulate information. Such programs need a place to put the data: variables.

C++ variable declaration consists of a type name followed by a variable name and a semicolon. The basic (or primitive) types include **int**, **short**, **long**, **float**, and **double**, among others. The following example declares two variables of type **int**.

```
int variable_name1;
int variable_name2;
```

The C++ variable-declaration syntax is simple. It doesn't involve any extra keyword, such as **Dim** or **var**.

You can create multiple data declarations on the same line. Separate each variable with a comma. The following example declares three variables of type **short** (i, j, k) and three variables of type **float** (x, y, z).

```
short i, j, k;
float x, y, z;
```

The basic syntax for data declarations in C++ has another interesting twist. You can initialize variables as they are declared. Doing so gives a variable a starting value but in no way prevents you from changing it later.

To initialize a variable, use the equal sign followed by a value. For example:

```
int my_var = 0;         // my_var initialized to 0
int your_var = 1;       // your_var initialized to 1
int a, b = 10, c = 12;  // b and c initialized, a is not
```

Before we proceed, now would be a good time to discuss comments. In C++, a *comment* consists of all the text starting with the double slashes (//) forward to the end of the line. A comment is ignored by the compiler. You can put any text in a comment, but people typically use comments to explain a part of their program. When they go back later and look at the source code, the comments help them recall how the program works.

 C++ also supports the begin- and end-comment symbols from the C language (/* and */, respectively). Not all C compilers support the C++ comment-to-end-of-line symbol (//), although many of them do.

Armed with the ability to declare and initialize data, we can now create a more interesting program:

```
#include <stdio.h>

void main () {
    int x = 1;
    int y = 2;

    printf("The sum of x + y is %d", x + y);
}
```

This use of the printf function here requires a little more explanation. The printf function supports formatted output, which means that it can take a numeric argument such as x+y and print the value of this number along with the rest of the string. The format character **%d** means "Print the value of the next argument." Here, **d** stands for decimal integer. Floating-point values are printed using **%f**.

All the primitive types are variations on just two kinds of data: integer and floating-point. An *integer*, as you may have learned in school, is a number that cannot hold fractions (but it can be negative). *Floating-point* values can have a fractional portion. Floating-point numbers are more flexible, but integers are more efficient. If you know that a certain variable will never need to hold a fraction—and there are a great many cases of this, as with a loop counter, for example—declare it as an integer.

The basic characteristics of the **int**, **short**, **long**, **float**, and **double** data types are summarized in Table 2.1.

Table 2.1 Characteristics of common data types.

TYPE	KIND OF DATA	TYPICAL SIZE	PRINTF FORMAT SYMBOL:	SCANF FORMAT SYMBOL:
short	integer	2 bytes	%d	%d
long	integer	4 bytes	%d	%ld
int	integer	2 or 4 bytes	%d	%d
float	floating point	4 bytes	%f	%f
double	floating point	8 bytes	%f	%lf

%ld and %lf are discussed under "Get Input" later in this chapter.

NOTE

The size of a data type determines its range. For example, the range of a **short** is -32,768 to 32,767. The range of a **long** is approximately plus or minus two billion.

For a more comprehensive list of data types and their ranges, see the topic "Data Types" in Part III.

More About #include

If you're like me, you don't like to place gobbledygook into your program without knowing what it's all about. I can hear you saying, "Why do I have to enter this **#include** thing? Shouldn't I just be able to tell C++ 'Print the darn string!'?"

I sympathize, particularly if you're coming from Basic and all you've had to do is to say PRINT X. However, the **#include** directive serves a very good purpose.

In C++, every function (except **main**) must be declared before being used. This goes for standard library functions, such as printf. Rather than declare printf yourself, it is easier to include a special file for this purpose (called a *header file*) that includes all the declarations you need. For example, the file **STDIO.H** has definitions for all the standard input/output functions, such as printf.

There are a couple of catches with **#include**. First, do *not* place a semicolon at the end. This rule seems a little arbitrary, although there are technical reasons for it. In any case, just commit to memory this Golden Rule of Directives: If a keyword begins with a pound sign (#), it is a directive, which means that you don't end the line with a semicolon (;). The second catch is that you have to know which header file to refer to. The solution is easy: when you look up the function in standard-library documentation, the first thing it tells you is which header file to use.

You never include the same header file more than once. If you call 10 functions but they are all declared in **STDIO.H**, for example, you need only one **#include** directive.

Once you're familiar with the C++ standard library, you can usually figure out which header file(s) you need without having to look up anything. The most common library functions fall into one of the following general categories shown in Table 2.2.

Table 2.2 Common C++ include Files.

HEADER FILE	INCLUDE DIRECTIVE	INCLUDES DECLARATIONS FOR THESE FUNCTIONS
STDIO.H	#include <stdio.h>	Standard input and output functions, including functions that perform file operations.
IOSTREAM.H	#include <iostream.h>	Stream operators (C++ only), which can be used to replace printf and scanf. Chapter 4 explains the use of these.
STRING.H	#include <string.h>	String-manipulation functions; for example, copy one string to another.
CTYPE.H	#include <ctype.h>	Functions for testing and changing the type of individual characters in a string.
MATH.H	#include <math.h>	Trig, logarithmic, exponential, and other fun things that engineers love to play with.
MALLOC.H	#include <malloc.h>	Functions for dynamically getting and freeing blocks of memory from the operating system.

The following syntax display summarizes the general pattern for a simple C program. It doesn't involve any functions except **main**, but later in the chapter later, we'll add functions to the syntax. Note that all the **#include** directives should come before anything else in the program.

```
include_directives

void main() {
    data_declarations_and_other_statements
}
```

The placeholder *data_declarations_and_other_statements* includes both data declarations, which you were introduced to in the previous section, and other statements. (These other statements are often called *executable statements*. In C++, however, data declarations can also involve executable code.) This last category is a large one, and I break it down somewhat in the next section.

 With C, all data declarations must appear before all other statements. C++ relaxes this restriction, letting you declare a variable any time (and almost anywhere) you want to.

What Can I Do with a Statement?

After declaring variables, you can use statements to perform a number of actions. These actions usually manipulate or use the variables in some way. In C++, you can mix declarations and other statements in any order. (You can't do that in C.) But it usually makes sense to declare variables first, because in both C and C++ you must explicitly declare a variable before using it.

Aside from control structures and functions, which I'll cover later, all the actions you can perform boil down to these three:

- Assign a value (optionally involving a calculation).
- Print output.
- Get input.

The next three sections discuss how you do each of these actions in C++.

Assigning Values

Assignment statements in C++ look similar to those in other languages, especially Basic. The main difference from Basic is that C++ statements are terminated by semicolons.

Before assigning data to a variable, make sure you declare the variable:

```
int amount, a, b, c;
```

To assign a value to one of these variables, place the variable name on the left side of an equal sign (=). On the right side, place a variable, a constant (such as 1 or -240), or a compound expression (such as 2 * c).

```
a = 1;
amount = -240;
b = 2 * c;
amount = a + 10 * b * -1;
```

Note that in C++, the asterisk (*) represents multiplication.

These statements look a lot like initialization inside a data declaration. In fact, in C++ there is very little difference between initialization and assignment except that initialization creates a variable and assigns it a value.

Initialization of variables is more restricted in the C language. You can use only constant values to initialize in a data declaration. In C++, this restriction is relaxed; you can use any valid expression to initialize.

Printing Output

You can use the printf function to print simple strings or to print formatted output displaying any number of numeric values. For example, the following lines of code print two lines, each displaying the value of certain variables. Note that you must first include **STDIO.H** and declare each variable before using it.

```
#include <stdio.h>

void main() {
    int date = 10, d2 = 15;
    float tmp = 45.0, t2 = 33.5;

    printf("On Dec. %d, temperature was %f.\n", date,
     temp);
    printf("On Jan. %d, temperature was %f.\n", d2,
     t2);
}
```

Note that **%d** should correspond to an integer argument and **%f** should correspond to a floating-point argument. These lines of code print the following results:

```
On Dec. 10, temperature was 45.0000.
On Jan. 15, temperature was 33.5000.
```

This example introduces another aspect of printing in C++: in a C++ string, the special character \n causes printing to start on a new line. (Not surprisingly, this character has the name *newline*.) The character could be omitted from the second string in this case, but if it were omitted from the first string, all the output would run together as shown next. Unlike the Basic PRINT statement, the printf function does not automatically append a newline.

```
On Dec. 10, temperature was 45.0000.On Jan. 15, tem-
    perature was 33.5000.
```

The newline character is an example of a C++ *escape sequence*, which begins with a backslash. Other sequences include \t, which prints a tab; and \", which prints a double-quotation mark. To print an actual backslash, by the way, use two backslashes: \\.

 With C++, but not C, you can choose to use stream operators to do input and output rather than use functions such as printf and scanf. Stream operators are at least as easy to use as printf, but I've put them off until Chapter 4. (By all means, skip ahead if you're interested.) As an example, the first line of output in this section could be printed this way:

```
#include <iostream.h>

void main () {
    int date = 10, d2 = 15;
    float temp = 45.0, t2 = 33.5;

    cout << "On Dec. " << date;
    cout << ",the temperature was " << temp <<
        ".\n";
}
```

Getting Input

The scanf function is a counterpart to printf, but scanf reads data rather than writes it. Like printf, scanf recognizes format symbols (such as **%d**), each of which corresponds to a numeric argument.

The scanf function has quirks all its own. First, all the arguments to scanf are addresses, so you must place the address operator (&) in front of your variable (unless it is a pointer; more about that in the next chapter). Second, scanf is finicky about types. A **long** argument must correspond to the **%ld** (long decimal) symbol, and a **double** argument must correspond to the **%lf** (long floating-point) symbol.

The following lines of code show how you could prompt for and retrieve four different kinds of data. You cannot print a prompt string using scanf: you must use printf to print the string. Note the format symbols used here: **%d**, **%ld**, **%f**, and **%lf**.

```
#include <stdio.h>


void () {
    int i;
    long lng;
    float flt;
    double dbl;

    printf("Enter a value for i: ");
    scanf("%d", &i);

    printf("Enter a value for lng: ");
    scanf("%ld", &lng);

    printf("Enter a value for flt: ");
    scanf("%f", &flt);

    printf("Enter a value for dbl: ");
    scanf("%lf", &dbl);
}
```

Some C++ Quirks

C++ has some syntactical quirks (and everything in this section applies equally to C). By "quirks" I mean features of the syntax that are not especially difficult, but that may throw you if your background is in another programming language such as Basic, FORTRAN, or Pascal. In any case, they are things to watch for.

Watch Out for That Semi!

When you're starting to program with C or C++ for the first time, probably the most common error is to forget to type the semicolon (;). It's also possible to type a semicolon where C++ doesn't expect one.

The rule for using semicolons is more complex than in Basic or FORTRAN (which don't use them) but a little more consistent and straightforward than in Pascal. Terminate every statement with a semicolon unless one of the following is true:

1. The statement is actually a directive, such as **#include** or **#define**, or

2. The statement is a compound statement. In practice, this means that you don't place a semicolon after a terminating brace (}) unless it is the end of a class or variable declaration. (You'll learn more about classes in Chapter 5, "A Touch of Class.")

The simple program shown in Figure 2.1 demonstrates the rule and the two exceptions.

29

```
                                        This does not end with
  #include <stdio.h>                    a semicolon because
                                        it is a directive.
  void main () {
       int  i = 5, j, k = 1;

       while (i > 0) {
            k = k * i;
            i = i - 1;                   Opening and closing
       }                                 braces do not end with
                                         a semicolon (unless ending
       printf("k is %d", k);            a class declaration).
  }
```

Figure 2.1 Using semi-colons in C++.

C++ uses a semicolon to indicate the end of a statement—
rather than rely on the end of a physical line—you don't
need line-continuation characters for statements. Any time
a statement threatens to grow wider than the physical
screen, you can simply spread the statement across multiple
lines. For example:

```
printf("On %d/%d/%d, the temperature was %f.\n",
    date,
    month,
    year,
    temp);
```

Another consequence of C++ syntax is that you can place
several statements on one line, as in the following four
assignments. Remember that a semicolon terminates each
statement, including the last one.

```
a = 0; b = 0; c = 0; d = 0;
```

There is an even more compact way to do all these assignments, as I explain in the next section.

Assignments Are Expressions, Too

One of the most fundamental units of grammar in the C++ language is that of the *expression*. Generally speaking, expressions evaluate to a value (although **void** expressions do not). An expression is either a variable, a constant, a function call, or a compound expression made up of smaller expressions connected by operators (such as +, -, *, /, and so on).

One of the most surprising things about C and C++ is that the assignment operator (=) is an operator just like any other, and an assignment expression is an expression just like any other. This probably means nothing to you until you consider that any assignment expression can be placed inside a larger expression.

This means that you can assign the same value to several variables using a single, compact statement.

```
a = b = c = d = 0;   // Initialize vars to 0.
```

To understand what this statement does, consider the rule for assignments: an assignment evaluates to the value of the left operand, *after* assignment (in other words, the value that was assigned). So an expression such as d = 0 first assigns 0 to d and then evaluates to 0. Associativity for assignment is right-to-left, so the rightmost assignments are evaluated first. Figure 2.2 shows how the complete statement performs each assignment, each time reusing the value 0 in the next assignment.

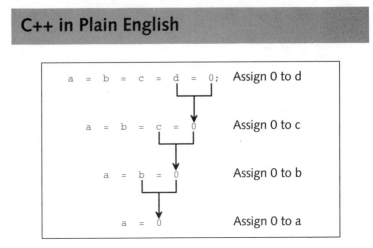

Figure 2.2 Multiple assignments in C++.

This feature of C++ is a useful convenience, but it has a side effect that can leap up and bite you. When an assignment appears inside a conditional test, it is still an assignment even though it *looks* like a test for equality. The problem is that the assignment, as always, evaluates to the value assigned. For example, in the following code, the assignment i = 5 unconditionally evaluates to 5, which indicates true (all nonzero values are "true").

```
if (n = 5)                    // ERROR! n gets 5.
    printf("n is equal to 5.\n"); // Always executes!
```

Here, the string is always printed no matter what value was in n previously, because n = 5 puts 5 into n and then returns 5. This is almost certainly not what was wanted. C++ does not assume that you wanted to test for equality here. After all, there are situations (though infrequent) when you might want to evaluate an assignment inside a conditional. To resolve this ambiguity, C and C++ provide a separate operator to test for equality (==). This operator performs a comparison and evaluates to true (1) or false (0) just as you would expect.

```
if (n == 5)                   // Test n against 5.
    printf("n is equal to 5.\n"); // Print if n eq. 5.
```

In the history of C and C++, many thousands of programmers have bashed their heads against their desks, trying to find an elusive bug that was caused by using assignment (=), instead of test-for-equality (==), in a conditional. This is by far one of the most common mistakes you'll make when you are first learning C or C++. Experienced C/C++ programmers usually learn (the hard way) to avoid it. In general, assignment (=) inside a conditional indicates an error, although there are times when it is exactly what you want. Most languages other than C and C++ simply wouldn't let you do this. (Here's an axiom for you: with greater freedom comes the mobility to step on your own foot.)

Adding Functions to Your Program

In any computer language, elements such as subroutines, procedures, functions, and GOSUB routines all have the same general purpose: to temporarily transfer control to another part of the program and then return to the same location. In C++, there is just one kind of subroutine: the *function*. Unless declared **void**, function calls evaluate to a value upon execution (that is, they return a value). Even when a function does return a value, the caller of the function is free to use that value or ignore it.

The practical implication of these features is this: in C++, one type of construct—the function—fulfills the role of functions and procedures in other languages. This fact helps to keep C++ syntax leaner and more streamlined. There is no need for a separate keyword like the Function keyword found in Visual Basic.

You've almost certainly encountered functions and procedures. A function takes zero or more arguments—depending on how it's declared—and evaluates to a single value that can be reused in a larger expression. Figure 2.3 illustrates how a call to the Pythagorus function might work.

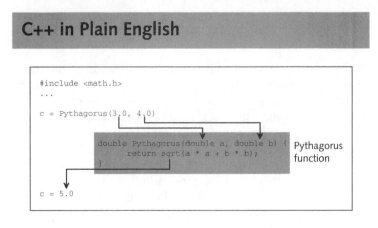

Figure 2.3 A function call in action.

In Figure 2.3, the expression Pythagorus(3.0, 4.0) results in a call to the Pythagorus function, passing the values 3.0 and 4.0 to the two parameters. The function uses the **return** statement to transfer control back to the caller and return the value 5.0.

General Syntax for Functions

When functions are taken into account, the general syntax for a C++ program follows the pattern shown in Figure 2.4:

Figure 2.4 General syntax of a C++ program.

Before you call or define a function, you must declare it; *function_prototypes* serves this purpose. A *function prototype* provides type information to the compiler so that it knows what type of arguments to expect. You may feel that the C++ compiler is being fussy, but it needs the type information to help catch errors before they happen at run time.

The format of a function prototype looks almost identical to that of the first line (the heading) of a function definition:

```
return_type   function_name(argument_list);
```

Note, however, that a function prototype ends with a semicolon (;). Do not—repeat, do not—place a semicolon after the terminating brace (}) of a function. Because prototypes end with semicolons and function definitions do not, it is easier for the compiler to tell them apart.

Prototypes and headings for a function definition are so similar that you can save effort by doing the following: after entering a prototype, make a copy, remove the semicolon, and then proceed to enter the rest of the function definition.

Function Example

Function syntax makes much more sense in the context of an example. Figure 2.5 illustrates each part of the function syntax, including prototype, function call, and function definition. Each part of this syntax has an important role: the prototype prepares for the function call (by letting the compiler know what types to check for), the function call executes the function, and the function definition tells the compiler how to execute the function.

```
#include <studio.h>                              Include directives
#include <math.h>

double Pythagorus(double a, double b);           Function prototype

void main() {
    double a, b, c;               Data declarations

    printf("Enter Angle 1: ");
    scanf("%lf", &a);
    printf("Enter Angle 2: ");
    scanf("%lf", &b);
    c = Pythagorus(a, b);
    printf("The hypotenuse is %f.", c);
}                                               Function
                                                definition
double Pythagorus(double a, double b) {
    double c;

    c = sqrt(a * a + b * b);
    return c;
}
```

Figure 2.5 An example program that calls a function.

For this example, you must include two header files (**STDIO.H** and **MATH.H**), because the program uses both I/O functions (printf and scanf) and a math function (sqrt), which takes the square root of a number.

A function with any return type other than **void** must transfer execution back to the caller at some point by using the **return** statement. A **return** statement also specifies the value that the function evaluates to.

Figure 2.6 analyzes the syntax of the Pythagorus function definition. The return type is **double**, indicating that the function evaluates to a double-precision floating-point number.

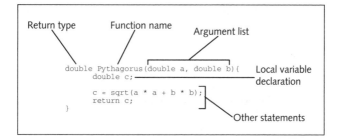

Figure 2.6 Breakdown of function-definition syntax.

Functions in the void

If a function does not need to return a value, declare it with the **void** return type. Unlike functions with other return types, a **void** function does not need a **return** statement. The function can use **return** to exit early, but it can also let execution terminate naturally at the end of the function definition. See the "return" topic in Part III for more information.

The following example calls a **void** function. Note that the function call is not used in a larger expression but instead terminates right away.

```
#include <stdio.h>

void print_vars(int i1, int i2, int i3);

void main() {
    int a, b, c;

    a = b = c = 1;
```

```
    print_vars(a, b, c);
    a = b = c = 2;
    print_vars(a, b, c);
}

void print_vars(int i1, int i2, int i3) {
    printf("The value of param1 is %d.\n", i1);
    printf("The value of param2 is %d.\n", i2);
    printf("The value of param3 is %d.\n\n", i3);
}
```

Local, Global, and Other Variables

One of the most important attributes of a variable is its *scope*, which determines how long a variable lasts and where it is visible (what part of the program can use it). The two fundamental kinds of scope in C++ are local and global. There are also the special kinds of scope: static and external.

These four kinds of scope—local, global, static, and external—are inherited from C. To these, C++ adds class scope, which attaches a variable to an object of a particular class.

Local Variables

A *local* variable is private to a function definition. Each function can have its own variable named variable X, for example, and can modify this variable without affecting the variable named X in any other function.

To declare a local variable, simply place the declaration inside a function definition. For example, the variable c is local in the following Pythagorus function definition. If another function had its own variable named c and if this function called Pythagorus, changes to c inside Pythagorus would not affect the other function.

```
#include <math.h>
...
double Pythagorus(double a, double b) {
    double c;

    c = sqrt(a * a + b * b);
    return c;
}
```

One of the important differences between C++ and certain other languages is that in C++, **main** is a function just like any other. It has only two unique features: it is the program entry point, and it doesn't need a prototype. Variables declared in main are local variables. For example, in the following definition of **main**, the variables a, b, c, and h are all local to **main**.

```
void main() {
    double a, b, c, h;

    a = b = c = 1;
    print_vars(a, b, c);
    h = Pythagorus(a, b);
    print_vars(a, b, c);
}
```

What's notable here is that the Pythagorus function operates on its own local variable c without affecting the value of c in **main**.

Global Variables

It's usually preferable to make a variable local, but sometimes you need scope that extends beyond a single function. *Global* variables have scope and lifetime that extend to the entire source file. One purpose of global variables is to enable communication between functions by letting them share information.

To make a variable global, simply define it outside all function definitions.

The example program in Figure 2.7 uses three global variables. All the functions in the program share common access to the variables a, b, and c, and any function can set or read their values.

```
#include <studio.h>                    Include directives
#include <math.h>

void Pythagorus(void);                 Global variable
void Setvars(void);                    declarations
                                       (Note these are declared
double a, b, c;                        before main.)

void main() {
    Setvars();
    Pythagorus();
    printf("\nThe hypotenuse is %f.", c);
}

void Pythagorus(void) {
    c = sqrt(a * a + b * b);
}

void Setvars(void) {
    printf("Enter value of Angle 1: ");
    scanf("%lf", &a);
    printf("Enter value of Angle 2: ");
    scanf("%lf", &b);
}
```

Figure 2.7 Global variable example.

Global variables are visible from the point where they are declared to the end of the source file. Generally, you should declare them near the beginning of the program unless you want them to be visible only to some functions.

Static Variables

A *static* variable combines the visibility of a local variable with the extended lifetime of a global variable. This capability is useful when you want to make a variable private to a single function (as with a local variable) but make it retain its value between function calls. For example:

```
void print_vars(int i1, int i2, int i3) {
    static int count = 0;

    printf("The value of param1 is %d.\n", i1);
    printf("The value of param2 is %d.\n", i2);
    printf("The value of param3 is %d.\n", I3);

    count = count + 1;
    printf("I've been called %d time(s).\n\n",
    count);
}
```

The variable count is initialized to zero just once. After each call to print_vars, the value increases by 1. At the same time, count is private to this function and is not affected by what happens to count variables in other functions.

External Variables

As a program grows in size, it's common to divide the code into multiple modules, compile them, and then link them. A *module* corresponds to one C++ source file.

Each function is automatically visible to all other modules in the project unless you declare it static (by placing the **static** keyword at the beginning of the prototype and the function-definition heading); in that case, the function is visible only within the module.

Variables are visible only in the module where they're declared unless you make them *external*. To make a variable external, first define it as a global variable in exactly one module. (By *defining* a variable, I mean to use a normal declaration that creates the variable.)

```
int  global_count;
```

All other modules that use this same variable need to include an **extern** declaration:

```
extern int global_count;
```

This declaration (which is not a definition) says to the compiler, "Recognize global_count as an external variable. It may be defined here or in another module."

Another way to use external variables is to throw all the **extern** declarations into a header file, which is then included in every source file. For example:

```
// ————————————————————————————-
// MYPROG.H — Extern declarations and function
// prototypes for myprog.

extern int global_count;
extern int current_checkno;
extern double accumulator;
...
```

Each of these variables must be defined in one—and only one—source-code module. For example, module A might define the first two variables:

```
// ————————————————————————————-
// A.CPP

#include "myprog.h"

int global_count;
int current_checkno;
...
```

Module B might define the third external variable:

```
// ———————————————————
// B.CPP

#include "myprog.h"

double current_accumulator;
...
```

No matter where they are defined, these three variables are shared by all functions in the program because of the **extern** declarations in the header file.

Fun with Control Structures

Control structures allow you to express decisions and loops in a readable way. This arrangement frees you from having to use the spaghetti-code style of programming seen in old versions of Basic and in most assembly language.

This section introduces the two most frequently used control structures: **if** and **while**. C++ also supports the **do**, **for**, and **switch** control structures, which are discussed as topics in Part III.

The if Statement

Here's the syntax for the C++ **if** statement:

```
if (expression)
    statement
[ else
    statement ]
```

Here, the brackets indicate that the **else** clause is optional. An **if** statement can appear without **else**, as in the following example.

```
if (age < 21 )
    printf(What you think you're doing?\n);
```

An **if** statement can also include an **else** clause, as in the next example.

```
if (age < 21 )
    printf(What you think you're doing?\n);
else
    printf(Eat, drink, and be computer literate.\n);
```

Technically speaking, there is no C++ "elseif" keyword like the one is in Visual Basic. However, the statement following **else** can itself be another **if** statement. This is a common example of *nesting* one control structure inside another:

```
if (age < 21 )
  printf("What you think you're doing?\n");
else
  if (age == 21)
    printf("Okay, just one drink.\n");
  else
    printf("Eat, drink, and be computer literate.\n");
```

Because C++ doesn't care about spacing, we can rewrite it this way:

```
if (age < 21 )
    printf("What you think you're doing?\n");
else if (age == 21)
    printf("Okay, just one drink.\n");
```

```
else
    printf("Eat, drink, and be computer literate.\n");
```

Control structures, such as **if**, are frequently used with compound statements. A *compound statement* consists of any number of statements placed between braces ({}). The interesting twist is that a compound statement can be used anywhere a single statement can be used. This gives us a nice, structured way to execute multiple statements in response to a condition:

```
if (age < 21 ) {
    printf("Hey! What do you think you're
    doing...?\n");
    printf("Serve minors? Just what kind of place ");
    printf("do you\nthink we run?\n");
}
else if (age == 21)
    printf("Okay, just one drink.\n");
else {
    printf("Eat, drink, and be computer literate.\n");
    printf("But we suggest that you be careful \n");
    printf("driving home on the information super-\n");
    printf("highway tonight...);
}
```

The test for equality used in conditions is the double equal sign (==). Confusing this with assignment (=) is a major cause of errors.

The while Statement

The **while** statement is another control structure frequently used with compound statements. Here's the syntax for **while**:

```
while (expression)
    statement
```

As with **if** statements, the conditional expression in the **while** statement can be any valid integer expression. All nonzero values are interpreted as true. Comparison operators (<, >, ==, <=, =>, and !=) return true (1) or false (0).

For example, the following code counts down from 5 to 1. The **while** statement executes the statement block repeatedly until the condition, n > 0, is false.

```
int n = 5;

while (n > 0) {
    printf(%d\n, n);
    n = n - 1;
}
```

The next example, which is slightly more compact, does the same thing:

```
int n = 5;

while (n) {
    printf("%d\n", n);
    n = n - 1;
}
```

There are a couple of ways to make this code even more compact, and one of them is introduced in the next section.

Impress Your Friends with Fancy C++ Operators

C++ has a number of fancy operators generally not found in any other language (except C). These operators include increment and decrement operators, assignment operators, and bitwise operators.

Increment and Decrement Operators

Among the easiest to use and most useful C++ operators are the increment and decrement operators. These operators simply add or subtract one from a variable. For example:

```
n++;            // Add 1 to n.
n--;            // Subtract 1 from n.
```

You can certainly use these operators inside a larger expression. So, for example, the decrement operator can be used to make the count-down-from-five example from the previous section even more compact:

```
while (n)
    printf("%d\n", n--);
```

There's a catch that you need to be careful about: increment and decrement come in a prefix variety (++n) and a postfix variety (n++). A *postfix* expression, used in this last example, evaluates to the current value of the variable. *Then* the variable is incremented or decremented.

With the *prefix* variety (such as --n), the change is made first. The expression evaluates to the new value. Consequently, the following code counts from 4 to 0 rather than from 5 to 1. In each iteration through the loop, n is decremented before *being* printed.

```
while (n)
    printf("%d\n", --n);
```

Assignment Operators

C++ assignment operators include not only the standard assignment operator (=) but also a range of other operators that combine assignment with another operation. These operators are similar to the increment and decrement operators, because they modify by performing an operation.

For example, addition-assignment (+=) performs both an addition and an assignment. The statement

```
n += 10;
```

is equivalent to the longer statement:

```
n = n + 10;
```

You can think of postfix increment and decrement operations as special cases of addition-assignment and subtraction-assignment. For example, these two statements are equivalent:

```
n--;           // Subtract 1 from n.
n -= 1; // Subtract 1 from n.
```

C++ supports a large set of assignment operators that work in a similar way, performing an operation and assigning the result to the variable on the left side of the assignment statement. These operators include *= (multiplication-assignment), /= (division assignment), and many others. For more information, see the topic "Assignment Operators" in Part III.

Bitwise and Logical Operators

To programmers new to C and C++, *bitwise* operators are often the most exciting part of the language. These operators enable you to test and modify individual bits.

A simple program has no need for such bit surgery, however, and even complex programs can usually get by without them. The major advantage of bit operations is that they make possible the most efficient use of space. Using bit operations, you can stuff data into individual fields within an integer, rather than use a series of different variables.

Table 2.3 summarizes bit-testing operations along with logical operators. C++ supports both. *Logical* operators are similar to the bit operators except that logical operators do not test individual bits. For example, ANDing together any two nonzero values results in the value true (1) when you use logical AND.

Table 2.3 Logical and bitwise operators.

OPERATOR	DESCRIPTION
&	Bitwise AND. Sets a bit in the result if both of the corresponding bits in the two operands are set.
|	Bitwise OR. Sets a bit in the result if either of the corresponding bits in the two operands is set.
~	Bitwise NOT (one's complement). Sets a bit in the result if the corresponding bit in the single operand is not set.
&&	Logical AND. If both operands are nonzero, evaluates to true (1). Evaluates to false (0) otherwise. Combines Boolean conditions as you would expect.
||	Logical OR. If either operand is nonzero, evaluates to true (1). Evaluates to false (0) otherwise. Combines Boolean conditions as you would expect.
!	Logical NOT. Evaluates to true (1) if operand is zero, and false (0) if the operand is nonzero. Reverses the true/false value of a Boolean condition as you would expect.

C++ also supports right-shift and left-shift operators, as shown in Table 2.4.

Table 2.4 Right-shift and left-shift operators.

OPERATOR	DESCRIPTION
>>	Right shift
<<	Left shift

To understand how bit operators work, you need to understand the binary numbering system, which I don't explain in detail here. You can use bit-test and bit-shift operators on any integer, but these operators work on the data as actually stored in the computer: the data is in binary form.

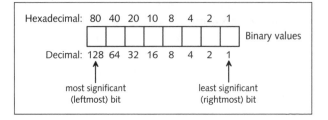

Figure 2.8 Binary representation.

For example, the number 18 is stored as 00010010, and the number 6 is stored as 00000110. Using binary AND on them tests each bit against the corresponding bit in the other operand; a bit is set in the result only if both of the corresponding bits in the operands are 1. The result here is 00000010 binary, or 2.

The following program uses the left-shift operator (<<) and bitwise AND (&) to print the binary representation of an integer. Note that 0x8000 is C++ notation for hexadecimal representation. 0x8000 is the value of the short integer that has the most significant bit set (equal to 1) and all the others off (equal to 0).

```
#include <stdio.h>

void print_binary(short input_field);

void main() {
    short n;
```

```
    do {
        printf("\nEnter a short integer ");
        prtinf("(0 to quit): ");
        scanf("%hd", &n);
        print_binary(n);
    } while (n);
}

void print_binary(short input_field) {
    int i = 1, bit_set;

    while (i <= 16) {
        bit_set = ((0x8000 & input_field) > 0);
        printf("%d", bit_set);
        input_field = input_field << 1;
        i++;
    }
}
```

This program takes advantage of the fact that, in C++, conditions evaluate to integers. Inside the **while** loop, 0x8000 is
ANDed with the argument. The result is either 0x8000 or
zero. The result is compared to zero, and the comparison
expression evaluates to either 0 or 1, which is then printed:

```
(0x8000 & input_field) > 0
```

C++ supports a left-shift-and-assignment operator (<<=) that
combines left shift with assignment. You can make the program more compact by using this operator.

3

Pointers, Strings, and Things

One of the things that most distinguish C and C++ from most other computer languages is their use of pointers. At first, pointers may seem difficult or exotic—but other languages use pointers all the time. The difference is that these other languages carry out pointer operations under the covers—you just don't see them. C and C++ are more transparent, and they give you more control.

What are pointers, anyway? I'll provide a more detailed description in the next section, but, in general, pointers are addresses: relatively small units of data (two bytes on 16-bit systems) that access other pieces of data indirectly. You can use an address to access an arbitrarily large chunk of data, often making significant gains in efficiency. In C and C++, pointers are closely related to arrays and character strings.

Pointers are, if anything, even more important in C++ than in C. C++ encourages the dynamic creation of objects through the use of the **new** operator, which returns a pointer. Moreover, certain operator functions (which I'll discuss in Chapter 7, "Operator Overloading") require understanding of pointers. In this chapter, we'll focus on the use of pointers with parameters, strings, and arrays.

A More Efficient Way to Pass Data

Simply stated, a *pointer* is a variable or an argument that stores an address in memory. Although this definition is technically complete, it is probably meaningless unless you understand what pointers are for—that is, how they are used. The important point is that, like a handle or a key, a pointer provides *indirect access* to data, and sometimes this arrangement is much more efficient than doing things the usual way.

Suppose you and I are two different functions (ok, I know that sounds silly, but stay with me on this) or, possibly, two separate objects. Suppose, further, that you have a large piece of data that you need to share with me. For example, you might need to pass me a long string of characters for me to display on the screen.

There are several possibilities for enabling this sharing of data. If the data structure is global, then sharing of data is automatic. But as I explained in Chapter 2, it's best to use as few global variables as possible. So you frequently need to pass a data structure as an argument in a function call. This leaves two possibilities:

- You could pass the data structure by giving me a copy of the entire data structure. This approach is fine in the case of small data types such as simple integers (**int**, **short**, and **long**) but can be inefficient when you start dealing with arrays, strings, and other large objects.

- You could give me the address of the data structure. An address (that is, a pointer) looks just like an integer, but it has a special meaning to the computer: an address tells the processor where to find something in memory.

To visualize these scenarios, try to picture the computer's *stack*, which is the area of memory reserved for passing data between functions. Passing a data structure directly causes an entire copy of the data to be placed on the stack. But passing an address causes a relatively small amount of data to be placed on the stack (typically, either two or four bytes, depending on the computer's address size). As the function being called, I need only the location of the data structure—its address—to gain access to all the data. Figure 3.1 illustrates these two approaches to passing data.

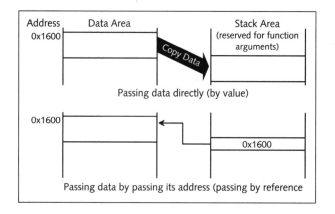

Figure 3.1 Passing data directly and passing its address (a pointer).

In the second scenario, I have only the address of the data. But this is all I need to access or modify the original data. Manipulating data through its address is called *indirection*. Modern processors are designed with a great deal of support for indirection.

The usefulness of pointers is not limited to saving memory on the stack. Among other things, pointers enable passing by reference, which is the topic we'll look at next.

Pointers and Passing by Reference

If you've used Basic, FORTRAN, or Pascal, to name only a few common languages, you're probably familiar with passing by reference and passing by value: a function can permanently change the value of an argument only if you pass by reference.

With languages such as Basic and FORTRAN, passing by reference is automatic or easily controlled by a simple keyword (such as "var" in Pascal). You may not have realized it, but these languages pass a pointer when you pass by reference. The language hides this fact from you, so you don't have to learn pointer syntax, as required by C.

C++, but not C, provides a special reference operator (&) that lets you use the same high-level pass-by-reference
T I P **technique that Basic, FORTRAN, and Pascal support. This operator is introduced in Chapter 6, "Another Look at Constructors." However, it's best to learn first how to pass by reference the hard way: with pointers. Even with C++, sooner or later you have to use pointers, and the best way to learn is to start with passing by reference.**

The connection between pointers and passing by reference should be clear if you look at Figure 3.1 again. If you pass by value, I get a complete copy of the original data. I can change the copy as much as I want, but this has no effect on the original data. When I finish execution, all the stack area I've been using is released. None of the changes I made to my copy have any effect on the program.

If, however, I get a pointer to your data, then changes I make affect you. A pointer is not exactly a new piece of data but instead is something that tells me the location of your data, which enables me to change it. It's as if you gave me the location and combination of the file cabinet containing your original records rather than make separate copies for me.

Therefore, passing a pointer (an address) is the same as passing by reference. In fact, that's literally what passing by reference means: a pointer *refers to* the original copy of the data.

Steps for Passing by Reference

To use pointers to pass by reference, you need to follow several steps:

1. In the prototype and function-definition argument list, declare the parameter using the pointer-indirection operator (*).

2. When passing an argument, make sure to pass an address. Typically, this means applying the address operator (&) to your argument.

3. Within the function definition, apply the pointer-indirection operator (*) when you want to access the data pointed to.

The rest of this section discusses each of these steps in a more detail.

First, you must apply the indirection operator (*) to declare your intention to use a pointer argument. The declaration is the same as it would be if the argument were not a pointer except that the indirection operator is placed to the immediate left of the argument name. For example, the following prototype declares a function taking one argument: a pointer to an **int**.

```
void double_it(int *n);
```

Second, you must pass an address argument. Typically, you apply the address operator (&) to a normal variable (in this case, an **int**). Alternatively, you can pass a pointer variable.

The following code gives an example of the first approach, that of using the address operator:

```
int amount;
...
double_it(&amount);   // Pass address of amount.
```

Finally, within the function definition, use the indirection operator (once again) to access the data pointed to. For example:

```
*p = *p * 2;
```

By using multiplication assignment (*=), you could instead write:

```
*p *= 2;
```

The two operators (* and &) are inverses of each other. The pointer-indirection operator (*) means "the object pointed to by," and the address operator says, "Get the address of." The first operator converts an address into the contents at that address (for example, it converts a pointer to an **int** into an actual **int**); the second operator converts a variable into the address of that variable.

NOTE Using p without the indirection operator (*) affects the pointer itself and not the thing pointed to. For example, (*p)++ increments the data pointed to, whereas p++ advances the pointer to the next address.

Two Complete Pass-by-Reference Examples

Both the indirection (*) and the address (&) operators are necessary for working with pointers, as the examples in this section demonstrate. To pass by reference, you first have to put an address on the stack (which involves &); later, in the function definition, you use that address to access the data pointed to (which involves *).

Figure 3.2 shows the complete context for the example code from the previous section. The example first defines a variable, amount, and sets it to 5. After calling the double_it function and passing the address of amount, the variable contains the value 10. If double_it were passed the normal way (by value), the double_it function would have no effect.

```
#include <stdio.h>                              Address of amount is
                                                passed to the
void double_int(int *p);                        parameter, *p.

main () {
    int amount = 5;

    printf("The value of amount is %d.\n", amount);

    double_it(&amount);

    printf("The value of amount is %d.\n", amount);
}

void double_int(int *p) {
    *p = *p * 2;
}
```

Figure 3.2 Passing the address of amount to the double_it function.

Figure 3.3 shows an example that passes two arguments by reference. (Incidentally, you can mix types of arguments; in a long argument list, some may be pointers and others may be simple data types.) Here, the function switches the value of two variables, a and b. The function can modify both a and b because the address of each is passed, enabling the function to access a and b themselves rather than copies of a and b.

```
#include <stdio.h>                       Addresses of a and b
                                         are passed to the
void swap(double *x, double *y);         parameters *x and *y.

main () {
    double a = 1.5, b = 3.9;

    printf("a = %lf, b = %lf\n", a, b);

    swap(&a, &b);

    printf("a = %lf, b = %lf\n", a, b);
}

void swap(double *x, double *y) {
    double temp;

    temp = *x;
    *x = *y;
    *y = temp;
}
```

Figure 3.3 Passing addresses of two variables, a and b.

Pointers and Arrays

In C++, pointers have a close connection to arrays. By using pointers, you can often process arrays more efficiently.

Arrays are an important element of almost every computer language—certainly of the major languages commonly used today. Arrays are essential in serious programming projects for two reasons:

- They provide a convenient way to allocate arbitrarily large chunks of data in program memory.

- They can be used to perform a large number of operations with a few lines of code. By combining an array with a loop, you can perform a series of statements and then repeat the operations on an arbitrarily large chunk of memory.

Chapter 3: Pointers, Strings, and Things

The importance of arrays and loop processing cannot be overestimated. Computer programming, and computers themselves, would be far less powerful without this single aspect of programming. C++ enhances this capability by providing pointer operations.

Array Basics

Here is the C++ syntax for declaring arrays:

```
type   name[length];
```

For multidimension arrays, the syntax is as follows:

```
type   name[length1][length2]...[lengthN];
```

In both cases, the brackets are intended literally. In the multi-dimension case, the number of dimensions can be two, three, or N, where N is as high a number as you want. (Bear in mind, though, that arrays with an unreasonably high number of dimensions are likely to eat up all your computer's memory.)

The rest of this example covers a single-dimension case, although multiple dimensions follow similar rules. The *length* in the declaration indicates the number of elements in the array. (For multiple arrays, the number of elements is *length* * *length* * ... *length*.) The lowest index is always 0, and the highest is always *length*-1.

A couple of examples should help make this clear. Consider the following declaration:

```
int  a[5];
```

This declaration creates not one, but five integers. The variables are referred to as follows:

```
a[0]
a[1]
a[2]
a[3]
a[4]
```

Notice that the highest index value supported here is 4, which is one less than the length (5). Similarly, we can declare an array 10 elements long:

```
int  b[10];
```

This declaration creates 10 integers. Again, the highest index, 9, is one less than the length (10).

```
b[0]
b[1]
b[2]
b[3]
b[4]
b[5]
b[6]
b[7]
b[8]
b[9]
```

T I P There's a reason I'm emphasizing that the highest index used is length-1. When you're working with arrays, one of the most common sources of bugs is to incorrectly set the initial and terminating conditions of a loop. Even experienced programmers occasionally set the terminating condition wrong, because they forget that the highest index is length-1. So check loop conditions carefully.

When I say that a declaration such as "int a[5]" creates five integers, I mean that literally. Figure 3.4 shows how the integers are laid out sequentially in memory. This illustration assumes that each **int** is two bytes even though on some systems (such as 32-bit systems), the **int** size is larger.

Figure 3.4 An array with five integers.

Declaring an array of five integers is similar in many ways to declaring each integer separately. We could declare five integers this way:

```
int a0;
int a1;
int a2;
int a3;
int a4;
```

How is this different from declaring the five-element integer array a, which generates the elements a[0], a[1], a[2], a[3], and a[4]?

Well, most obviously, the array declaration saves effort. Declaring integers individually is not so tedious when there are only five, but think of how many lines of code are saved when there are a thousand integers:

```
int a[1000];
```

And there's another reason. Elements can be indexed by either a constant or a variable. For example:

```
int a[5];

a[0] = 10;
a[1] = a[0] + 1;

int n = 2;
a[n] = a[1];    // Assign a[1] to a[2]
```

Using variable indexes with arrays is a powerful technique. It enables loop processing of arrays, as in the following example.

```
// Initialize all 1,000 elements of the array to
//   contain the value 100.

int a[1000];
int i = 0;
while (i++ < 1000)
    a[i] = 100;
```

Loop Processing with Pointers

Pointers provide another way to perform loop processing. The pointer version is generally more efficient than a version using array indexes. (This is particularly true with multidimension arrays.) For instance, the example at the end of the last section could be written this way:

```
// Initialize all 1,000 elements of the array to 100.

int a[1000];
int i = 0;
```

```
int *p = a;
while (i++ < 1000)
    *p++ = 100;
```

Some of these statements require a closer look. The third statement declares a pointer, p, and initializes it to the starting address of the array, a. The declaration works this way because when an array name appears without an index, it is translated into the address of the first element. This is one reason pointers and arrays are closely connected—both are address expressions.

```
int *p = a;
```

The loop statement relies on C++ rules of precedence to do things in a certain order.

```
while (i++ < 1000)
    *p++ = 100;
```

Parentheses help clarify the effect of the loop statement. Note that postfix increment ++ has a higher precedence than indirection (*). Because it is a *postfix* increment, the increment is applied after the rest of the statement is evaluated (so p++ is equivalent to p except for a side effect that is resolved later).

```
while (i++ < 1000)
    *(p++) = 100;
```

The loop could have been made even more self-evident, but less compact, by writing it this way:

```
while (i++ < 1000) {
    *p = 100;    // Assign 100 to element pointed to
    p++;         // Point to next element
}
```

The first statement inside the loop (*p = 100) is an operation on the data pointed to. But the second statement (p++) is an operation on the pointer itself. Adding one to a pointer always advances it to point to the next element regardless of the size of the base type.

Figure 3.5 illustrates how this loop processes the array by assigning a value and then advancing to the next element.

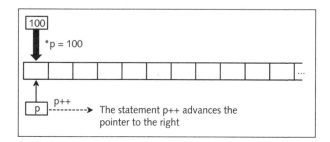

Figure 3.5 Using a pointer for loop processing on an array.

Similar code can be used to copy all the members of one array, b, to all the members of another array, a:

```
int a[1000], b[1000];
...
int i = 0;
int *pa = a;
int *pb = b;
while (i++ < 1000)
    *pa++ = *pb++;
```

Again, the precedence of postfix increment (++) is higher than that of indirection (*), so the loop has the same effect as the following, less compact version:

```
while (i++ < 1000) {
    *pa = *pb;      // Copy element from b to a
    pa++;           // Point to next element in a
    pb++;           // Point to next element in b
}
```

Figure 3.6 illustrates how this loop processes the array by assigning a value and then advancing to the next element.

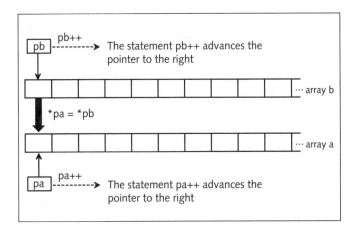

Figure 3.6 Using pointers for loop processing on two arrays.

C++ Strings

Array-handling techniques, especially those involving pointers, are useful in handling C++ character strings. If you are not well versed in how pointers can be used to process array elements, it's a good idea to go back and review the preceding section.

In C++, a character string is an array of **char**. Technically, a **char** is an integer, one byte in length. (Note, however, that there is no necessary connection between strings and one byte; the wide-character format, used in products intended for international distribution, uses two bytes per character.) When printed on screen, each **char** value is mapped to a printable character. The mapping system most widely in use today is the ASCII coding convention.

Simply stated, a character string is implemented as an array of one-byte integers, in which each integer represents an ASCII character code.

If you are used to string handling in Basic, you may at first find that string handling is not as easy in C++. For example, you have to call a library function (strcpy) just to assign one string value to another. In Chapters 5, 6, and 7, I use object-oriented C++ features to create a string class every bit as easy to use as Basic strings. This class demonstrates much of the power of C++ object orientation. But to understand the code for Chapters 5, 6, and 7, it's important to first understand the underlying mechanics of C++ strings.

Incidentally, character strings are never simple values— no matter what the language. A language such as Basic simply hides the underlying array-handling mechanics from you. C and C++ give you more control by not hiding what's going on.

C++ strings have one special characteristic in addition to being arrays. This is the first cardinal rule of string handling: **A string is terminated with a null byte ('\0'), which is a value of zero (as opposed to a printable character "0").**

The location of the null-terminating byte determines the effective length of the string. This is a potential point of confusion for people who are new to C/C++ strings. You can allocate as many bytes for a string as you want, but the current length depends on the location of the first null byte. If you pass a string to the printf function, for example, only the characters up to the first null are printed; everything past that character is ignored. This can be stated as the second cardinal rule of string handling: The array dimension of a string determines its maximum length (minus one for the null terminator) and not its current length.

The following simple example should clarify. Suppose you declare a string as follows:

```
char str[10] = "Hello";
```

The name str is declared as a **char** array. It is therefore a string with maximum length of nine (10, minus one for the null-terminating byte). The declaration initializes the string with the value "Hello," so it is represented in memory as shown in Figure 3.7.

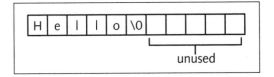

Figure 3.7 A string with unused bytes.

The last four bytes are not currently in use. But they could be used if a new set of characters were to be copied into the string (by using the strcpy function, as you'll see later). In no case, however, should more than 10 bytes be copied to this string location. Doing so would overwrite data areas reserved for other variables or even other programs. This is another way in which C++ differs from a language such as Basic. You need to pay attention to the maximum lengths you have set.

By the way, an alternative way to create a string is to omit an explicit array dimension. In that case, C++ allocates just enough bytes to store the initial string, and no more. This approach is fine as long as the string will never grow in length.

```
char str[] = "Hello";
```

Figure 3.8 shows the resulting byte layout in memory.

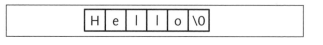

Figure 3.8 A string with no unused bytes.

When creating C++ strings, you can initialize them with any string constant, as was done in the last two examples. Note that this use of the equal sign (=) is initialization and not assignment; it is limited to the same statement that declares and defines the string.

But after a string is declared, you must use the strcpy function to copy a new string value (or write a strcpy function yourself, which is easy). You can't simply assign one string to another as if they were numbers or simple objects. This can be stated as the third cardinal rule of C++ string handling: **Because strings are arrays, they can't be directly assigned to each other. You must call a function or use a loop to copy one character at a time.**

This is where string handling in C++ seems more difficult than in other languages. You can't write statements such as A$ = B$ as you can in Basic. The following code produces an error:

```
char string1[10] = "One";
char string2[10] = "Two";
string2 = string1;        // ERROR! Cannot assign to
                          // string
```

Your compiler would probably give you an unhelpful, unfriendly message such as "Cannot assign to a constant,." although this message makes sense when you consider that C++ array names are actually constants that translate into the address of the first element.

To copy the contents of one string to another, use the strcpy function:

```
#include <string.h>

char string1[10] = "One";
char string2[10] = "Two";
strcpy(string2, string1);   // Correct way to copy
                            //string
```

Note the use of the **#include** directive to support the strcpy function, which requires the declaration in **STRING.H**. Include this file whenever you use any string-handling functions from the C++ standard library. Other string-handling functions are shown in Table 3.1.

Table 3.1 C++ string-handling functions.

FUNCTION	DESCRIPTION
strlen(char *s)	Return the number of characters up to, but not including, the first null byte.
strncpy(char *dest*, char *src, int *n*)	Copy at most *n* characters.
strcat(char *dest, char *src)	Concatenate contents of *src* onto the end of *dest*.

The following code uses the strcpy and strcat functions from the standard library:

```
#include <stdio.h>
#include <string.h>
...
```

```
char *name[81];     // Max. length is 80 characters,
                    //plus one for the null

strcpy(name, "Archie");
strcat(name, " ");
strcat(name, "Leach");

printf("%s, he my friend.\n", name);
```

The **%s** format character specifies that the corresponding argument is the address of a string. Remember that an array name (in this case, an array of characters) translates into the starting address. This code prints the following string:

```
Archie Leach, he my friend.
```

Pointers are convenient for writing string-handling functions. For example, you could write your own version of the strcpy function. In practice, this is not necessary, because the standard library provides this function. However, it is useful to see how easy such a function is to write in C++.

```
char *strcpy(char *dest, char *src) {
    while (*src != '\0') {
        *dest = *src;
        dest++;
        src++;
    }
    *dest = '\0';  // Add terminating null
    return dest;
}
```

There are at least a couple of ways to make this code more compact, although this version is probably the easiest to understand. (However, as an exercise, you can apply some of the techniques in the previous section to reduce the size by at least a couple of lines.) In any case, Figure 3.9 illustrates how the function works.

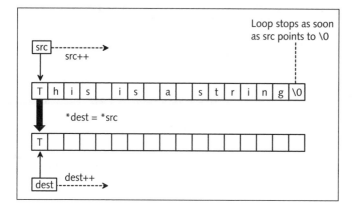

Figure 3.9 How the strcpy function works.

Pointers and Dynamic Memory

Dynamic is one of those terms that get tossed around (even abused) a lot in the programming world. In general, *dynamic* means "in motion" or "changing."

Dynamic memory is used when your memory requirements may change during running of the program. If you're reading the contents of a file into memory, for example, the amount of memory you need depends on the size of the file. If you're building a linked list of structures, you need to allocate new memory every time you add a new structure.

C++ provides two approaches to dynamic memory. You can use the malloc family of functions inherited from the C standard library, or you can use the **new** and **delete** operators, which are supported in C++ only.

In both cases, you have to understand and use pointers. With ordinary data structures, the compiler assigns an address to the variable or object. You never need to know this address; instead, you just use the variable's name.

Using malloc and free (C and C++)

Calling the malloc function is a way of asking the operating system to give you a chunk of memory of a specific size. The operating system will oblige you if it possibly can (but note that in serious programs, you should test for error conditions). The result is that you get a pointer to this chunk, which consists of consecutive bytes in memory.

Using the malloc and free library functions involves the following steps:

1. Include the header file, **MALLOC.H**:

```
#include <malloc.h>
```

2. After declaring a pointer of the appropriate type, call the malloc function, specifying as the argument the number of bytes needed. Apply a pointer cast, which changes the type to the appropriate kind of pointer, and then assign the result to the pointer:

```
pointer = (type *) malloc (elements * sizeof(type));
```

3. When you are finished with the memory, call the free function and give the pointer as the argument:

```
free(pointer);
```

In terms of programming techniques, the use of dynamic memory differs from using ordinary variables in one important way: when using dynamic memory, you have no direct access to the data. You have access only through a pointer. Fortunately, it is easy to refer to any part of a memory block through a pointer. In C++ (and in C), pointers and array names are almost interchangeable. Once the operating system allocates the chunk of memory, the operating system returns a pointer giving the starting address of this chunk.

74

Don't lose this pointer (or change its value without first saving it), because otherwise all ties to the memory are lost.

For example, the following code allocates a memory block of 500 integers (**int**). After malloc returns successfully, you can refer to any of the integers as members of an array. Use array indexing on the pointer itself.

```
#include <malloc.h>
#include <stdio.h>
...
int *p;

p = (int *) malloc(500 * sizeof(int));

if (p) {
    p[0] = 5;           // Assign 5 to first element
    p[50] = -33;        // Assign -33 to 51st element
    printf("The 51st element is %d.\n", p[50]);
    ...
    free(p);
}
```

The malloc statement takes one argument: the number of bytes requested. Because room for 500 integers is wanted, the appropriate size is 500 times the size of each integer. The **sizeof** operator (which admittedly looks like a function) is a special built-in operator in C and C++ that returns the size of a type.

```
p = (int *) malloc(500 * sizeof(int));
```

This statement also uses a data cast, (int *), to change the type of the value returned. The malloc function returns a pointer of type **void***, which is a generic pointer type. In C++, you must change this data type before assigning it. The data cast changes the type from **void*** to **int*** so that it matches the type of the pointer p.

```
(int *) expression
```

As another example, the following code allocates a block of 100 double-precision floating-point numbers (**double**):

```
double *p;

p = (double *) malloc(100 * sizeof(double));
```

 Requiring the data cast is one area where C++ adds restrictions to C. In C, you can be sloppy and freely assign between pointers of different types. In C++, you must explicitly change the data type of a void* pointer before assigning it to another type of pointer. The C++ approach is safer, because it prevents you from accidentally assigning between different kinds of pointers. Using an int* pointer to access an array of double, for example, is guaranteed to cause errors unless you are doing it deliberately and for good reason.

After the malloc function returns, it is a good idea to test the result. If the function was successful, the pointer contains a valid address. Otherwise, the pointer is assigned the null value, which is numerically equal to zero. An **if** statement interprets a null value as false. The pointer value is zero (false) if the malloc function failed because of insufficient memory. A "true" value therefore indicates success.

```
if (p) {
    p[0] = 5;           // Assign 5 to first element
    p[50] = -33;        // Assign -33 to 51st element
    printf("The 51st element is %d.\n", p[50]);
    . . .
    free(p);
}
```

The final thing the code does is to explicitly free the memory block by calling the free function. This is the other key difference between dynamic memory and ordinary variables. If you don't get into the habit of freeing dynamic memory blocks, then your code is likely to eat up memory without returning it, resulting in memory leaks to the system. You don't want to do that!

Using new and delete (C++ Only)

The **new** and **delete** operators can be effectively used wherever you use the malloc and free functions. If you understand how to call malloc, using **new** is easy. The use of **new** and **delete** also offers other advantages:

- You don't have to include a header file just to declare **new** and **delete**.

- You don't have to use a type cast before assigning to a pointer. The **new** operator automatically returns the right kind of pointer.

- Most important, **new** and **delete** do more than simply allocate chunks of memory. When you allocate an object using **new**, it automatically calls the object's constructor, if any. Similarly, freeing memory using **delete** automatically calls a destructor if appropriate. In Chapter 5, you will work with objects that have constructors and destructors.

In summary, then, you need to use **new** and **delete** if you are going to work with classes and object orientation in C++; otherwise, you can use malloc.

To allocate memory using **new**, place the type of the object after **new**. This type can be a primitive type, a class, or an array.

```
pointer = new type;
```

So, for example, you could allocate a single integer or an array of 500 integers:

```
int *p1, *p2;

p1 = new int;          // p1 points to a single integer
p2 = new int[500];     // p2 points to first of 500
                       //    integer
```

In C++, you can combine initialization with operators and function calls so that you can use **new** in the same statement that declares the pointer:

```
int *p2 = new int[500];
```

To free memory allocated with **new**, use the **delete** operator followed by a pointer name. If the memory involved the creation of an array (as in the immediately preceding example), then place empty brackets ([]) before the pointer name.

Therefore, use one of the following two statements, as appropriate.

```
delete pointer;    (if one object was created with new)
delete [] pointer; (if array was created with new)
```

The example in the previous section could have been written this way using **new** and **delete**:

```
#include <stdio.h>
...
int *p = new int[500];

if (p) {
```

```
p[0] = 5;           // Assign 5 to first element
p[50] = -33;        // Assign -33 to 51st element
printf("The 51st element is %d.\n", p[50]);
...
delete [] p;
}
```

Note that the **new** operator returns a null value if there is insufficient memory, just as malloc does. For best results, you should test this value before using or deleting the new memory.

4

Input, Output, and C++

In Chapter 2, I introduced input/output techniques to help you write simple programs. But there's a good deal more to C++ input and output.

C++ is object-oriented, and it provides an object-oriented approach to input and output through *stream objects*, which are supported by the C++ standard library and header files. Stream objects are not supported in C. If you have a C background, stream objects may be the first C++ extension you use regularly. On the other hand, introducing these objects into your programs is entirely optional.

Not all input and output involves the keyboard and screen. Just as important, particularly in serious programs, is the process of reading and writing to data files. This chapter examines different file reading and writing techniques.

Going with the Flow: Introduction to Streams

In this chapter, you're going to see the term *stream* a good deal. It is often used in systems programming generally. What is a stream?

Speaking literally, a stream is a flow of water. In computer programming, a *stream* is a flow of data. One of the chief characteristics of a stream is that it is a one-direction-al flow. Although you might argue that this isn't absolutely true (even a small stream can have whirlpools and backflows), it's true enough to hang a metaphor on. An input/output stream is a sequence of bytes continually flowing in one direction or another, either input or output.

Another characteristic of a stream is that it is nearly inexhaustible. Streams sometimes run dry, but you don't expect this to happen often. An output stream, in particular, will always accept another byte (except under rare error conditions such as a full disk).

The two most commonly used streams in programming are standard input and standard output, and they do not run dry. You can always ask standard input to provide another ASCII character from the keyboard, and you can always print another character on the screen (see Figure 4.1).

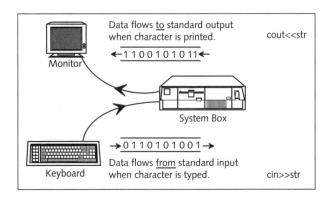

Figure 4.1 Input and output streams.

Files are also considered streams. When you perform file input or output, you can always put or get the next byte. "The next byte" is always valid, except under error conditions. An example of something that holds data but is *not* a stream is an array or data structure. An array, for example, always has a specific size and cannot grow as an output file can.

To some extent, the concept of streams is a fiction created by computer scientists. An area of random access memory (RAM), for example, can be treated as a large array, or it can be used as virtual disk memory, which in turn can support streams. It's the same hardware in either case. As with many other concepts in programming, what makes something a stream is how it is treated. In the final analysis, a stream is a context in which the idea of "the next byte" makes sense.

A stream is either an input or an output stream. The following statements are true, barring error conditions such as end-of-file or disk full:

- With an input stream, you can always read the next byte.

- With an output stream, you can always write another byte.

The ability to read or write the next byte implies the ability to read or write any number of bytes. Writing a two-byte field, for example, is the same as writing one byte and then writing another byte. Of course, the bytes must be read and written in a consistent order.

Stream Operators (<< and >>): A First Look

Stream operators (<< and >>) provide an alternative to using printf, scanf, and the other functions defined in **STDIO.H**. The stream operators provide two advantages: you don't have to use format specifiers if you are happy with the

83

default formats, and it's possible to extend the operators so that they work with your own classes. (The next chapter introduces the subject of classes.) For information on how to extend the operators, see the topics "istream Class" and "ostream Class" in Part III.

This chapter presents several input/output techniques: printf and scanf, stream operators, and line-based input. You should not mix these techniques in the same program. You can pick any kind of input technique and any kind of output technique (for example, mixing printf with line-based input), but don't switch between two different kinds of input. The C++ standard library uses different I/O buffers for each technique, so mixing them causes unpredictable results.

Here is a simple program that gets two floating-point numbers and then prints their sum:

```
#include <iostream.h>

void main() {
    double a, b;

    cout << "Enter the first number: ";
    cin >> a;
    cout << "Enter the second number: ";
    cin >> b;
    cout << "The total is ";
    cout << a + b;
}
```

This program behaves the same way as the following program, which uses **printf** and **scanf**:

```
#include <stdio.h>

void main() {
```

```
   double a, b;

   printf("Enter the first number: ");
   scanf("%lf", &a);
   printf("Enter the second number: ");
   scanf("%lf", &b);
   printf("The total is %s", a + b);
}
```

Note the following important points about the version that uses the stream operators, **cin**, and **cout**.

- The file **IOSTREAM.H**, rather than **STDIO.H**, is included.

- No format specifiers are needed. C++ uses the type of the object (a and b in the example) to determine how to perform the data transfer. In this respect, the stream operators are like the Basic PRINT statement and are a little easier to use than **printf** and **scanf**.

- The address operator (&) isn't used to get input, as it is in scanf. (Here, input streams act more like Basic by using reference arguments, which you'll learn more about in Chapter 6.)

- Data flows toward standard output (**cout**), which usually represents the display screen:

  ```
  cout << "Enter the first number: ";
  ```

- Data flows from standard input (**cin**), which usually represents the keyboard:

  ```
  cin >> a;
  ```

The direction of the arrows may seem arbitrary at first. Think about the direction in which data flows, and you'll remember which way the arrows should go. Refer to Figure 4.1 for an illustration.

NOTE The stream operators look suspiciously like the left and right bit shift operators. In fact, that's exactly what they are! This use of left and right shift is an example of operator overloading, a technique that Chapter 7 discusses in detail. The behavior of the shift operators is redefined for istream and ostream classes (these classes are defined in IOSTREAM.H) so that the shift operators become "put to" operators for these classes.

Programmers who overload operators usually strive to maintain the operator's general meaning. For example, you'd want the plus sign (+) to indicate some kind of addition operation in any situation (although what it means to add two strings is quite different from what it means to add two numbers). The use of << and >> as stream operators is an exception to this general design principle. Sending data to and from I/O streams has nothing to do with shifting bits. The << and >> operators were overloaded for stream operations because they had syntactic advantages as well as the advantage of being visually appropriate (they suggest data flows).

In the example at the beginning of this section, the last two lines can be rewritten as one. These two lines print two pieces of data—a string and a number:

```
cout << "The total is ";
cout << a + b;
```

The two lines can be replaced by the following, more compact statement:

```
cout << "The total is " << a + b;
```

The associativity of the shift operators is left-to-right, meaning that the following expression is evaluated first:

```
cout << "The total is "
```

As is common in C and C++, this expression does two things: it sends the string to **cout** (this is its side effect, if you will), and then it evaluates to a value. It so happens that expressions that combine **cout** with a value always evaluate to **cout** itself. This is true regardless of the actual output string. Evaluating to cout is, in effect, a syntactic trick that enables you to output or input any number of items using a single statement. You can perform the same trick to input several numbers with one statement, because each subexpression evaluates to **cin**. For example:

```
cin >> a >> b >> c >> n;
```

Figure 4.2 shows how C++ breaks down this statement, each time performing an input operation as the expression's side effect.

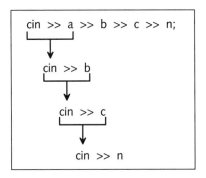

Figure 4.2 How C++ evaluates multiple input to cin.

The Joy of Formatting

One of the attractions of using **cin** and **cout**, especially for beginners, is that you don't have to use the funny symbols that you use with **printf** and **scanf**. Each data type is recognized by the operator, and each data type has a reasonable default behavior. For example, by default the following statement prints the decimal representation of n, which is the most common format.

```
cout << n;
```

But what if you want to print in hexadecimal or octal format? For example, you could do the following with the **printf** statement:

```
int n = 16;
printf("n is %x hex, %o octal, and %d decimal.", n, n,
    n);
```

This code prints the following text:

```
n is 10 hex, 20 octal, and 16 decimal.
```

The following example, using the C++ stream operators, prints the same results:

```
int n = 16;
cout << "n is " << hex << n << " hex, ";
cout << oct << n << " octal, and ";
cout << dec << n << " decimal.";
```

Just what are **hex**, **oct**, and **dec**? They're objects (which you'll learn more about in the next chapter). When sent as "output" to **cout** or as "input" to **cin**, they have the effect of changing the integer format of the stream until further notice.

When complex formatting is involved, using the C++ stream objects makes for less readable code than using good old reliable **printf** and **scanf**. This is especially true if you have a background in C.

On the side of the stream operators, however, there is a pleasant alternative. Instead of using objects such as hex, oct, and dec, you can use the format function (declared in **IOSTREAM.H**), which duplicates the behavior of printf format characters and returns a string that can be passed to **cout**. For example:

```
int n = 16;
cout << format("n is %x hex, %o octal, and %d decimal.",
          n, n, n);
```

Line-Based Input with STDIO.H

Some C++ programmers prefer to use the I/O library functions declared in **STDIO.H** and inherited from C. If you have a C programming background and are accustomed to using these functions or if you are maintaining legacy code written in C, it may make sense to continue using them. You'll probably encounter problems if you attempt to mix different input techniques or different output techniques. Therefore, if you have existing code, it may be best to continue using **STDIO.H** functions throughout the program.

There is more to the input and output functions than I described in Chapter 2. For one thing, **printf** and **scanf** support a wide variety of format specifiers, which are particularly useful with **printf**. For example, you can use **%x** to print integers in hexadecimal format. You can also control the spacing and precision of floating-point numbers as well as left-justify or right-justify your output fields. See the topics on **printf** and **scanf** in Part III.

Some of the most useful functions declared in **STDIO.H** support line-oriented input and output. You can use puts, for example, as a more efficient way of printing strings. The statement

```
printf("%s\n", string);
```

behaves the same way as

```
puts(string);
```

The latter version is more efficient, however, because it avoids the overhead of the more elaborate printf function. At the same time, the puts function is less flexible, because it prints a new line whether or not you want one.

One of the most useful functions declared in **STDIO.H** is gets ("get string"). When you call this function, it waits until the user types something and then presses the **Enter** key. Then the function places the entire line of input—spaces and all—into the string argument. For example:

```
#include <stdio.h>
...
char str[81]; // Allow for max. chars on screen

gets(str); // Get line of input and place in str.
```

I have found using gets far preferable to using scanf in all but the simplest programs. Once you read a line of input into a string, you are free to analyze it or interpret its contents any way you choose. This capability is useful in writing a compiler or other sophisticated tool, because you can lexically analyze the input as you wish. In plain terms, this means that you have total control over which characters divide different fields and how sequences of spaces should be interpreted. When you use **scanf** or **cin**, you have no control over how a numeric or string field is defined. The scanf function gives you input when and if it decides that the user has typed something valid.

As a simple example of line input, you might decide that your program accepts input delineated by the at sign (@):

```
Here is some input@1234@More input@34.0005
```

The following code uses gets to input this entire line. Then the code assigns each input field—delineated by @—to a different string. Although this example may seem odd, it does show how you could choose to input embedded spaces in strings, something that scanf and cin don't support.

```
#include <stdio.h>
...
char str[81]; // Allow for max. chars on screen
char array[40][81];

gets(str); // Get line of input and place in str.

int i = 0;
char *p = str;
char *s;
while(*p != '\0') {

// Set s equal to next string in array.
    s = array[i++];

// Read chars into string, up to next @.
    while (*p != '\0' && *p != '@')
        *s++ = *p++;

// Stop reading — terminate string and advance
//   pointer past the @.
```

```
    *s = '\0';
    p++;
}
```

When you have isolated a numeric field (for example, "1234") as input to one of these strings, you can optionally convert it to a numeric value by calling the atoi or atof function. These library functions are also declared in **STDIO.H**.

File Operations with STDIO.H

The line-oriented I/O functions of the previous section—gets and puts—are put to good use in the next example, which demonstrates sequential file I/O. This example prompts the user for a file name, but he or she has the option of just pressing **Enter**. The gets function responds in a reasonable way, inputting an empty string.

File input and output is almost as easy in C++ as it is in any other language. If you use standard library functions declared in **STDIO.H**, you should follow these four basic steps (which I also outlined in *C in Plain English*):

1. Include the **STDIO.H** header file and declare a file pointer of type FILE*. (Repeat this last part for each separate file you want to open.)

2. Open the file by calling the fopen function. This function returns a value you assign to the file pointer.

3. Read or write to the file as appropriate. You use file I/O functions such as fprintf, fscanf, fputs, fgets, and so on. These functions work the same way as their counterparts printf, scanf, puts, and gets, except that they take a file pointer as an additional argument.

4. Close the file by calling the fclose function.

Figure 4.3 illustrates the first three steps. This figure is a bit oversimplified. In step 2, the fopen function actively checks the file system. (The function does more than simply associate a file with a name.) If the requested file is not found or for some reason cannot be opened, the program must stop and respond to the error condition.

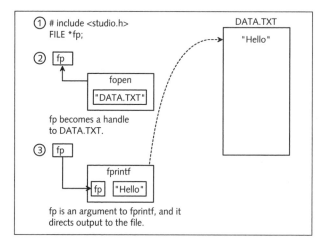

Figure 4.3 Summary of file I/O programming.

The following example program illustrates each of these steps, although it calls fgetc rather than fprintf. Note that **main** has a return value in this program. This technique enables **main** to return a code to the operating system: 0 (for success) or -1 (for error).

```
// Sample program to print out the contents of a text
//   file, converting all lowercase to uppercase.
//   The program prompts for the file name.

#include <stdio.h>
#include <ctype.h>
```

```
int main()
{
    int c;
    FILE *fp;
    char filename[81];

    printf("Enter file name, please: ");
    gets(filename);
    if ((*filename) == '\0') { // Test for empty string
        puts("No file name entered.\n");
        return -1;
    }

/* Open for reading; "r" specifies read mode. */

    fp = fopen(filename, "r");
    if (!fp) {
        puts("Error: file name not found.\n");
        return -1;
    }
    while ((c = fgetc(fp)) != EOF)
        putchar(toupper(c));

    fclose(fp);
    return 0;
}
```

In the example, the file is treated as an input file, so it is opened for read mode in line 23. The second argument is a string containing "r," for read mode. Write mode is "w," and read-write mode is "rw."

```
    fp = fopen(filename, "r");
```

The example program calls the fgetc function to read from the file. This function reads a single character from the input stream and is the file-input version of getchar, which reads a single character from standard input. The character read is compared to EOF, a constant defined in **STDIO.H** that indicates the end-of-file condition.

Line 28 calls fgetc. This complex line of code does the following: it calls fgetc to get a character; it assigns the result to the integer variable, c; and it compares that value to EOF. As long as the value returned is not EOF (the end of file has not yet been reached), the loop continues.

```
while ((c = fgetc(fp)) != EOF)
. . .
```

NOTE All the file operations in this chapter assume sequential access with text-based I/O. Such access techniques treat files as streams similar to the screen and keyboard. This access mode is often easiest to program, because it grows out of the standard I/O techniques (printf, scanf, and so on) that most beginners start with.

However, the logic of some programs requires random access: reading and writing fixed-length records to numbered or indexed locations in a file. (Note that there is no underlying hardware difference between a random access file and a sequential file; they are simply treated a little differently by a program.) Random access is not intrinsically more difficult. Generally, you open a random access file in binary mode and use the following library functions: fread, fwrite, and fseek. Although C++ has no notion of a record number, you can easily seek (move) to the appropriate position in a file by multiplying the record number by the size of each record. Records, in turn, are implemented as C++ structures or classes.

Files and Stream Operators

The stream concept can be applied to disk files as much as to the screen and keyboard. C++ supports objects of type ifstream (input-file stream) and ofstream (output-file stream). You create these objects by specifying the name during initialization. First, however, include the file **FSTREAM.H**. This file automatically includes all the contents of **IOSTREAM.H**.

```
#include <fstream.h>
```

To create file-stream objects, specify the name in parentheses when you define the object. For example:

```
ifstream inf("C:\\TXT\\DATA.TXT");
ofstream outf("C:\\TXT\\OUTPUT.TXT");
```

As always when specifying full path names, remember to use double backslashes inside C quoted strings whenever you're indicating a single backslash. Once the objects are defined and initialized with full or relative path names, you can use them just as you can cin and cout.

```
outf << "Here is a string written to a file."

long n;
inf >> n;
```

Stream objects evaluate to null values if an error condition, such as end-of-file, is present. So you can write loops such as the following, which stops after text has been exhausted.

```
while (inf)
    inf.getline(string, 80);
```

The getline function is a *member function* of the inf object; getline provides the same functionality that gets and fgets do. The first argument is a character string; the second is the maximum number of characters to read.

The following program prints the contents of the file **DATA.TXT**:

```
#include <fstream.h>

void main() {
    char buffer[81];

// Open input file DATA.TXT, in current directory.

    ifstream inf("DATA.TXT");

// While end of file not reached, get and print
//  a line of text, appending a newline each time.

    while (inf) {
        inf.getline(buffer, 80);
        cout << buffer << "\n";
    }
}
```

The Great Controversy: To Stream or Not to Stream

The major theme of this chapter has been that when it comes to input and output, there is more than one way to do things. Most books on C++ are strongly oriented toward one or the other approach and tend to dismiss the approach not used as either wrong-headed or old-fashioned.

There's a good reason for this (it's not only that authors are a stubborn, biased lot!) as I've pointed out, you should not mix different input/output techniques, such as using **cin** on one line and **scanf** on the next. Doing so is almost guaranteed to cause errors. Generally, C++ authors find it easiest to take the position that one approach is much better and stick with that. That way they don't encourage the errors that would arise from mixing the approaches.

The truth is that you can write equally efficient, readable, and elegant code either way. The stream operators are, arguably, simpler to use in trivial cases (although they introduce objects, which may confuse beginners). Using printf and scanf usually makes for more-readable code when significant formatting is involved, although the format function brings the blessings of printf format specifiers to cout.

If you have a C background and are comfortable with printf and scanf, there's no reason not to go on using them. For the next several chapters, I'll stick with printf and scanf in examples. I easily could have used **cin** and **cout** instead, but I went with printf and scanf to make the material a little more accessible to C programmers.

The stream objects are interesting because they quickly introduce classes and objects into the daily, routine tasks of programming. If you don't have piles of C legacy code to maintain and you are chomping at the bit to be object-oriented, you will likely want to begin using cin and cout immediately. The advantage of stream operators is that you can overload them for your own classes; this capability demonstrates how the object-oriented approach is inherently more extensible than traditional functions such as printf are. You cannot write a new format specifier for printf, for example, but using operator overloading, you can extend C++ so that it knows how to print objects of your own classes (by sending them to cout):

```
CMyClass myobject;
cout << "Here is my object: " << myobject << "\n"
```

We've gotten way ahead of the story. Before I can explain how to overload the operator, you need to confront the mysteries of classes, objects, constructors, and member functions, which lie ahead in the next few chapters. This has been a transitional chapter. With any luck, it has aroused your curiosity about objects and their role in C++.

 Once you understand operator overloading, see the topics "istream Class" and "ostream Class" in Part III. for an explination of how to extend your classes to support stream operations.

5

A Touch of Class

One of the key ideas in C++ is *active types*: you define a type in terms of what you can *do* with it. You can specify built-in operations and functions for the type. Because the operations are built into the type, certain kinds of programming are much easier.

If you create your own string type, for example, what would it mean to add two strings? How might they be initialized? If you have a mathematical bent, you could define a complex-number type and build in the ability to do complex-number arithmetic. Or you might have a pizza-shop program and define all the operations you can perform on a pizza.

In C++, the word *class* describes any kind of user-defined type. Classes can include built-in function support and virtually become part of the language once declared. You can freely define new items with a class name, just as you can with **int**, **float**, **double**, and so on. This is one of many ways in which C++ is programmer-friendly.

Developing Class: A Better String Type

One of the major complaints that people have when they learn C is that character strings are cumbersome. In Basic, for example, you can do this:

```
str1 = "My name is "
str2 = "Bill."
str3 = str1 + str2
```

And now str3 contains the message "My name is Bill." In standard C, this operation would take more work:

```
strcpy(str1, "My name is ");
strcpy(str2, "Bill.");
strcpy(str3, str1);
strcat(str3, str2);
```

In this chapter and in the two that follow, we'll build a new string type that is every bit as good as the string type in Basic. In many ways, the new string type will be better than anything in Basic, because you have ultimate control over the fate of the type. When you work with classes in C++, you can add new capabilities any time you want to.

From now on, I'll follow C++ terminology in using *class* whenever I talk about a user-defined type. (This term applies to structures, by the way, as well as to anything created with the **class** keyword.) When you see the term *class*, you should think of a new type that has its own characteristics and capabilities.

To create a class, use the **class** keyword with the following syntax:

```
class class_name {
    declarations
};
```

In C++, the declarations can include function declarations as well as data declarations. First, let's look at the simplest possible string class:

```
class CStr {
    char sData[256];
};
```

The name CStr is the class name, and sData is its contents. This simple class stores the string data. Now let's add some functions:

```
class CStr {
    char sData[256];
public:
    char *get(void);
    int  getlength(void);
    void cpy(char *s);
    void cat(char *s);
};
```

The four functions—get, getlength, cpy, and cat—operate on data stored in the class. What's the big deal? Why is it better to define functions inside the class rather than use functions—such as C's strcpy function—that operate externally on the class?

This is a simple class, and at this point it doesn't provide many practical advantages. There is one benefit, however: the string data, sData, is private to the class. No one can touch it except the class's own functions. If you later rewrite the class so that its internal implementation is completely different—and later in this chapter we will do that—code that uses this class won't break. This is a big advantage of classes.

Member Functions: A Class Act

You can write definitions for these functions just as you would for any other function, with one difference: the function name must be preceded by a special prefix.

class_name::

The two colons (::) form a single operator, called the *scope* operator. This operator, along with the class name, clarifies which function you're talking about. More than one class could have a function with the same name. For example, a class named CMyclass could also have a function named *get*. Outside the class declarations,

```
CMyclass::get
```

refers to the version of the get function belonging to CMyclass, and

```
CStr::get
```

refers to the version of the get function belonging to CStr. The complete syntax for a class-member function definition is as follows:

```
return_type  class_name::function_name  (arguments) {
      statements

}
```

In this case, the class name is CStr. In the function definitions that follow, remember that "CStr::" is simply part of the function name. Aside from this name prefix, these function definitions look just like those you might write for ordinary functions.

```
#include <string.h>
char *CStr::get(void) {  // Return ptr to string data.
    return sData;
}

int  CStr::getlength(void) { // Return length.
    return strlen(sData);
}

void CStr::cpy(char *s) {   // Copy string arg
    return strcpy(sData, s);
}
```

```
void CStr::cat(char *s) {     // Concatenate string arg
    return strcat(sData, s); //  onto object.
}
```

Don't get thrown by the pointer syntax in these function definitions. Remember that *any* function that returns a pointer is declared with the indirection operator (*) to the left of the name:

```
char *strcpy(char *s1, char *s2);
```

With CStr member functions, "CStr::" is simply part of the name. So the declaration of the get function has an asterisk to the left of CStr::.

Figure 5.1 summarizes how declarations and function definitions are linked by the class name, which in this case is CStr.

```
class CStr {
        char sData[256];
public:
        char *get(void);
        int getlength(void);
        void cpy(char *s);
        void cat(char *s);
};

#include <string.h>
char *CStr::get(void) {  // Return ptr to string data.
        return sData;
}

int CStr::getlength(void) {  // Return length.
        return strlen(sData);
}

void CStr::cpy(char *s) { // Copy string arg to object.
        strcpy(sData, s);
}

void CStr::cat(char *s) { // Concatenate string arg
        strcat(sData, s);   //  onto object.
}
```

Figure 5.1 CStr class declaration and function definitions.

The Deadly Semi: Watch Out for That Syntax!

One syntax error you're sure to make a few times—unless you're careful—is to use too many or too few semicolons. Class declarations end with them; function definitions do not.

As a general rule, C and C++ statements do not follow a terminating brace (})with a semicolon. All function definitions follow this rule:

```
char *CStr::get(void) {
    return sData;
}
```

However, **class**, **struct**, and **union** declarations require a semicolon after the brace.

```
class CStr {
    char sData[256];
public:
    char *get(void);
    int  getlength(void);
    void cpy(char *s);
    void cat(char *s);
};
```

This rule may seem one of the more arbitrary rules in C and C++, but it does have the benefit of helping the compiler to distinguish between declarations and function definitions. All declarations except function definitions require the terminating semicolon. So a function prototype ends with a semicolon whether or not it's inside a class:

```
char *get(void);
```

What's an Object, Anyway?

Together, a class declaration and function definitions, define how the string type works. The next step is to use the CStr declaration to create some strings:

```
CStr   str1, str2, str3;
```

In C++, as soon as you have successfully declared a class, you can use the class name to declare variables, just as you can with **int**, **long**, **float**, **double**, and so on. The class name takes on the same status in the language that data-type keywords have.

 The ability to define variables extends to the struct and union keywords. In C++, as soon as you declare a structure Mystruct, you can use it to declare variables:

```
Mystruct a, b, c, d;
```

In C, you would have to use the struct keyword:

```
struct Mystruct a, b, c, d;
```

Alternatively, you could use a typedef declaration to skip this step. In either case, C requires extra work. For the sake of compatibility with C, C++ supports this same use of struct and typedef. But once you start using C++, you can adopt the practice of declaring variables directly.

Once we have declared the strings, what do we call them? What are the entities a, b, c, and d in the following declaration?

```
CStr a, b, c, d;
```

These variables are all objects. If you have been listening to the dogma of object orientation, this may be an exciting moment for you: you finally have *objects*! To some people, the appearance of objects may seem deserving of a Nobel prize. ("Now that I have objects in my program, I'm going to save the world!")

Before you go out and celebrate, you should realize that you've been using objects all along. Technically speaking, an object in C++ is just a variable or other piece of data. Yet the term *object* does communicate something meaningful. An object is something that, through its class declaration, may be given behavior. C has variables but doesn't really have objects in the sense that C++ has them.

Calling a Member Function

Without further ado, let's look at behavior in the string objects. These objects know how to respond to the get, getlength, cpy, and cat functions:

```
CStr string1, string2;

string1.cpy("My name is ");        // Copy string to
    string1
string2.cpy("Bill.");         // Copy string to string2
string1.cat(string2.get());   // Concat string2 onto
                              // string1
puts(string1.get());          // Get string1 data and
                              // print
```

Each of the last four lines involves a call to a member function. Note the use of the dot (.) in a function call:

object.member_function(arguments)

If you've used structures in C, this syntax should look familiar. It's a natural extension of the syntax used to refer to a structure member:

object.member

Let's look more closely at one of these function calls. This first function call gives a command to the string1 object, in effect saying, "Copy the given string to yourself."

```
string1.cpy("My name is "); // Copy string to string1
```

This function call tells string1 to copy the data "My name is " to itself. The string1 object knows how to copy other strings this way because it has a built-in cpy function. Poetically, we can say that cpy is part of the object's behavior.

In actuality, here's what happens. The compiler recognizes string1.cpy( ) as a function call. It knows that string1 is an object of the class CStr. The function call is therefore resolved as a call to CStr::cpy.

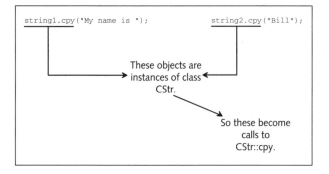

Figure 5.2 Resolving calls to member functions.

Earlier in the program, string1 and string2 were defined as objects of class CStr. So calls to string2.cpy( ) also result in calls to CStr::cpy. Objects of the same class share all their function code and in this sense have the same behavior.

What happens in the CStr::cpy function call? Control passes to the CStr::cpy function, just as it would with any normal function call.

109

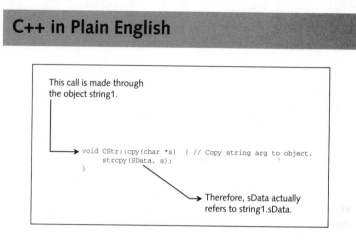

Figure 5.3 Member function access to data members.

But something interesting is going on here, as Figure 5.3 shows: the variable sData is a CStr *data member*. This data member belongs to the object string1.

Each object of class CStr has its own copy of the data member, sData. In this example, the statement calls CStr::cpy through the string object, string1. Therefore, when the function refers to sData, it is *string1's* copy of sData that is referenced. Figure 5.3 illustrates this connection.

Code and data work differently in objects. The following rules hold true regardless of what's public and what's private:

- Objects of the same class share function code. You resolve a call to a member function by determining the object's class and then calling *class::member_function*.

- But each individual object has its own copy of the data members.

One way to understand the distinction between code and data is to remember that objects are just packets of data. If you've worked with structures in C, records in Pascal, or user-defined types in Basic, the fact that C++ objects have data members is nothing new. And because these packets are collections of variables, they can vary from one another. Each C++ object can assign different values to its data members, so each object must have its own copy of these members.

Member functions are what's new. But member functions are just functions restricted to working on data of a particular type (i.e., a particular class). A member function works equally well on any object in its class. Functions, therefore, exist at the class level.

Figure 5.4 illustrates the class/object relationship and how it involves code and data. Assume that you define four string objects: str1, str2, str3, and str4.

```
CStr  str1, str2, str3, str4;
```

Each of these objects shares code created for the CStr class while also having its own copy of the CStr data member, sData.

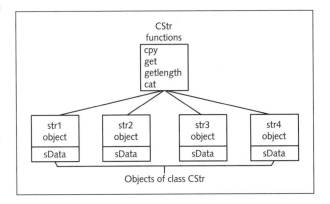

Figure 5.4 Code and data in the CStr class.

In this case, there is only one data member, but most classes have more than one. For example, we might create a class

111

CTemp_point, which locates a point in three-dimensional space and a temperature value:

```cpp
class CTemp_point {
    int    x, y, z;
    double temp;
public:
    void  set_point(int x, y, z);
    void  get_point(int *x, *y, *z);
    void  set_temp(double new_temp);
    double get_temp(void);
};
```

Assume, also, that you define four objects of this class:

```cpp
CTemp_point  pntA, pntB, pntC, pntD;
```

Here, all the instances of this class—that is, the individual points—share the CTemp_point function code in common, just as string objects share the CStr function code. But each point has its own copy of the four data members: x, y, z, and temp. (See Figure 5.5).

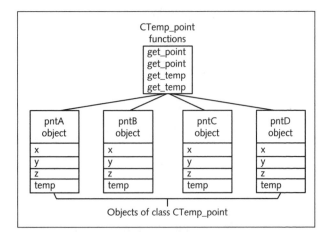

Figure 5.5 Code and data in the CTemp_point class.

Member Functions: A Walk-Through

If its clear to you how member functions work, you can skip to the next section. This section gives you an additional perspective on the working of member functions by walking through a series of function calls. Consider this code:

```
CStr   string1, string2;

string1.cpy("My name is "); // Calls CStr::cpy
string2.cpy("Bill.");       // Calls CStr::cpy
string1.cat(string2.get()); // Calls CStr::cpy and
                            // CStr::get
puts(string1.get());        // Calls CStr::get
```

The first function call results in a call to CStr::cpy, because string1 is an object of type CStr. The result of this call is to set string1's copy of the data member:

```
string1.cpy("My name is "); // Calls CStr::cpy
```

The next line of code results in a call to the same function, CStr::cpy. However, this time the call is made through the object string2, so it is string2's data member that gets changed:

```
string2.cpy("Bill.");       // Calls CStr::cpy
```

The next two statements result in calls to CStr::cat and CStr::get (the latter is called twice).

```
string1.cat(string2.get()); // Calls CStr::cpy and
                            // CStr::get
puts(string1.get());        // Calls CStr::cpy
```

As a final example, consider another class declaration, CTemp_point. Assume that the function definitions are provided elsewhere in the program.

```
class CTemp_point {
    int     x, y, z;
    double temp;
public:
    void    set_point(int x, y, z);
    void    get_point(int *x, *y, *z);
    void    set_temp(double new_temp);
    double get_temp(void);
};
```

With this declaration, we might declare two objects:

```
CTemp_point  mypoint, point_break;
```

The following function call results in a call to CTemp_point::set_point. If any data members are affected, they will be mypoint's copy of these members.

```
mypoint.set_point(0, 0, 0);
```

Pointers to Objects

Just as you can have pointers to structures and pointers to variables, you can have pointers to objects in C++. (Remember that structures and variables should be considered to be kinds of objects.)

Many C++ programs make heavy use of pointers to objects. To create objects dynamically, you have to use pointers. This means creating objects on the fly, allocating and freeing them at will, without having to give them the lifetime of a program or even the lifetime of a function call (unlike local variables which must be given the lifetime of a function call).

Although you can create and free objects with the malloc and free library functions, C++ supports the **new** and

delete keywords for dynamic object creation. The **new** keyword returns a pointer. When you use it, you follow it with a type or class name.

```
CStr *pString;
pString = new CStr;
...
delete pString;            // free memory allocated
```

The use of new and delete is strongly preferred over the use of malloc to create objects, because new and delete automatically call constructors and destructors of the class as appropriate. You'll learn about constructors and destructors later in this chapter.

The syntax for using pointers to objects in C++ is a natural extension of that for pointers to structures in C. To refer to a data member, use the -> operator:

ptr->member

Not surprisingly, you can use a similar syntax to call member functions for the object pointed to:

ptr->member_function(args)

Reaping the Benefits of Private Data

If you're reasonably cynical, you may be wondering what's so wonderful about classes and member functions. After all, isn't the member-function technology just so much syntactic sugar? What is the difference between these two function calls?

```
strcpy(string1, "hello");
string1.cpy("hello");
```

The next chapter will show a much more dramatic contrast, but I can describe a major benefit right now: in the standard approach, rewriting any code that implements string handling is dangerous and likely to cause programs to fail. But in the second case, you can rewrite the internals of string objects without causing any errors.

One of the most pressing of all problems in software development is this: how do you fix, update, or alter one part of a program without disrupting all the other parts that interact with it? To some extent, object orientation helps to solve this problem, but only if you follow the Golden Rule of Classes: as long as the type information of public members (both functions and data) is unchanged, you can freely rewrite member-function implementations and any and all private members. By member-function implementations, I mean the function definitions. You can freely rewrite these function definitions as long as you don't change the argument or return types.

The original class declaration of CStr was far from optimal. It can be improved for efficiency and flexibility. The problem is that the current implementation of CStr fixes maximum size at 256 bytes. This limitation may be too small in some cases and overkill in others.

```
class CStr {
    char sData[256];
public:
    char *get(void);
    int  getlength(void);
    void cpy(char *s);
    void cat(char *s);
};
```

Enough of this inefficiency. A superior implementation uses a pointer that can be set to any address. It also stores length as an integer for more efficient reporting of length.

```
class CStr {
    char *pData;
    int  nLength;
public:
    char *get(void);
    int  getlength(void);
    void cpy(char *s);
    void cat(char *s);
};
```

The internal members of CStr have changed dramatically. But because the public declarations haven't changed, the rest of the program won't be affected.

Because sData is gone, all the function definitions must be rewritten. In this implementation, strings are created and re-created as needed through dynamic memory allocation.

```
#include <string.h>
#include <malloc.h>

char *CStr::get(void) {  // Return ptr to string data.
    return pData;
}


int  CStr::getlength(void) { // Return length.
    return nLength;
}


void CStr::cpy(char *s) {   // Copy string arg to
    object.
    int n;

    n = strlen(s);
    if (nLength <> n) {
        if (pData)
                free(pData);
        pData = (char*) malloc(n + 1);
```

```
        nLength = n;
    }
    strcpy(pData, s);
}




void CStr::cat(char *s) {      // Concatenate string arg
    int n;
    char *pTemp;

    n = strlen(s);
    if (n == 0)
        return;
    pTemp = (char*) malloc(n + nLength + 1);
    if (pData) {
        strcpy(pTemp, pData);
        free(pData);
    }
    strcat(pTemp, s);
    pData = pTemp;
    nLength += n;
}
```

Even though many changes were made, all the code that uses the CStr class still works. For example, the following code, used with the previous version of CStr, continues to work correctly without any change:

```
CStr string1, string2;

string1.cpy("My name is ");  // Copy string to string1
string2.cpy("Bill.");        // Copy string to string2
string1.cat(string2.get());  // Concat string2 onto
                             // string1
puts(string1.get());         // Get string1 data and
                             // print
```

But even though the externals of CStr haven't changed, the change to the class has been profound. CStr behaves the same way as before and looks the same to the outside world, but the way it goes about doing things is a thousand times more efficient. The new CStr implementation uses the malloc library function to allocate exactly the amount of bytes needed for the data at any given moment. The next section walks through how these functions work.

We've had a taste of object-oriented magic: you can alter large parts of the class-definition code all you want without worrying about introducing unforeseen errors into the rest of the program.

This magic is called *encapsulation*. It means that certain parts of the object are encapsulated, or protected, from the outside. There must be some interaction with the outside world, of course, or the class is useless. This external part is usually called the *interface*.

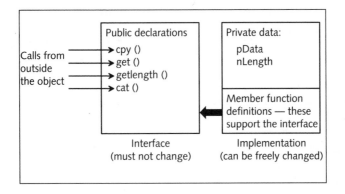

Figure 5.6 Encapsulation in the CStr class.

In standard C, any statements can reach into the internals of a data structure and access any part of it. That's fine until you rewrite the data structure in some way. At that point,

119

your debugging nightmares begin, because all the code any-where that refers to the structure must be rewritten—and in a big program, you've probably forgotten all the places that refer to your data structure! Encapsulation prevents these nightmares.

The Dynamic-Memory Implementation: A Walk-Through

In the last section, I claimed that the new implementation for CStr is much more efficient. This is true even though there is more code to execute.

Specifically, the new class is far more efficient in its use of string memory. Every string occupies exactly the memo-ry it needs at every moment. This memory management is not free: more statements are needed to manage the memo-ry. Yet on the whole, the result is a much better string class. Probably the single greatest benefit is that there is no arbitrary limit of 256 bytes of storage. Beyond that, efficient storage is usually more important than execution speed when you make intensive use of strings.

The cpy and cat functions make use of the malloc library function. This function requests a number of bytes from the operating system; if successful, the function reserves a block of memory for use by the program and then returns a pointer to the beginning of the block. Calls to mal-loc should use this general form:

```
pointer = (base_type *) malloc(total_size_requested);
```

After the memory is no longer needed, you can free this same block by calling the free function:

```
free(pointer);
```

Under our new implementation, the cpy member function copies a new string into the current string data area. But it has an important side effect. If the new string data is longer or shorter than the current string, the current string must grow or expand in size. This is particularly crucial if the new string is longer, because there are no unused bytes in this implementation. Strings cannot grow without corrupting other data.

The solution is to allocate a new block of memory and copy the new data there. The steps are as follows:

1. Get the length of new string data.

2. If the new length is different from the current length, then free the current memory block and allocate a new memory block of the same size as the new string.

3. Copy the new string data into this memory block.

First, the function gets the length of the new string data and stores it in the local variable n:

```
n = strlen(s);
```

Next, this length is compared to the current length, and, if they are not equal, the current string data must grow or shrink to the new size—plus one for the null terminator. The easiest way to do that is to simply throw away (free) the current block and then allocate a new one of the correct size. Finally, the class variable nLength is updated to the new length.

```
if (nLength <> n) {
    if (pData)
            free(pData);
    pData = (char*) malloc(n + 1);
    nLength = n;
}
```

The rest of the function copies the new string data to the object's current string data (pointed to by class variable pData).

```
strcpy(pData, s);
```

The cat (concatenate) member function is a little more complicated. It must create a new memory block but also copy data from the current string data, all before finally concatenating the new string. Without this preliminary work, there would be no room for the object's string data to grow without corrupting other data. The steps are as follows:

1. Get the length of the new string data. Return immediately if this string is zero length, because there's nothing more to do.

2. Allocate a memory block large enough to hold the combined strings.

3. If there is current string data, copy this data to the new memory block. Then free the old memory block.

4. Finally, concatenate the new string and update pData to point to the new memory block. Update nLength as well.

The first three lines get the length of the new string data and return immediately if the length is zero:

```
n = strlen(s);
if (n == 0)
    return;
```

The function then allocates a memory block large enough for the combined strings. Note that one extra byte is allocated to hold the null terminator.

```
pTemp = (char*) malloc(n + nLength + 1);
```

We now have a new memory block, pointed to by pTemp, big enough to hold the combined strings. The next thing to do is to copy the current string data into this block. Then the memory block that held that data is freed:

```
if (pData) {
    strcpy(pTemp, pData);
    free(pData);
}
```

At this point, there is a memory block containing the current string, and it has the extra room needed to concatenate the new string data onto the end. After performing the concatenation, the function ends by updating pData and nLength:

```
strcat(pTemp, s);
pData = pTemp;
nLength += n;
```

Life and Death of an Object: Constructors et al.

The CStr class has a couple of problems. First, until string data is assigned, the pData member doesn't point to anything. This is risky, because the user may expect always to get a meaningful address even if it is only the address of an empty string. But the get function simply returns pData, which might be a null pointer.

```
char *CStr::get(void) {  // Return ptr to string data.
    return pData;
}
```

The best solution is to initialize pData when an object is created. I've been relying on the fact that by default, member variables are initialized to zero or (in the case of pointers) to NULL. But this is not good programming practice.

There's a worse problem. Nothing frees the current memory block when the string is destroyed. The result is a memory leak: every time a string is created, initialized, and destroyed, it leaves behind a hole in memory. If you don't have infinite memory, this could be a problem.

 When an object is defined as local to a function, it's destroyed as soon as the function terminates. Global objects terminate when the program ends.

N O T E

The general problem is that there's a need to take certain actions when the object is created and later when it's destroyed. Fortunately, C++ makes object initialization and cleanup easy by providing *constructors* and *destructors*. These special member functions control how an object is created or destroyed. The naming syntax is unusual: for a given *class*,

- the name of a constructor is *class*, and

- the name of a destructor is ~*class*.

Our string class is named CStr, so the constructor and destructor are named CStr and ~CStr, respectively:

```
class CStr {
    char *pData;
    int  nLength;
public:
    CStr();          // Constructor
    ~CStr();         // Destructor

    char *get(void);
```

124

```
int   getlength(void);
void cpy(char *s);
void cat(char *s);
};
```

Constructors and destructors have some quirks. One quirk is that they have no return type of any kind—not even **void**. This is an apparent exception to the rule that every C++ function must have a return type. Another quirk is that the argument lists are left blank rather than using **void**.

The function definition for the constructor initializes the two class variables as well as allocates a one-byte string that consists of a single null terminator:

```
CStr::CStr() {
    pData = (char *) malloc(1);
    *pData = '\0';
    nLength = 0;
}
```

Odd, isn't it? The name "CStr" appears twice in the function heading. The first occurrence of CStr should be taken together with the scope operator (::) as an indicator that this function is a member of the CStr class. So "CStr::" is a prefix. The second occurrence of CStr is the name of the function itself.

The destructor is simpler. All it has to do is to give the current memory block back to the system by calling the free function. Remember that the name of the function is ~CStr.

```
CStr::~CStr() {
    free(pData);
}
```

Destructors tend to be somewhat cut and dried: all a destructor does, generally, is to free any loose system resources hanging around; then it ends. Constructors, however, have more interesting possibilities. You'll learn more about them in the next chapter, "Another Look at Constructors."

Function Inlining for Fun and Profit

OK, you say, encapsulation sounds wonderful, but it's too inefficient. Remember, encapsulation is the idea that internals such as pData and nLength cannot be accessed from outside. The user of an object has to call public functions to get at the values.

Encapsulation has many benefits, but it also means that you often end up with one-line functions such as these:

```
char *CStr::get(void) {  // Return ptr to string data.
    return pData;
}

int  CStr::getlength(void) { // Return length.
    return nLength;
}
```

There's a certain overhead associated with each function call, so calling a function rather than just getting a value slows down performance. Fortunately, C++ provides an optimal solution: inline functions. The term *inline* refers to expanding something directly into the body of the code (that is, placing it inline) rather than executing a jump via the processor's CALL instruction. For extremely short functions, the inline approach is ideal. In this case, if getlength were an inline function, then the compiler would, in effect, replace this statement:

```
x = string1.getlength();
```

with this:

```
x = string1.nLength;
```

This arrangement eliminates function-call overhead and preserves execution speed.

Normally, this second C++ statement would be illegal (nLength is private and can't be accessed), but because nLength was accessed through a public member, getlength, there is no problem. The inline function approach preserves both encapsulation and efficiency.

In C++, functions are automatically inlined when you place them inside the class declaration. Here this is done for get and getlength:

```
class CStr {
    char *pData;
    int  nLength;
public:
    CStr();              // Constructor
    ~CStr();             // Destructor

    char *get(void) {return pData;}
    int  getlength(void) {return nLength;}
    void cpy(char *s);
    void cat(char *s);
};
```

Despite their brevity, get and getlength are functions and obey almost all the same syntax rules as normal functions do. Each of them could have had more than one statement if you chose, although most inline functions are very short. Note that, as with standard function definitions, the closing brace in these function definitions is *not* followed by a semicolon.

C++ also supports an **inline** keyword so that you can selectively make any function an inline function. But, as I said, it's automatic inside a class declaration.

Structures as a Special Case of Classes

How is a class different from a structure? If you've used structures in C, you'll recall that they're collections of data that can be of varying types. How is this different from a class?

It's tempting to give the answer that classes can have member functions and structures can't—but that's not true. C++ will not only compile all your code that uses **struct**, but it will also let you add member functions to those same structures!

Strangely enough, the only difference between a data type declared with **struct** and one declared with **class** comes down to what's public and what's private. It is not a matter of whether or not it has member functions. In a type declared with **struct**, all the members are public. This is necessary to give C++ maximum compatibility with C. In C, there is no concept of private data, so it's as if everything in C were declared public.

The situation is potentially confusing because the word *class* refers not just to things created with the keyword **class**, but also to things created with **struct** and **union**. Think of structures and unions as special cases of classes in which everything is public. When you use the **class** keyword, everything is private by default—which is the preferred way of creating classes in a language (namely C++) that tries to encourage encapsulation.

Classes in Perspective

This has been a long chapter, yet classes are a simple and elegant idea. A class is a user-defined type in which part of the definition of that type can include the operations that it supports. In other words, you tell me what something is by what it can *do*.

Encapsulation

One of the most important features of C++ classes is encapsulation. This means a clean separation between the interface of a class, which is public to the world, and the internals, which cannot be accessed by anything outside the class. Such a separation is immensely useful, because it means that you can rewrite the internals of the class without messing up the rest of the program. (The revisions must not have obvious errors, but that goes without saying.) In the old world of C, intricate connections between internals throughout a program meant that any revisions at any time—no matter how correct they were in and of themselves—could destabilize the entire system.

I'd like to report that object orientation has eliminated all causes of bugs, but you'd know I was kidding (or drinking something strong). Assiduous use of encapsulation, however, does prevent some causes of bugs.

Classes, Objects, and Instantiation

Another of the key concepts in this chapter is the distinction between classes and objects. A class is a user-defined type; an object is a *thing of that type*. This is not as abstract as it sounds. The class is the general mold or assembly line for a set of objects. The class determines the size, the shape, and all the properties and built-in behavior for each object. Once the class is defined, any number of objects of that class may then be defined and used for whatever purpose the program sees fit.

For each class, the number of objects of that class can range from zero to infinity.

The process of creating an object of a certain class is referred to as *instantiation* (an ugly word). Usually it's easiest to replace the word *instantiation* with the phrase "creating objects of a particular class." A class with zero objects has not been instantiated. The word instantiation is occasionally useful, though, for if a class has not been instantiated it normally has no effect on a program—it's just a Platonic form, a product specification without a prototype. Certain actions are never carried out until a class is instantiated. Yet uninstantiated classes can affect a program indirectly by their relation to other classes. That's something we'll consider in Chapter 8 "Inheritance: C++ and Good Genes."

But, in general, a class without an object is an idea without concrete representation. Or a factory mold that has not yet produced anything.

Classes: Reusing and Publishing

Before concluding this chapter, I should emphasize that classes become truly useful when you are dealing with large programs or creating a new type that is so powerful it can profitably be used in one program after another.

We're on our way to creating just such a useful class with CStr. Once it's finished, it will become a useful language extension that you can use in many programs. There is still work to do, however.

A class is most useful when you can give it to someone else and say, "Here, use this in your own programs." To enable this class-distribution, you should organize your code as follows:

- Place your class declaration in a header file. Header files traditionally contain type information that is needed by every module in a program, so programmers use an **#include** directive to read this type information into each module.

- Place your function definitions (except those that are inline) into a separate file, which you compile. This file called an *implementation* file, typically has a **.CPP** or **.CXX** file extension. Compiling the file produces an object file, which the class user links into his or her program.

The beauty of this division is that you need not share most of your source code with people who use your class if you choose not to. You need only provide the header file and object files containing compiled code. The class users include the header file with each of their modules and then add your object file to the linker command line. They can automate the latter step by the use of make files, projects, or batch files.

With this introduction to classes, you know almost enough to write useful classes you can reuse in many programs. However, even mildly sophisticated classes such as CStr need carefully written copy constructors and operators, topics that are the subject of the next two chapters.

6

Another Look at Constructors

The name is perfectly apt: a *constructor* is a function that manufactures an object. Constructors are as vital to you as factories are to a captain of industry. You may think of constructors simply as initialization functions, but they have important subtleties.

To write your classes correctly, you often need special constructors. One of the most important functions is the *copy constructor*, which tells the class how to pass the object as an argument or return value. As you'll see in the next chapter, code that extends the CStr class is likely to cause errors without a correctly written copy constructor.

This chapter is shorter than Chapter 5. There are only a few key facts you have to keep in mind about constructors, but these facts are vital to your C++ health!

Overloading: Constructors and More Constructors

When you define a string object, you may want to initialize it in a variety of ways. For example, wouldn't it be nice to be able to place any and all of the following in your programs?

```
CStr a, b, c;              // Define with no initial
                           //value.
CStr name("Joe Bloe");     // Initialize from char*.
CStr name2(name);          // Initialize from another
                           //CStr.
```

Or even to combine them on the same line:

```
CStr title("The Big Show");
CStr a, name("Joe"), b(title);
```

Each of these declarations invokes a different constructor. C++ lets you write any number of constructors for the same class, in which each constructor takes a different type of argument or arguments. This is an example of the technique of *function overloading,* which means that the same function name can be reused in different contexts.

Remember that the name of the constructor is always the same as the name of the class itself. Here are the prototypes for the three constructors we need:

```
CStr();             // No initializer.
CStr(char *s);      // Initialize from char*.
CStr(CStr &str);    // Initialize from another CStr.
```

Let's look at the first two constructors first. The third introduces a new operator—the reference operator (&)—and requires special commentary.

The term overloading occurs a good deal in C++ literature. In general, almost any C++ function—not just class functions—can be overloaded. Overloading means that you can reuse the same name and rely on differences in the argument list to distinguish them. Either the number of arguments or the types of arguments (or both) must differ. (Argument names are irrelevant in this case.) For example, C++ considers the following two functions to be different, and each must have its own definition:

Display(int);

Display(char*);

In case it's not obvious, C++ calls a different function—Display(int) or Display(char*)—depending on which type of argument it finds in source code at compile time.

A Tale of Two Constructors

The first constructor is the one originally shown in Chapter 5. This constructor has the task of initializing an empty string:

```
CStr::CStr() {
    pData = (char *) malloc(1);
    *pData = '\0';
    nLength = 0;
}
```

The CStr(char*) constructor, which initializes from a standard C string, is roughly the same length. The basic requirements for CStr constructors are always the same: allocate memory to hold string data, initialize the data, and initialize the nLength data member.

```
CStr::CStr(char *s) {
    pData = (char *) malloc(strlen(s));
    strcpy(pData, s);
    nLength = strlen(s);
}
```

In both cases, the scope operator (CStr::) is used to prefix the constructor name, because these are function definitions and occur outside the CStr declaration.

These constructors are invoked in the following example definitions:

```
CStr string1;               // Invoke CStr()
CStr string2("Hello, C++.");// Invoke CStr(char*)
```

Interlude with the Default Constructor

Before we move on to the third constructor, CStr(CStr&), let's look at a special kind of constructor, the *default constructor*. Surprise! This is actually the first constructor we looked at: the constructor with no arguments.

```
CStr::CStr() {
    pData = (char *) malloc(1);
    *pData = '\0';
    nLength = 0;
}
```

Every class has, or should have, a default constructor. In every class, the default constructor is simply the constructor with no arguments. C++ has an interesting quirk in regard to its handling of constructors:

- If a class declares no constructors of any kind, the compiler supplies a default constructor for free. This is a *hidden constructor*. This function is not sophisticated; it simply initializes all data members to zero. In the case of CStr, this behavior would not be adequate, but it might be sufficient for simpler classes.

- But if you go back and add *any* constructors to the class declaration, the compiler-supplied default constructor goes away. It simply vanishes!

The moral of the story should be clear: you should always include a default constructor, even if that constructor doesn't do anything. This is a form of defensive programming. It ensures that if you go back later and add other constructors, the default constructor won't vanish. (It *will* vanish if you rely on the compiler-supplied default constructor, but it won't vanish if you write your own, no matter how simple.)

Such a default constructor might well do nothing. For example:

```
class CHorse {
    BREED horse_breed;
    char *name;
public:
    CHorse();
};

CHorse::CHorse() {
}
```

The importance of having a default constructor cannot be overemphasized. It so happens that the default constructor is invoked in a number of situations: defining variables with no initial values (already mentioned) as well as declaring an array with uninitialized members.

```
CHorse  posse[30];
```

Default constructors are also invoked when you use the **new** operator—this operator (introduced in the previous chapter) is important in C++ and occurs frequently. If the default constructor is missing, all these situations result in an error.

Given the way I've described the behavior of C++ (making the hidden default constructor vanish as soon as you add your own constructors), it may sound as though the compiler is trying to play a nasty trick on you. Yet the behavior makes sense if you think about it. C++ is designed to be as compatible as possible with C. This includes porting structures from C and considering them classes.

C has no notion of member functions or constructors, but simplistic classes (namely, C struct types) must be ported to C++ and work correctly. This is why the compiler supplies a hidden default constructor: to handle backward-compatibility cases where there are no member functions at all. Once you start defining new classes and writing member functions, however, you should supply your own default constructor.

The Copy Constructor and the Reference Operator (&)

The copy constructor CStr(CStr&) turns out to be another constructor that's difficult to live without. As mentioned earlier, the copy constructor is invoked when you use one object to initialize another object:

```
CStr name("Joe Bloe");
CStr name2(name);          // Call copy constructor.
```

In the first line of code, name is defined and initialized from the string "Joe Bloe". C++ calls the constructor CStr(char*) to initialize this string. Then in the second line, name2 is initialized as a *copy* of name. The object name2 is the same kind of object as name and is to be initialized to contain the same information.

The constructor that tells how to make a copy from the same kind of object is the class's copy constructor. This constructor is very important, because, in addition to variable definition, it is automatically invoked in the following situations:

- When an object of the class is passed by value. C++ calls the class's copy constructor to create a copy of the argument, which is then placed on the stack:

```
void Print_string(CStr str);
```

- When a function returns an object of the class—that is, the class is the return value type. C++ calls the copy constructor to create an object that is handed back to the function caller:

```
CStr Generate_a_name(void);
```

These situations are all too common, so the compiler supplies a hidden copy constructor if you don't provide one. However, this compiler-supplied constructor is simplistic. All it does is to perform a simple member-by-member copy. In some cases, this is fine.

But CStr is a good example of a class in which a simple member-by-member class is inadequate. In fact, the results can be disastrous. Figure 6.1 shows what happens when this approach is used to copy one CStr object to another.

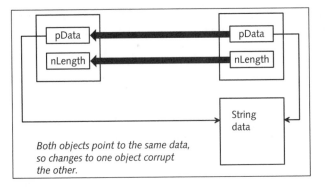

Figure 6.1 Effects of simple a member-by-member copy on CStr objects.

After the member-by-member copying is performed, the second object (name2) has a pointer to the *same memory block* that the first object points to. Such a situation works for now, but any change to either object could invalidate the other object. There are many ways this could happen, but the most obvious occurs if one of the objects is deleted?

```
pString = new CStr;
pString->cpy("John Q. Public");
CStr name2(*pString);
...
delete pString;
puts(name2.get());    // What happens now?
```

The basic idea of copying, I think you'll agree, is that if you lose or destroy the original, the copy should live on and be fully usable. But that's not what happens here. When the copy constructor is invoked (in the third line of this example), it initializes the pointer name2.pData to the same address as pString->pData. When *pString is deleted, the memory block is freed. But name2.pData still points to this same memory block, which is now invalid! What happens with the last line, then, is an illegal memory reference.

Clearly, the copy constructor should do what the CStr(char*) constructor does: allocate a *new* memory block and then make a physical copy of the string data. This copy constructor is easy to write, because it should look almost exactly like CStr(char*). First, however, you need to understand what the reference operator (&) is and how it's used in copy construction. Figure 6.2 illustrates correct copy construction.

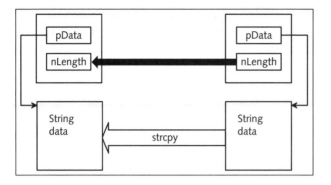

Figure 6.2 Correct implementation of copy construction for CStr.

References: The Address Operator (&) Used in a New Way

To write a copy constructor, you must use the reference operator. This operator uses an ampersand (&), just as the address operator does.

The reference operator isn't the same as the address operator, although both operators have a strong relationship to pointers. C++ may be confusing here because there are a total of three different uses for the ampersand. In addition to being the reference operator and the address operator, it's also used for bitwise AND, a binary operation.

But the reference operator is easy to identify because it occurs in only one place: declarations. The syntax is similar to that of pointers: the ampersand occurs just to the left of a variable or argument name, just as would a pointer symbol (*).

141

In a simple variable definition, the reference operator indicates that one variable is to be used as an alias for another variable.

```
int a;
int & b = a; //b is an alias for a
a = 10;
b++;    // This increments a
```

In this example, the reference operator is used to make b an alias for a. This code is functionally equivalent to the following example, using pointers:

```
int a, *b;
a = 10;
b = &a; // *b is an alias for a
(*b)++; // This increments a
```

If you compare the code examples closely, you'll see one critical difference: when b is defined as a reference (&b), it is not treated as a pointer in the source code. The compiler may implement b as a pointer, but this fact is hidden by the C++ syntax; b looks like a normal integer.

You can use the reference operator (&) simply to create aliases for variables, but the most important uses tend to occur in function calls. Look at the prototype for CStr's copy constructor:

```
CStr(CStr &str);
```

This constructor takes one argument, str, of type CStr&. This indicates that the argument is actually passed as a pointer, but the language syntax pretends that a pointer is not involved. Avoiding the pointer syntax in this case keeps the C++ code much cleaner and simpler.

In simple terms, to make a copy of an object, the copy constructor gets a pointer to the original object and accesses members through that pointer. The object is passed *by reference*, without explicit pointer syntax, just as you might do in Basic, Pascal, or FORTRAN. If you think about it, this passing by reference is required here. If the copy constructor had to get a copy of an object before it could create a copy, then it would have to invoke itself before it ever got started! The result would be a self-defeating infinite regress.

Writing the Copy Constructor

At this point, all you need to remember about the reference operator is this: treat the argument as a value and not a pointer, even though you know it's being passed by reference. The correct copy constructor for CStr is as follows:

```
CStr::CStr(CStr &str) {
    char* s = str.get();
    int n = str.getlength();
    pData = (char *) malloc(n);
    strcpy(pData, s);
    nLength = n;
}
```

This function is similar to the CStr(char*) constructor. The principal difference is that the string data, s, is extracted first. The length is also extracted, because this is more efficient than making a call to strlen.

By the way, the header of the function definition may seem confusing at first. The class name, CStr, is used three times, each time in a slightly different way. Figure 6.3 analyzes and explains each occurrence. The three uses are closely related, but each fulfills a different role in the syntax—scope qualifier, name, or argument type.

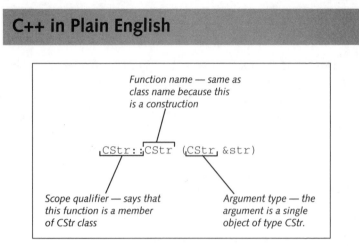

Figure 6.3 Syntax of a copy constructor definition.

The Finishing Touch: The const Keyword

One of the effects of passing by reference is to enable the function to change the argument's value. If you've studied Basic, FORTRAN, or Pascal, you've no doubt learned that this is the main reason for passing an argument by reference.

But the last thing the copy constructor should ever do is to change its argument. Here, passing by reference is for efficiency's sake. One would like to pass by reference but prevent the possibility of ever changing the argument.

Fortunately, C++ provides such a technique—place the **const** keyword in front of the argument declaration:

```
class CStr {

    CStr(const CStr &str);
...
};

// Copy constructor with const arg.
// All the code is the same except for arg declaration.

CStr::CStr(const CStr &str) {
```

144

```
    char* s = str.get();
    int n = str.getlength();
    pData = (char *) malloc(n);
    strcpy(pData, s);
    nLength = n;
}
```

Now the copy constructor cannot change the value of any member of str. Any attempt to assign values to str or any of its data members would be flagged as an error by the compiler. Nor can str be passed to any other function unless that function also takes a **const** argument. Using a **const** argument is the preferred way to write a copy constructor, because it prevents a cause of run-time errors.

Unfortunately, if you attempt to compile the code with this use of **const**, you'll get errors. The problem is that the first two lines of the body of the function make calls through the argument, str: how does the compiler know that these function calls won't corrupt str? The solution is to declare these functions, get and getlength, as **const** functions. Doing so means that these functions have a contract to not change any data members (a condition that does hold in these cases), so they are safe to call for a **const** object:

```
    int getlength(void) const {return nLength;}
    char *get(void) const {return pData;}
```

Whew! This extra work may make **const** seem like more trouble than it's worth, but all the rules make sense, if you think about them. For more information on the fine points of the **const** keyword, see Part III.

Other Constructor Examples

As another example, consider the CTemp_point class introduced in Chapter 5. This class produces objects that record a point on a three-dimensional grid and a temperature at that point. Along with the code in Chapter 5, I've added several constructors:

```
class CTemp_point {
    int     x, y, z;
    double temp;
public:
    CTemp_point();
    CTemp_point(int xx, yy, zz);
    CTemp_point(CTemp_point& pt);

    void set_point(int xx, yy, zz);
    void get_point(int *xx, *yy, *zz);
    void set_temp(double new_temp);
    double get_temp(void);
};
```

The first and third constructors in this declaration are, respectively, the default constructor and the copy constructor. The CTemp_point class is much simpler than the CStr class—there is no dynamic memory to allocate, reallocate, or clean up—so in this case, there is nothing for the default constructor to do. However, for reasons explained earlier, you must include the default constructor. Otherwise, C++ assumes that there is no default constructor and prevents you from (for example) using the **new** operator or declaring uninitialized objects.

The default constructor is easy to write, to put it mildly:

```
CTemp_point::CTemp_point() {
}
```

The next constructor is slightly more interesting. Note that it has three arguments. Constructors may have any number of arguments.

```
CTemp_point::CTemp_point(int xx, int yy, int zz) {
    x = xx;
    y = yy;
```

146

```
    z = zz;
}
```

Finally, the copy constructor initializes an object by copying the data members of its argument, pt. This argument is another object of type CTemp_point. This constructor could be omitted from the program code with no effect, because it performs the same actions (member-by-member copy) as the compiler-supplied copy constructor:

```
CTemp_point::CTemp_point(CTemp_point& pt) {
    x = pt.x;
    y = pt.y;
    z = pt.z;
    temp = pt.temp;
}
```

Each of the following three statements makes a call to one of the three constructors:

```
CTemp_point pt1;
CTemp_point pt2(100, 101, 200);
CTemp_point pt3(pt2);
```

How C++ Calls Constructors (Conversion)

C++ calls constructors in ways you might not expect. Consider the following declarations:

```
CStr name1("John Doe");
CStr name2 = name1;
CStr name3 = "Jane Doe";
```

Clearly, the first declaration results in a call to the constructor CStr(char*). More surprising, the second declaration also calls the copy constructor. This is not obvious. You might think that the second statement creates name2 by calling the default constructor and then performs an assignment from name1 to name2. However, it doesn't do either of these things. The following declarations are exactly equivalent, not only in ultimate effect but also in the way constructors are called:

```
CStr name2 = name1;
CStr name2(name1);
```

In C++, assignment and initialization are sharply distinguished (there is no overlap) even though they look much the same. Except in a variable definition, the equal sign (=) always indicates assignment. Within a variable definition, however, the equal sign always indicates initialization, which results in a call to the appropriate constructor and not to the assignment operator.

As you'll discover in the next chapter, assignment is an operator whose behavior you can define. It is not the same as the copy constructor. One would expect the copy constructor and the assignment operator to do the same thing, but this is not true in all cases. (The main difference is that a copy constructor cannot assume that an object was previously initialized and may therefore have to do a little more work.)

Similarly, the final declaration calls the constructor CStr(char*):

```
CStr name3 = "Jane Doe";
```

There's another case in which constructors are called: conversion from other data types to the class in question (in this case, CStr). A constructor does double duty as a conversion function whenever the following conditions are met: there is exactly one argument, and the type is not the same as the class itself. (In other words, the copy constructor is not a conversion function.)

The constructor CStr(char*) tells the compiler how to convert a **char*** string into a CStr object. Consequently, you can use a **char*** string wherever a CStr object is expected, and the compiler will convert it for you. For example:

```
CStr make_uppercase(CStr s);   // prototype

CStr string1;
string1 = make_uppercase("cia/fbi");
```

The last line of this code sequence makes a call to the constructor CStr(char*) to create a CStr object from the string "cia/fbi". The resulting object is then passed to the function convert_to_upper.

Summary: the Key Points of Construction

Constructors may seem like a trivial topic at first, but as it turns out, there are important things to say about them. The major points are summarized in the next few sections.

Overloaded Constructors

The name of a constructor is always that of the class itself. So for the CStr class, every constructor is named CStr. There is no return type, not even void.

As with most C++ functions, constructors can be overloaded. This means that you can reuse the same name with different argument lists (in this case, only the number and types of the arguments matter). The significance for this chapter is that you can create a number of constructors, each of which uses a different argument or arguments to initialize an object.

The Default Constructor

class( );

One of the most important constructors is the default constructor—which for any given class is the constructor that has no arguments. This constructor is called when you define an object without initialization, create an uninitialized array of objects, or use the **new** operator. The compiler is a little deceptive because it creates a hidden default constructor for you, unless you add any constructors of your own, in which case the hidden default constructor goes away. This is why, you should write your own default constructor, even if it doesn't do much.

The Copy Constructor

class(*class***&**);

The copy constructor is another constructor of great importance for each class. Its most obvious use is to initialize an object from another object of the same type. But this constructor is also called when you pass the type by value or you use the type as the return value in a function call. The compiler always supplies a hidden copy constructor if you don't. Remember, though, that this compiler-supplied constructor performs a simple member-by-member copy that for a class such as CStr, is inadequate. If in doubt, write your own constructor.

The argument to a copy constructor uses the reference operator (&), which means to pass by reference as in Basic or FORTRAN—without pointer syntax.

Initialization and Conversion

Object definition and initialization always invoke constructors, even when they use the equal sign (=). In this context, the equal sign does not mean exactly the same thing as assignment.

```
CStr string1 = "Hi world!";  // Call CStr(char*)
```

Another case in which constructors are automatically invoked is in type conversion. Given the constructor CStr(char*), you can pass a **char*** argument where CStr is expected, and the compiler performs the conversion for you.

With preliminaries such as classes and constructors out of the way, we can move on to one of the most interesting, time-saving aspects of C++: operator overloading.

7

Class Operations
(Operator Overloading)

Operator overloading enables you to define the meaning of operators such as +, -, *, and / when applied to your class. There are few C++ operators you cannot define for your class, a fact that makes C++ perhaps more flexible than any other programming language you've ever seen.

In general, *overloading* is the reuse of a name or a symbol in a new context. For example, the compiler handles integer addition and floating-point addition differently, although you may not be aware of it. With the CStr class, addition should mean something different from both integer and floating-point addition. This chapter will define CStr addition to mean concatenation of strings.

With C++, you write *operator functions* to define how each operator works. If you don't write an addition operator function for the class, attempting to use the plus sign (+) with objects of the class results in an error.

The Basic Syntax

There are a number of subtle twists and turns when it comes to operator functions, but the basic syntax is simple. For a given operator @, the name of the operator function is:

```
operator@
```

So, for example, operator functions for +, -, *, and / have the following names:

```
operator+
operator-
operator*
operator/
```

This looks deceptively simple, and you probably suspect that there's more to this operator business. To begin with, what are the arguments? The answer depends on a couple of factors:

- Is the operation binary or unary? (Note that some operators, such as the minus sign, can go both ways.)

- If the operation is binary, do you want to support the occurrence of objects on either side of the operator? For example, do you want to support both *string + cstr_object* and *cstr_object + string*? If you do, you need to use friend functions. (These global functions are given access to the class through use of the **friend** keyword.)

It's beginning to get more complicated, but this chapter will explain esoteric concepts such as friend functions. In any case, here is the proper syntax for the addition functions:

```
class CStr {
...
    CStr friend operator+(CStr str1, CStr str2);
    CStr friend operator+(CStr str, char *s);
    CStr friend operator+(char *s, CStr str);
};

CStr operator+(CStr str1, CStr str2) {
...
}

CStr operator+(CStr str, char *s) {
```

```
...
}

CStr operator+(char *s, CStr str) {
...
}
```

You should be able to see a strong connection between function overloading and operator overloading here. There can be many functions named operator+. What differentiates these functions is their argument lists. The operator+ functions that have one or more CStr arguments are the ones that define how addition works with CStr objects.

Writing the Addition (+) Operator Function

The following definition successfully implements the addition of two CStr objects. Each of the arguments represents an operand in the expression *str1+str2*.

```
CStr operator+(CStr str1, CStr str2) {
    CStr new_string(str1);
    new_string.cat(str2.get());
    return new_string;
}
```

CStr appears at the beginning of the function heading as the return-value type. To return a CStr result, the operator+ function definition creates an entirely new CStr object in the first line:

```
    CStr new_string(str1);
```

This statement calls the copy constructor to initialize new_string as an exact copy of str1, the first operand. The next statement concatenates the second operand, str2, onto the end of new_string. This process produces the very string we wanted to build.

```
new_string.cat(str2.get());
```

The final task is to pass the new string as the return value.

```
return new_string;
```

This statement makes a copy of new_string before it goes out of scope and is destroyed. As explained in Chapter 6, the compiler automatically invokes the copy constructor, CStr(CStr&), to create the return-value copy. This same return-value object is placed on the stack, where the caller can access it.

With a sophisticated class such as CStr, returning a value would fail without a correctly written copy constructor. The hidden copy constructor supplied by the compiler would perform a straight member-by-member copy that would result in errors. That's why I introduced the subject of copy construction first (in Chapter 6) before describing how operator overloading works.

The Mechanics of Calling an Operator Function

When C++ sees an expression such as str1 + str2, it translates the expression into the appropriate function call. Figure 7.1 illustrates how this works. If the function call did not exist, it would report an error at compile time saying that the operation was not defined.

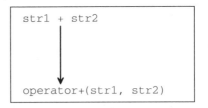

Figure 7.1 Translation of an expression.

The following code shows an example of how string addition might be used. Each of the following statements is an object definition. The last uses statement carries out an addition operation (calling the operator+ function) to produce a CStr value. That value is then used to initialize the object name by means of the copy constructor.

```
CStr first("Archie ");
CStr last("Leach");
CStr name(first + last);
```

Figure 7.2 illustrates how the addition operation works. Note that the value of the expression, first + last, is stored in a separate CStr object. The operator+ function creates this object and then returns it as a CStr object containing "Archie Leach". This is a temporary object, and the compiler will destroy it when it is no longer needed.

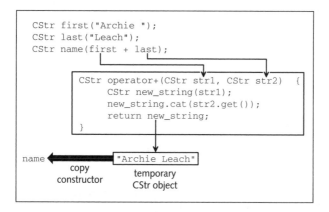

Figure 7.2 Mechanics of a call to operator+.

And the Rest... (Other Addition Functions)

The other operator+ functions for the CStr class look similar to the first operator+ function shown in the previous two sections.

157

```
CStr operator+(CStr str, char *s) {
    CStr new_string(str);
    new_string.cat(s);
    return new_string;
}

CStr operator+(char *s, CStr str) {
    CStr new_string(s);
    new_string.cat(str.get());
    return new_string;
}
```

All these operator+ functions look similar. In every case, the general procedure for evaluating string addition is basically the same:

1. Create a new CStr object, initialized with the contents of the first operand.

2. Concatenate the contents of the second operand.

3. Return the resulting CStr object.

Who Needs Friends?

All the operator functions discussed so far have been declared with the **friend** keyword within the CStr class. Normally, functions not declared in a class have access only to the public members. The **friend** keyword offers a way around this restriction. A function declared as a friend to a given class has access to all members in the class and not just to those that are public. The function may be a global function—that is, not declared within any class—or a function that is a member of a different class.

For example, the function setbk is a friend of the class CBook; this enables it to access private members of the class: a, b, and c.

```
class CBook {
    int a, b, c;
    friend void setbk(CBook bk, int x, int y, int z);
};

void setbk(CBook bk, int x, int y, int z) {
    bk.a = x;
    bk.b = y;
    bk.c = z;
}
```

The purpose of friend functions is to make possible functions such as operator+(char*, CStr). You can implement operator functions as member functions, but such functions assume that an object of the class appears on the *left* side of the operator. Along this line, the function operator+(CStr, char*) could have been written this way:

```
class CStr {
...
    CStr operator+(char *s);
}

CStr CStr::operator+(char *s){
    CStr new_string(*this);
    new_string.cat(s);
    return new_string;
}
```

The first statement in the body of the definition initializes the new string with an object referred to as ***this**. The value of ***this** is none other than the left operand. To understand how the code works, remember that this approach to defining addition translates an expression as shown in Figure 7.3.

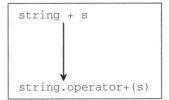

Figure 7.3 Translation of operation into a member function call.

With this approach, addition is translated into a member function called *through the left operand*, which is a CStr object. In C++, the **this** keyword is a pointer to the current object, and ***this** refers to the object itself. So the first statement initializes new_string to the contents of the left operand by referring to ***this**.

```
CStr new_string(*this);
```

I'll have more to say about the **this** keyword later in this chapter and in Part III.

In any case, the problem with writing operator functions this way is that it restricts you to always having your class object on the left side of the operator. Only with nonmember functions is it possible to write a function that tells how to evaluate

```
s + string
```

reversing the operands shown earlier. For this reason, binary operators are usually implemented as friend functions and not member functions. (Binary operators should be friends so that the function can access private data if needed.) That's the approach I adopted at the beginning of the chapter:

```
class CStr {
...
```

```
CStr friend operator+(CStr str1, CStr str2);
CStr friend operator+(CStr str, char *s);
CStr friend operator+(char *s, CStr str);
};
```

An exception to the use of friends is the assignment operator, which must be implemented as a member function and not a friend—as you'll see in the next section.

Writing the Assignment Function

Assignment (=) is another one of those operations for which the compiler supplies a default, hidden function. As a general rule, assignment between objects of the same type is always supported in C++, just as direct assignment between structures is supported in standard C. Therefore, statements such as the following are valid:

```
CStr string1, string2;
...
string1 = string2;    // Assign value of string2 to
                      // string1
```

 It's possible to avoid assignment altogether if you want to: define an assignment operator function and then NOTE make it private to the class.

However, as with copy construction, the compiler-supplied assignment behavior is inadequate for a class such as CStr, which uses dynamic-memory allocation. This default behavior is a simple member-by-member copying. As pointed out in Chapter 6, this behavior can lead to major errors.

Therefore, when you write a class such as CStr, defining the behavior of the assignment operator is important. The assignment operator function must be a member of the class, with the following prototype within the class declaration:

```
class& operator=(const class &arg);
```

The argument name is optional. The corresponding function definition has the following syntax:

```
class& class::operator=(const class &arg) {
    statements
}
```

In the CStr class, the assignment operator function could have the following prototype. The only aspect of this declaration that you have a choice about is the argument name.

```
class CStr {
...
    CStr& operator=(const CStr &source);
};
```

The assignment operator declaration can be intimidating to C++ beginners, because so much of it uses syntax elements not found in C. All the syntax elements have been introduced in this and previous chapters. But it may help a to review them. Figure 7.4 analyzes the syntax of the CStr-to-CStr assignment function.

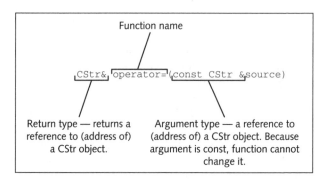

Figure 7.4 Analysis of an assignment operator declaration.

The Assignment Function Definition

The assignment function turns out to be trivial to write once you understand all the syntax. Here's the shortest version of this function:

```
CStr& CStr::operator=(const CStr &source) {
    cpy(source.get());
    return *this;
}
```

The function doesn't need to be any longer than this; it works perfectly well. In fact, this function is so short that it is a good candidate for function inlining. The definition can be given in the CStr declaration.

```
class CStr {
...
    CStr& operator=(const CStr &source)
        {cpy(source.get()); return *this;}
};
```

In either case, the two statements in the body of the function definition are almost trivial. The first statement calls the cpy function, which already exists, to do the copying. The second statement returns the object itself—that is, the same CStr object that is the target of the assignment. In effect, the statement **return *this** says:

```
Return myself!
```

Figure 7.5 illustrates how C++ translates an assignment expression. Note that this function is called through str1, the left operand. This fact becomes important in the next section, when we look more closely at the **this** keyword.

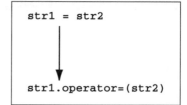

Figure 7.5 Translation of an assignment expression.

The this Pointer and Its Uses

Within a member function, the **this** keyword is a pointer to the current object. (By "current object," I mean the object through which the function was called.) Every time you call a member function, C++ passes a hidden **this** pointer as an argument (see Figure 7.6).

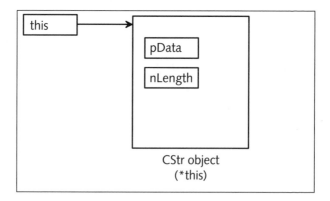

Figure 7.6 The "this" pointer as used with the CStr class.

Within the member-function definition, references to a data member are automatically translated into object-member references using the **this** pointer, as shown in Table 7.1. Many member functions never use the **this** pointer, because its use within the function is implicit.

Table 7.1 Implicit use of "this" pointer.

DATA MEMBER REFERENCE	TRANSLATED IN A MEMBER FUNCTION TO:
pData	this->pData
nLength	this->nLength

Sometimes you need to refer explicitly to the object, and then using **this** is necessary. Such is the case with assignment functions. Assignment expressions in C and C++ return a value: that of the left operand. The fact that assignments return a value makes possible the following kinds of statements:

```
int     x, y, z;
CString stringA, stringB, stringC;

x = y = z = 0;
stringA = stringB = stringC = "hello!";
```

After "hello!" is assigned to stringC, the expression stringC = "hello" returns the resulting value of the stringC, which is then assigned to stringB. An assignment function must therefore return the value of the left operand after it is assigned a value. The consequence for writing the code is this: the final task of the assignment function must do is return the value of the left operand.

But remember that the assignment function is called as *a member function of the left operand*. The left operand is the current object (the object through which the function was called). Therefore—if you're still following me—in implementing assignment, the final task of an object is to return itself. Here's how you express this idea in C++:

```
return *this;
```

Earlier I said that **this** is a pointer to the current object. Therefore, ***this** refers to the object itself.

Assignments and the Reference Operator (&)

The reference operator (&) is necessary in assignment operator syntax, because it is the only way to support assignment operator syntax (which uses values and not pointers to the objects) and yet do so efficiently. C++ carries out a multiple assignment statement by transferring data from one object to another without creating extra copies. Were it not for the reference operator, many extra copies would have to be made and then thrown away.

Figure 7.7 illustrates how assignment between two CStr objects would work. The return value is a pointer to the object on the left. (In source code, a value is returned, but the reference operator causes the compiler to implement this by returning a pointer.) In multiple assignment, the pointer returned would immediately become the argument for the next assignment to be performed.

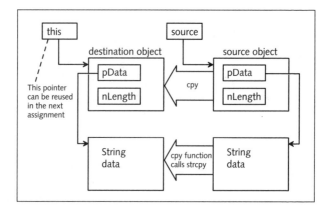

Figure 7.7 Mechanics of a CStr assignment.

Writing a Conversion Function

The CStr class is now extremely flexible and easy to use. You can, for example, use it to concatenate and assign expressions, just as with strings in Basic.

```
CStr first = "Norma"
CStr middle = "Jean"
CStr last = "Baker"
CStr name;

name = first + " " + middle + " " + last;
```

Before we leave the CStr example, there's at least one other ability it would be useful to give it. In the best of all worlds, you should to be able to use the class wherever **char*** is expected. For example, puts is one of many standard library functions that take a **char*** argument. It would be convenient to pass a CStr object to this function and have it print the contents, just as it would with a **char*** argument.

```
#include <stdio.h>

CStr warn = "This is your final warning";
puts(warn);             // puts takes a char* argument
```

In C++, you can get this functionality by writing a *conversion function*. This function tells the compiler how to convert an object of the class to another type. It's easy to get confused here, because as I pointed out in Chapter 6, constructors also perform conversion. But there's no contradiction. Whether the compiler calls a conversion function or a constructor depends on the *direction* of the conversion.

For any given class, conversion functions handle outgoing conversions (convert *to* another type). Constructors handle incoming conversions (convert *from* another type).

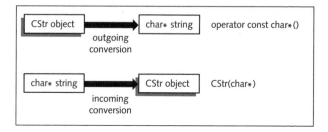

Figure 7.8 Conversion and constructor functions compared.

The conversion function is a member function declared as follows within the class declaration. The declaration has no return type and no arguments.

```
operator type ()
```

Converting from a CStr object to **char*** is easy, because all the function has to do is to extract the data pointer. The following code declares a conversion function within the CStr class declaration. Function inlining is used because the definition is so short.

```
class CStr {
    ...
    operator const char*() {return get();}
};
```

I used **const char*** as the conversion type here rather than **char***. These types are the same except that the result of a **const char*** conversion cannot be modified in code, and it can be passed only to a function taking a **const char*** argument. The bottom line is that CStr objects can be given as arguments where **const char*** is expected but not where a simple **char*** is expected.

Most string-handling functions in the standard C++ library (including puts) take a **const char*** argument unless they write to the string, in which case they take a **char*** argument. Because of the way memory allocation works in CStr, it would be dangerous to allow direct modification of the string data through the pointer to the actual memory block (pData). The fact that the conversion is to **const char*** prevents such direct modification.

The CStr Class in Summary

We've come a long way been through a lot with the CStr class, gradually building it up over the course of three chapters. I've used the CStr class to introduce many of the core concepts in C++. If you understand these concepts, the CStr class is not difficult to write.

You might question whether writing such a class is worth all the work involved. If you were going to create only a few instances of this class and then never use it again, you probably wouldn't want to spend the time to create such a class as CStr, with its feature set that includes memory management, multiple constructors, and built-in operators.

But if you design such a class carefully enough, you can use it in many programs. If you think of the class as an extension to the C++ language, Cstr becomes highly cost-effective. You can define CStr objects in any program, as long as you do the following:

- Include the appropriate header file, **CSTR.H**, in each source module that refers to the CStr class.

- During a build, link in **CSTR.OBJ** (or an appropriate object file name), which should contain the implementations for CStr member functions in compiled form. Alternatively, you can use your system's library-management utility, if one is available, to link **CSTR.OBJ** into the standard library.

Here are the final contents of the **CSTR.H** file, declaring all the members of the CStr class presented until now.

```
// CSTR.H — Declaration of the CStr class

class CStr {
    char *pData;
    int  nLength;
public:
    CStr();             // Constructors
    CStr(char *s);
    CStr(const CStr &str);
    ~CStr();            // Destructor

    char *get(void) const {return pData;}
    int  getlength(void) const {return nLength;}
    void cpy(char *s);
    void cat(char *s);

    friend CStr operator+(CStr str1, CStr str2);
    friend CStr operator+(CStr str, char *s);
    friend CStr operator+(char *s, CStr str);

    CStr& operator=(const CStr &source)
        {cpy(source.get()); return *this;}
};
```

Three of the member functions are defined in the CStr declaration as inline functions. Because they are defined in the class declaration, they don't need to be defined in **CSTR.CPP**, the implementation file for the class.

CSTR.CPP contains the remaining definitions. You would compile this code and link the resulting object file into any project that needed to use the class.

```
// CSTR.CPP — implementation of CStr class

#include "cstr.h"
#include <string.h>
#include <malloc.h>

CStr::CStr() {
    pData = (char *) malloc(1);
    *pData = '\0';
    nLength = 0;
}

CStr::CStr(char *s) {
    pData = (char *) malloc(strlen(s));
    strcpy(pData, s);
    nLength = strlen(s);
}

CStr::CStr(CStr& s) {
    char* sz = s.get();
    int n = s.getlength();
    pData = (char *) malloc(n);
    strcpy(pData, sz);
    nLength = n;
}

CStr::~CStr() {
    free(pData);
}

void CStr::cpy(char *s) {    // Copy string arg to
    object.
    int n;
```

```
        n = strlen(s);
        if (nLength <> n) {
            if (pData)
                free(pData);
            pData = (char*) malloc(n + 1);
            nLength = n;
        }
        strcpy(pData, s);
}


void CStr::cat(char *s) {    // Concatenate string arg
    int n;
    char *pTemp;

    n = strlen(s);
    if (n == 0)
        return;
    pTemp = (char*) malloc(n + nLength + 1);
    if (pData) {
        strcpy(pTemp, pData);
        free(pData);
    }
    strcat(pTemp, s);
    pData = pTemp;
    nLength += n;
}


CStr operator+(CStr str1, CStr str2) {
    CStr new_string(str1);
    new_string.cat(str2.get());
    return new_string;
}


CStr operator+(CStr str, char *s) {
    CStr new_string(str);
    new_string.cat(s);
    return new_string;
}
```

```
CStr operator+(char *s, CStr str) {
    CStr new_string(s);
    new_string.cat(str.get());
    return new_string;
}
```

Another Class Operator Example

Before leaving the subject of operator overloading, let's look at another example that uses operator functions: the CTemp_point class first introduced in Chapter 5. This class specifies a point on a three-dimensional grid, along with a temperature value. Some of the member functions are much easier to implement than CStr is, because the CTemp_point class does not involve memory allocation.

```
class CTemp_point {
    int    x, y, z;
    double temp;
public:
    CTemp_point();
    CTemp_point(int xx, yy, zz);
    CTemp_point(CTemp_point &pt);

    void set_point(int xx, yy, zz);
    void get_point(int *xx, *yy, *zz);
    void set_temp(double new_temp);
    double get_temp(void);

    CTemp_point operator+(double temp_diff);
    CTemp_point operator-(double temp_diff);
    CTemp_point& operator=(const CTemp_point &pt);
};
```

When you design a class, one of the most important tasks is to decide which operations make sense. In the case of the CStr class, it made sense to define addition as an operation between two strings that produces another string. In the case of the CTemp_point class, it isn't so clear what addition should do. What would it mean to add together two points on a grid? (The operation would be meaningful if one of the points were interpreted as a vector or a size, but you might consider creating a separate vector class for that purpose.)

For the CTemp_point class, I defined only one simple operation each for addition and subtraction. These operations add or subtract from the temperature data member (temp) and leave the grid coordinates untouched. Note that these functions support only the adding or subtracting of floating-point numbers (or values, such as integers, that the compiler knows how to convert to floating point):

```
pt1 = pt2 + 33.3;     // Ok; addition to flt pt defined
pt2 = pt2 + 1;        // Ok: 1 can be converted to
                      //floating pt
pt2 = pt1 + pt3;      // ERROR! Operation not defined
```

Like the CStr addition functions, these operator functions return an object by value. Consequently, they follow the same basic steps: create a new object, set some values, and return the object as a value. (The last step implicitly calls the class's copy constructor.)

```
CTemp_point CTemp_point::operator+(double temp_diff) {
    CTemp_point new_pt(*this);
    new_pt.temp += temp_diff;
    return new_pt;
}
CTemp_point CTemp_point::operator-(double temp_diff) {
    CTemp_point new_pt(*this);
    new_pt.temp -= temp_diff;
    return new_pt;
}
```

The last function I added to the class is the assignment operator. This function is unnecessary, because it implements assignment in the same way that the compiler would implement assignment by default. However, it's still useful as an example. This approach uses a simple member-by-member copy from the right operand (translated into the argument, pt) to the left operand (the object through which the function is called). As with almost all assignment functions, the last line of the function is **return *this**.

```
CTemp_point& CTemp_point::operator=(const CTemp_point
    &pt) {
    x = pt.x;
    y = pt.y;
    z = pt.z;
    temp = pt.temp;
    return *this;
}
```

Forging Ahead with Operator Overloading

Believe it or not, we've only started covering the subject of operator overloading. The subject has a number of fine points (some of which you may not use for years) that I'll leave for Part II. But there are some major points that you should keep in mind when experimenting with operator functions. This section is both a summary and an overview of some points not yet covered.

Using the this Pointer

Many operator functions use **this**, a C++ keyword not supported in C. Within a member function, **this** is a pointer to the current object. (In this context, "current object" is the object through which the function was called.) The keyword is often useful in operator functions, because it provides a way to apply the copy constructor to the current object or return the current object as a value.

Naming an Operator Function

Operator functions follow a simple naming scheme. For any given operator @, the name of the function is **operator@**. The exception is conversion functions, for which the name is:

```
operator type
```

Binary Operators

When the compiler evaluates an expression of the form *obj1@obj2*, it translates the expression into the function call:

```
obj1.operator@(obj2)
```

if this function is defined within *obj1*'s class, or the compiler translates the expression into the function call:

```
operator@(obj1, obj2)
```

in which the function is defined outside any class. Declaring it as a friend of a class gives the function access to all members.

The advantage of using the latter form is that it makes it possible to implement the same operation regardless of whether *obj1* appears on the right or the left of the operator. To support the reverse order, write a separate function:

```
operator@(obj2, obj1)
```

If the declaration of *obj2*'s class is supplied by someone else (for example, if *obj2* has a standard type such as **int** or **char***), this is the only way to define this operation.

Unary Operators

When the compiler evaluates an expression of the form @*obj1*, it translates the expression into the function call:

```
obj1.operator@()
```

if this function is defined within *obj1*'s class, or the compiler translates the expression into the function call:

```
operator@(obj1)
```

in which the function is defined outside any class. Declaring it as a friend of a class gives the function access to all members.

As an example, unary minus (-) can be defined for the CTemp_point class, in which the effect is to reverse the sign of the temp data member:

```
class CTemp_point {
    ...
    CTemp_point operator-();
};

CTemp_point CTemp_point::operator-() {
    CTemp_point new_point(*this);
    new_point.temp *= -1;
    return new_point;
}
```

As with all operator functions (except conversion), the return type must be declared explicitly. The compiler can make no assumptions here. You can define an operation on class A, for example, so that it returns an object of any type you wish.

The Assignment Operator

The assignment operator defines how to assign an object from another object of the same class. Although assignment is a binary operator like any other, it has some special restrictions. The assignment function must be defined as a member function with the following declaration:

```
class& operator=(const class &arg)
```

The function is called as a member function of the left operand of an assignment, and the right operand is the argument. The final task of an assignment function is to return the left operand, which it does by using the **this** pointer:

```
return *this;
```

Assignment from Other Types

An assignment function determines how the compiler assigns a value to an object from another object of the same class. There is no valid assignment function that involves assignment from another type. Instead, the compiler calls the appropriate constructor or conversion function, if available, to convert from one data type to another.

```
CHorse stacy, sugar;

stacy = sugar;        // Calls CHorse::operator=
stacy = "fast";       // Calls CHorse::CHorse(char*)
*char name = sugar;   // Calls CHorse::operator char*
```

Other Assignment Operators (+=, -=, etc.)

You might think that if you define both addition (+) and assignment (=) for a given class, the addition-assignment operator (+=) is automatically defined, but this is not the case. Each assignment operator (such as +=, -=, *=, and so on) is considered a separate operator, and if you want to support it, you need to write another function. For example, the following code implements += for the CStr class. (Because of its small size, by the way, it is a good candidate for function inlining.)

```
class CStr {
    ...
    CStr& operator+=(CStr &str);
};

CStr& CStr::operator+=(CStr &str) {
    cat(str.get());
    return *this;
}
```

Associativity, Precedence, and Commutativity

The rules of *associativity* and *precedence* determine which operations are performed before others. C++ follows the standard rules when you define operators for your own classes—in other words, C++ applies the same associativity and precedence rules to your class that it applies to standard types such as **int** and **float**. For example, suppose you have defined both addition (+) and multiplication (*) between CStr objects and that the compiler is evaluating the following statements:

```
CStr stringA, stringB, stringC;
stringA = stringA * stringB + stringA * stringC;
```

The compiler evaluates this last statement as though it were written as:

```
stringA = (stringA * stringB) + (stringA * stringC);
```

Commutativity is a property some operators have in which the left-to-right order of the operands does not matter. Not all C++ operators have this property, but addition and multiplication do when applied to the standard types. However, commutativity of addition and multiplication does not automatically extend to user-defined classes. These operations are commutative only if you write them that way. Furthermore, you have to write operations such as operator+(CStr, char*) and operator+(char*, CStr) as separate functions, although it is legal to save space by having one function call the other.

```
CStr operator+(char* s, CStr &str) {
    return operator+(str, s);
}
```

8

Inheritance: C++ and Good Genes

Inheritance is all about software reuse, C++'s greatest promise. Never write the same piece of code twice! Make exponential gains in productivity! Of course, it's not quite that easy. But if you're thinking about reusable components, inheritance provides a convenient, time-saving way of packaging them.

Beyond that, inheritance provides the underlying structure for *virtual functions*. I'll talk about virtual functions in the next chapter.

As much as any C++ buzzword, *inheritance* seems to metaphorically endow objects with life. After all, isn't inheritance a property of living things? That would be going too far, but inheritance, as you'll see, does allow you to develop a useful hierarchy that goes from the general to the specific—much like a deity or Darwin (take your pick).

Return to CStr: A Software Dilemma

If you've been reading the chapters of this book sequentially, you know about the CStr class and how to write it. Let's assume for a moment, though, that someone else developed the CStr class and then sold you the right to use the software. Typically, here's what you are provided with:

- A header file containing the class declaration.

- An object-file (**.OBJ** file) containing the implementations of member functions of the class in compiled form.

The second item includes implementations of all functions except those defined in the class declaration. The latter are inline functions.

Most of the source code is not available. The provider or vendor of a class is under no obligation to provide the C++ code beyond the class declaration. There are often good reasons for not providing the source code for functions. Vendors may not wish others to see all the details of their programming techniques.

All this is fine as long as the class does exactly what you want it to do. But suppose you want to modify or add to some aspect of the class behavior. What do you do with the CStr class? Must you limit yourself to the behavior of the class or write your own CStr class from scratch? Fortunately, better alternatives are available. One alternative is to create a class that contains a CStr object as a member; in such an approach you're essentially building an outer class around the CStr class.

But a better alternative, in light of the amount of work required, is to use inheritance. This means creating a new class and deriving it from CStr. In *deriving* one class from another, you include all the members of the first class (called the *base class*) and then add more members. Another term for this is *inheriting* from the base class.

Ultimately, deriving a class has an effect similar to building one class around another: you get all the built-in functionality and add your own. The effect is about the same, but the inheritance syntax potentially saves you a great deal of work.

Son of CStr (Or Is It "Daughter"?)

The final version of the CStr class—summarized in Chapter 7, "Class Operations"—supported a number of useful functions and operations, including those shown in Table 8.1.

Table 8.1 Functions and operations of the CStr class.

FUNCTION OR OPERATION	DESCRIPTION
get	Return pointer to null-terminated string data.
getlength	Return length of string data.
cpy	Copy string from **char*** argument.
cat	Concatenate **char*** argument onto current string data.
+	Concatenate two strings, of which at least one is a CStr object. The other may be a CStr object or a **char***.
=	Copy string data from another CStr object.

The class also supports a number of useful constructors. Let's assume that you'd like to retain all this functionality as well as add the following:

- output, which would print string data to standard output.

- input, which would input a string from standard input.

Deriving a class through inheritance makes it easy to add this functionality without access to the original CStr code and without having to rewrite any of the CStr class. The next section introduces the syntax.

Derived Class Syntax

Assume that a class *Parent_class* has already been declared. The following syntax derives *Class_class* from *Parent_class*; this means that *Child_class* has all the members defined in *Parent_class* in addition to any declarations of its own.

class *Child_class* : **public** *Parent_class* {
    declarations

};

The only part that is new here is the colon (:) and the syntax that follows:

public *Parent_class*

In this context, **public** is the base-class access specifier. Alternatively, you can specify either **private** or **protected**. In the majority of cases, **public** suffices. For information about the effect of the other keywords, see the topic "Base-Class Access" in Part II.

The declarations for *Child_class* include the new members to be added to the declarations in *Parent_class*. For example, the following declaration creates CIoStr as a class derived from CStr. CIoStr contains all the CStr members in addition to the member functions input and output.

```
// CIOSTR.H — declaration of the CIOStr class

#include "cstr.h"

class CIoStr : public CStr {
public:
    void input(void);
    void output(void);
};
```

Note that the file **CSTR.H** is included, which results in CStr being declared before CIoStr. A class must be declared before you can derive another class from it.

Given this declaration of the CIoStr class, you can use CIoStr to declare objects just as you can with CStr. These objects support two new functions—input and output—in addition to all the functions supported by a CStr object. For example:

```
CIoStr iostring1, iostring2, iostring3;

iostring1 = "This is a new string";
iostring2 = iostring1 + ".";
iostring2.output();
iostring1.input();
iostring3.cpy(iostring1);
```

Writing Functions for the New Class

CIoStr follows the same rules that any class follows for implementing member functions: for each member function, you can either define the function inside the class declaration (in which case it is automatically an inline function), or you can define the function outside the declaration. In the latter case, you use CIoStr:: to prefix the name.

The definitions of the new CIoStr functions are simple.

```
#include <stdio.h>
#include "ciostr.h"

void CIoStr::output(void) {
    printf("%s", get());
}
```

```
void CIoStr::input(void) {
    char buffer[256];

    gets(buffer);
    cpy(buffer);
}
```

Only two functions (input and output) are defined here; these functions are defined with the CIoStr:: prefix. Many other functions are inherited from the base class CStr, all of them were defined with the CStr:: prefix. For example:

```
void CStr::cpy(char *s) {    // Copy string arg to
    object.
    int n;

    n = strlen(s);
    if (nLength <> n) {
        if (pData)
                free(pData);
        pData = (char*) malloc(n + 1);
        nLength = n;
    }
    strcpy(pData, s);
}
```

So CIoStr supports two kinds of functions: those contributed by the base class, CStr, and those added by CIoStr itself. The prefix varies depending on where the member function is declared and defined—in the base class or in the derived class.

Overriding Functions and Clarifying Scope

You've already seen inheritance at work, whether or not you've noticed it. The definitions of the CIoStr functions use functions from the base class. Take another look at the input function:

```
void CIoStr::input(void) {
    char buffer[256];

    gets(buffer);
    cpy(buffer);
}
```

The last statement in the definition calls the CStr::cpy function. As in other member-function definitions, the function can be referred to as cpy, because it is a member of CIoStr (by virtue of inheritance from CStr).

The situation gets more complex, though, if the derived class, CIoStr, *overrides* one or more functions in the base class. In this example, there is little motivation to override any of the CStr functions, but it is still perfectly valid. For example:

```
class CIoStr : public CStr {
public:
    void input(void);
    void output(void);

// Overridden from base class CStr
    void cpy(char *s);
};

void CIoStr::cpy(char *s) {
  // Alternative implementation of cpy function
}
```

Now there are two versions of cpy: one defined in the CIoStr class and a second one defined in its base class, CStr. Member functions of CIoStr can call either of these functions. But now, to call the original version of cpy, you must use the scope operator (::) to specify that the CStr version should be called. Otherwise, the new version (CIoStr::cpy) is assumed.

```
void CIoStr::input(void) {
   char buffer[256];

   gets(buffer);
   CStr::cpy(buffer);   // Call base-class version
                        //  of cpy.
}
```

In general, when the compiler sees a name, it attempts to resolve the scope in the following order:

- If the context is within a member-function definition, the compiler checks whether the name is declared within the same class. If it is, the compiler uses that version.

- Next, the compiler checks the declaration of the base class. (This is done recursively, so if the base class has its own base class, all the base classes are checked.)

- Finally, if the name is not declared within the class hierarchy, the compiler checks to see whether it is declared globally.

NOTE If a member function is intended to be overridden by derived classes, then the function should usually be declared virtual, for reasons explained at the end of the chapter. However, you can ignore virtual functions for now.

Inheritance Hierarchies

As the last section hinted, base classes can have their own base classes, and derived classes can have derived classes.

This arrangement may sound complex, so let's take a simple example. Suppose you want to declare a class that has even more functions available than CIoStr has. You can derive a class from CIoStr even though CIoStr itself was derived from CStr.

```
#include "ciostr.h"

class CFontIoStr : public CIoStr {
    int  ptsize;
public:
    void clr(void) { cpy(""); }
    void setchar(int c, int n);
    void set_font(int size);
};
```

This new class, CFontIoStr, inherits all the members of CStr *and* CIoStr, because each successive generation adds or overrides members from the previous class. Nothing is ever lost (although access rights can sometimes change, as explained later in this chapter). CFontIoStr has one new data member (ptsize) and three new member functions that the other classes do not have.

The three classes—CStr, CIoStr, and CFontIoStr—create a class hierarchy, albeit a simple one. The original string class, CStr, is indirectly a base class of CFontIoStr, the most recent class. Through inheritance, CStr passes its contents all the way down to CFontIoStr, much as grandparents pass genes to a grandchild. Figure 8.1 illustrates this simple class hierarchy.

Much more complex class hierarchies are possible. You can derive several classes from any given base class, and the result can be a family tree of classes as elaborate as you like.

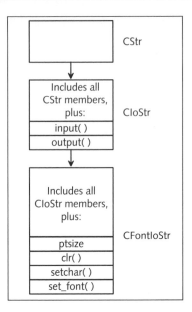

Figure 8.1 A class hierarchy.

Without Inheritance: Doing It the Hard Way

Although inheritance is not the only technique for creating reusable software (nor is it automatically the best technique in all cases), it's useful to see how inheritance can save a good deal of work in many cases.

Suppose you don't have access to the original CStr source code except for the class declaration. (Consequently, you don't have access to source code for function definitions.) But you want to write a new class, CIoStr, with all the capabilities of CStr plus a couple more. How would you create a CIoStr class without using inheritance and without rewriting all the CStr functions from scratch?

You could write such a class without inheritance, but you would have to do the following: write a new class that forms, in effect, a shell around a CStr object; then translate calls to the outer class into calls to the CStr object. Figure 8.2 illustrates this scheme conceptually.

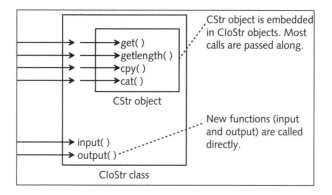

Figure 8.2 Object containment, simulating inheritance.

The difficulty of this approach is that every call to a CStr function must be explicitly translated into a call to the CStr object. Here's what the code would look like:

```
#include "cstr.h"

class CIoStr {
    CStr   str;
public:
// New functions
    void input(void);
    void output(void);

// Old functions, simulating CStr inheritance
    char  *get(void) const {return str.get(); }
    int    getlength(void) const
         {return str.getlength(); }
    void   cpy(char *s) {str.cpy(s);}
    void   cat(char *s) {str.cat(s);}
...
```

In addition to these functions, a complete implementation would also include the operator and conversion functions for the CStr class.

Now compare the version of CIoStr you've just seen to the earlier one:

```
#include "cstr.h"

class CIoStr : public CStr {
public:
    void input(void);
    void output(void);
};
```

The effect is the same with either approach: the CIoStr class supports all the same member functions that CStr does and then adds two new functions (input and output). Clearly, the version that uses inheritance has a much simpler, cleaner, and more elegant syntax.

In theory, you can think of inheritance and object *containment* —declaring one object inside another—as being different. Inheritance, according to object-oriented theory, should be used in situations of the form "A is a kind of B." A, the derived class, is simply a more specialized version of B, the base class. Adopting this approach, we would say that CIoStr is a more specialized kind of string than CStr, and therefore it adds new functions. But both are strings.

With object containment, on the other hand, one class uses—or is a *client* of—the other class. For example, you might create a CAddress class that contains several strings (CStr objects), among other data.

```
class CAddress {
    CStr   name;
    CStr   line1;
    CStr   line2;
    int    months_at_residence;
};
```

You wouldn't consider CAddress to be simply a more specialized type of string; it is a fundamentally different type from CStr.

These cases are fairly clear-cut. But in some cases it can be more difficult to decide whether one class should be derived from another (inheritance) or whether one class should contain the other. The best policy is to remember that inheritance is a convenient bit of syntax for including all the members of one class in another and is therefore not very different from containment. (Inheritance also has a critical role in virtual functions, a fact we'll look at in the next chapter.)

Another way to simulate inheritance, by the way, is to use object containment but rely on the user of the object to adjust function calls.

```
#include "cstr.h"

class CIoStr : public CStr {
public:
    CStr    str;

    void input(void);
    void output(void);
};
```

It's easy to write this class, but it's not as convenient to use. Most functions have to be called through the data member str. For example, the following code fragment calls the cpy function:

```
CIoStr  Iostring;
...
iostring.str.cpy("Let's go to the Oscars.");
```

If you had used inheritance, the call to cpy would be made more directly. The moral of the story is that in situations such as this one, inheritance can often be more convenient than other techniques.

Public, Private, and Protected Access

So far I have introduced one member-access keyword: **public**. In certain respects, this keyword is the most useful. But C++ has three member-access keywords: **public**, **private**, and **protected**.

Within class declarations, **private** is the default member access level. Because it is the default, you can usually get away with not using it. However, making private access explicit is a good idea because it makes the class declarations easier to read. For example, here is the CFontIoStr declaration with the **private** keyword used to clarify the access level of ptsize:

```
#include "CIoStr.h"

class CFontIoStr : public CIoStr {
private:
    int ptsize;
public:
    void clr(void) { cpy(""); }
    void setchar(int c, int n);
    void set_font(int size);
};
```

The third access level, **protected**, is an intermediate level between **private** and **public**. A member with protected access can be accessed with the scope of the class and its derived classes but is private in any other scope.

Look at the CIoStr declaration again. This class inherits from CStr, the original class, and adds two new functions.

```
#include "cstr.h"

class CIoStr : public CStr {
public:
    void input(void);
    void output(void);
};
```

In the declaration of CStr, the two data members (pData and nLength) were declared **private**. This was done by default, because they were not declared with the **public** keyword. This is fine unless you want the new functions in CIoStr to be able to refer to the data members. At that point, there is a problem:

```
void CIoStr::print(void) {
    printf("%s", pData);    // ERROR! No access to pData
}
```

Earlier, I said that a derived class inherits all the members of its base class. This is true, even here. The data member pData is present in every instance of CIoStr and can be accessed indirectly through a CStr member function such as get or cpy. However, pData is not visible in function definitions for the derived class CIoStr.

If pData and nLength had been declared with the **protected** keyword in the CStr declaration, then they could be accessed in CStr function definitions and in CIoStr function definitions.

```
class CStr {
protected:
    char *pData;
    int  nLength;
public:
    CStr();              // Constructors
    CStr(char *s);
    CStr(const CStr &str);
    ~CStr();             // Destructor

    ...
```

Figure 8.3 summarizes the three levels of member-access rights—public, protected, and private.

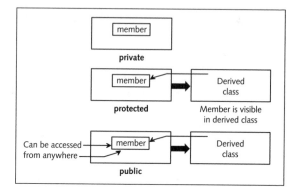

Figure 8.3 Member-access levels summarized.

Is it better to declare data members as protected or as private? The answer depends on the purpose of the members. In the case of the CStr class, it probably isn't necessary to declare pData and nLength as protected, because a series of public functions—get, getlength, cpy, and cat—provide complete access to the data.

In this case, the *interface* (the set of public functions) completely encapsulates the data. If you were to give the class to other programmers, there would probably be no reason to let them directly alter nLength in their derived classes. Instead, they should set data properly by using the cpy function. Providing direct access to pData or nLength could result in errors.

Yet in other cases, it might be useful to make members visible to derived classes. Declaring members as protected provides maximum flexibility to derived classes while retaining most of the advantages of private access.

Member functions can be declared public, private, or protected, just as data members can. You can also declare data members as public. Bear in mind, though, that public data members become part of the interface; if the class is already being used, changing the interface can potentially introduce errors in the rest of the program.

Another Example: Fast Cars and Inheritance Trees

One of the central ideas of inheritance is that you can declare a general type and then derive any number of more specific types from it. These types can be the basis for even more specific types, so a family tree of classes can be as elaborate as you like.

For example, you might define a general class to store information about various cars:

```
class CAuto {
public:
    char    make[20];
    char    model[20];
    int     year;
    int     color_selection;

// Constructors
    CAuto() {}
    CAuto(char mak[], char mod[], int y, int c);
};


#include <string.h>
```

```
CAuto::CAuto(char mak[], char mod[], int y, int c) {
    strcpy(make, mak);
    strcpy(model, mod);
    year = y;
    color_selection = c;
}
```

T I P Here, I've included two arrays of char (make and model) to store character strings. I've used the char type so that the example can be entered easily from scratch. However, if you have declared and compiled the code for the string class, CStr, this would be an ideal place to use it. The declarations of the first two CAuto members could be replaced by:

```
CStr   make;
CStr   model;
```

Then assignments to make and model could be made through simple assignments rather than a call to strcpy. To use the CStr class, remember that you would have to include the CSTR.H header file in your source code and link in CSTR.OBJ.

For cars in general, this information might be adequate. But for certain kinds of cars, you might want to store more information. With a sports car, you are interested in everything in the CAuto class (make, model, year, and color), but you might also want to keep track of horsepower and acceleration time from 0 to 60 mph. The following CSportsCar definition inherits CAuto members and adds some members of its own.

```
CSportsCar : public CAuto {
public:
    double horse_power;
    double accel_0_60;
```

```
// Constructor
   CSportsCar() {}
};
```

You can say that sports cars (CSportsCar) are one subspecies of cars in general (CAuto). Another subspecies of CAuto might be station wagons (CWagon). With this class, other information might be appropriate, such as storage capacity and maximum number of passengers.

```
CWagon : public CAuto {
public:
   double storage;
   int passengers;

// Constructor
   CWagon() {}
};
```

So far, we have one base class (CAuto) with two derived classes (CSportsCar and CWagon). To make things more interesting, let's add one more class: CRaceCar.

The first thing to do in designing the CRaceCar class is to decide where it fits in the inheritance hierarchy. (This is one of the basic principles of object-oriented design, by the way.) You can consider race cars, for the sake of this example, a subspecies of sports car. The most interesting difference is that a race car is driven on a racing track and is entered into competitions. For a race car, you want to store all the information that you would for sports cars in general as well as one other piece of information: the number of racing competitions won.

```
CRaceCar : public CSportsCar {
public:
   int  races_won;
};
```

Because the class is designed as part of an existing inheritance hierarchy, the amount of code to write is quite small. Most CRaceCar data members are simply inherited from existing classes.

You may have noticed that I didn't include a constructor here, although I did for the other classes. As I pointed out in Chapter 5, "A Touch of Class," usually it is a good idea to add a default constructor, particularly if there is any chance that you will add other constructors later. However, CRaceCar is a simple class and I won't be adding any functions to it.

Figure 8.4 shows the resulting inheritance hierarchy.

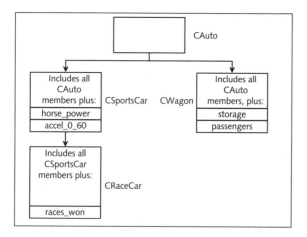

Figure 8.4 A class hierarchy for automobiles.

Base-Class Constructors

As you've seen in this chapter, inheritance is a way of including class members (both data and functions) previously declared in another class. C++ supports a special feature—base-class constructors—to support efficient initialization of these inherited members.

The previous section introduced a sports-car class, CSportsCar, that inherits members from the CAuto class and adds its own. To this declaration, it would be nice to add a second constructor to initialize all the data members, including those inherited from CAuto.

```
CSportsCar : public CAuto {
public:
    double horse_power;
    double accel_0_60;

// Constructors
    CSportsCar() {}
    CSportsCar(char mak[], char mod[], int y, int c,
      double hp, double a);

};
```

The new constructor initializes all the data members, one by one.

```
#include <string.h>

CSportsCar::CSportsCar(char mak[], char mod[], int y,
    int c,double hp, double a)
    {
    strcpy(make, mak);
    strcpy(model, mod);
    year = y;
    color_selection = c;
    horse_power = hp;
    accel_0_60 = a;
}
```

There are couple of problems with this function. First, it is inefficient. It is not obvious here, but C++ always constructs an object by first calling the constructor for the base class, if any. Because no base-class constructor is specified, the compiler generates a call to the CAuto default constructor.

Consequently, all the original members of CAuto are already initialized—in this case, to zero—before the first statement in this function starts executing. The function initializes all CAuto members twice.

The second problem is potentially much worse. The CAuto members were declared public, but had they been declared as private, this CSportsCar constructor would be impossible to write at all!

The solution is to specify the appropriate base-class constructor in the CSportsCar constructor function definition. Here is the syntax:

```
class::class(arglist1) : base_class(arglist2) {
    statements
}
```

In this syntax, *arglist2* contains a subset of arguments from *arglist1*. These arguments are passed through to the base-class constructor. This base-class constructor must match, by number and type of arguments, a constructor defined in *base_class*.

In the following function definition, the CSportsCar argument list is followed by a colon (:) and the appropriate CAuto constructor. The first four arguments are passed through to the base CAuto class constructor, which takes four arguments. If you review the CAuto declaration, you'll see that CAuto has such a constructor.

```
CSportsCar::CSportsCar(char mak[], char mod[], int y,
    int c, double hp, double a) : CAuto(mak, mod, y, c)
    {
    horse_power = hp;
    accel_0_60 = a;
}
```

Now the four data members inherited from CAuto are initialized only once. You probably also notice a fringe benefit: the resulting CSportsCar constructor is shorter and therefore easier to write.

Base Classes and Pointers

Our final look at inheritance sets up much of the rationale behind virtual functions, the subject of the next chapter. Many programmers consider the virtual-function capability to be at the heart of object orientation, so it's worth taking a few minutes to understand the problem it addresses.

Inheritance creates a kind of one-sided relationship between types in C++. Generally speaking, C++ does not allow you to assign pointers of one type to pointers of a different type without using a data cast. But you can assign an object of a derived type to a pointer of base-class type. Figure 8.5 illustrates this rule.

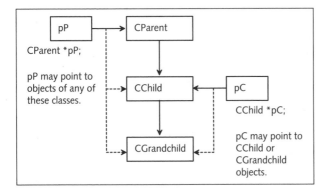

Figure 8.5 Pointer assignment between base and derived types.

Interestingly, this pointer assignment is allowed in only one direction: a pointer of base type can point to a derived type. This arrangement makes sense if you think about it. Consider the following case:

```
CStr    *pBase;
CIoStr DerivedObj;

pBase = &DerivedObj;    // Assgn. to base-class ptr OK.
```

203

When the pointer pBase is declared, the compiler assumes that it will point to an object of type CStr. Errors could arise if pBase is made to point to an **int** variable, for example, because the **int** type does not support CStr members. But there is no problem in making pBase point to an object of a derived type (in this case, CIoStr), because the derived type must include *at least* the same members that CStr does. The following statement works equally well whether pBase points to a CStr object or to a CIoStr object:

```
pBase->cat(" blah blah blah");
```

But the converse does not hold. Consider what would happen if C++ let you freely assign the address of an object of base type (CStr) to a pointer to the derived type (CPrStr):

```
CStr    BaseObj;
CPrStr pDerived;

pDerived = &BaseObj;    // ERROR! Cannot assgn. to
                        // derived type without cast
```

The problem is that the base type, CStr, is a subset, and not a superset, of the type pointed to by pDerived. The object pointed to by pDerived should include at least all the members that CIoStr does, but CStr does not include everything in CIoStr. For example, what happens when the following function call is made?

```
pDerived->input();
```

In the CIoStr declaration, the input function is a new member above and beyond those declared by CStr. This operation would be invalid if pDerived points to a CStr object.

In summary, a pointer to a class can be assigned the address of something in the same class or a derived class. The pointer's type controls which members can be accessed. You could declare an array of pointers to CStr, for example, and each pointer could point to a different type: CStr, CIoStr, or CFontIoStr. But, assuming that you don't recast the pointer, you can use the pointer to refer only to members, such as the cpy function, that are declared in CStr itself.

```
CStr *pStr[10];
pStr[0] = new CStr;
pStr[1] = new CIoStr;
pStr[2] = new CFontIoStr;
```

An interesting question arises when one of the member functions is overridden. Suppose that CPrStr overrides the cpy function with its own implementation, as described earlier in this chapter. This operation creates two versions of the function: CStr::cpy and CIoStr::cpy. Which version of cpy do the following statements call?

```
CIoStr prstr;
CStr pStr = &prstr;
pStr->cpy("Initialize me.");
```

The last statement calls CStr::cpy (the base-class version) and not CIoStr::cpy! When the compiler scans the code and attempts to resolve this function call to an address, the compiler must use the type information it has. In this case, all it knows is that pStr points to something of type CStr. It therefore calls CStr::cpy.

```
pStr->cpy("Initialize me.");
```

But wait a minute, you say, that can't be right! The *object* knows that it is an object of type CIoStr and not CStr. The object should be able to call the version of the function found in the CIoStr class.

But that determination cannot be made until run time. The problem is that at compile time, the compiler cannot know the precise type pointed to, but it must make a determination of the function's address. Its only choice is to use the type information given and assume CStr scope.

For example, in the following code, the expression pStr[n] could point to any object of type CStr, CIoStr, or CFontIoStr, but the compiler has to assume CStr as the type.

```
CStr *pStr[10];
...
pStr[n]->cpy("hi!");
```

During running of the program, the precise type pointed to by pStr[n] is finally determined. If the decision of which function to call could be delayed until run time, then the expression pStr[n]->cpy("hi!") could call the right function, either CStr::cpy or CIoStr::cpy, as appropriate.

This is just what happens with virtual functions, which are the subject of the next chapter. Virtual functions use *late binding*, which means that a reference to a function, such as pStr[n]->cpy, is not bound to an actual address in code until run time.

9

Virtual Functions and Why They're Good

Here's one of the best ways to understand object orientation: imagine a set of independent objects that communicate to each other by sending messages. The C++ virtual-function/ capability fits neatly into this picture. Virtual functions enable different kinds of objects to respond to the same message (actually, a call to a member function) in different ways. Different objects are like different kinds of printers. Each is sent the same message: "Print this page." But the two printers—one a dot-matrix printer and the other a laser printer—respond with different behavior.

None of this is a dramatic break from earlier concepts in this book. Virtual functions are vaguely similar to function overloading, but there is a difference: with overloading, the exact behavior of a name or operator is determined at compile time. With virtual functions, the exact behavior is determined at run time. Overloading is a nice convenience, but virtual functions extend the flexibility of what an object can *do*.

When you're starting out with objects and C++ programming, it's not entirely clear what virtual function are or why you'd use them. After explaining syntax and usage, I'll spend much of the chapter on a simple menu command example. Through this example, I hope to show you how virtual functions can make your life easier by strengthening the independence and self-reliance of objects. In simple terms, it's a way of decentralizing program control.

 What does the virtual in virtual function mean, anyway? In computer terms—such as virtual memory and virtual reality—virtual usually describes something that isn't quite real but works as if it were. In the case of functions, virtual describes a function call that, at run time, could refer to any number of different function calls. It is not a "real" function call in that it doesn't correspond to a specific code address. In some ways, the name is misleading, because virtual functions are entirely real. They are simply called through indirect function calls rather than standard function calls.

Applying the virtual Keyword

To make a member function into a virtual function, precede the function declaration with the **virtual** keyword. The keyword must appear at the beginning of the declaration, before the return-value type.

```
virtual   return_type   name(arguments);
```

As a result, the function is declared virtual, meaning that it is late bound. In *late binding,* the address of the function does not have to be determined until run time. (I devote most of the rest of the chapter to explaining when this is useful.)

Once the **virtual** keyword is used in the function declaration, you don't need to use it again either in the function definition, in derived class declarations, or in derived class function definitions. The function remains virtual in all derived-class declarations using the same name and type.

For example, suppose you have a class CTimePiece that has a ShowTime function. This function is declared virtual.

```
class CTimePiece {
public:
    virtual void ShowTime(void);
    ...
};
```

The function definition for ShowTime does not need to include the **virtual** keyword.

```
#include <iostream.h>

void CTimePiece::ShowTime(void) {
    cout << hours << ":" << minutes;
};
```

In any classes derived, directly or indirectly, from CTimePiece, the ShowTime function is virtual—including the following class, which overrides the ShowTime function.

```
class CClock : public CTimePiece {
public:
    void ShowTime(void); // Override function
    ...
};

void CClock::ShowTime(void) {
    paint_clock_face(hours, minutes);
}
```

There is no requirement that a virtual function be overridden by derived classes or that it be called through a pointer. A virtual function can be called in the same ways as any other member function is called. There is no difference in the syntax, either in declaration or in usage. (This is to say that the syntax in the C++ source code looks the same as for normal member functions, even though there are differences under the covers.)

```
CTimePiece time;
CClock clock;
```

```
time.ShowTime();
clock.ShowTime();
```

Virtual functions do have a few minor restrictions. Inline functions cannot be virtual, for example.

The effect of making a function virtual most often shows up when you access objects through base-class pointers. (You might want to review the last section in Chapter 8 "Inheritance: C++ and Good Genes" if you haven't read it.) With the ShowTime function, you could use the same line of code to call different function implementations. In the following example, assume that CClock and CDigital are both derived classes of CTimePiece.

```
CTimePiece *pTime;

pTime = new CClock;
pTime->ShowTime();   // Calls CClock::ShowTime

pTime = new CDigital;
pTime->ShowTime();   // Calls CDigital::ShowTime
```

When Should You Make a Function Virtual?

As I mentioned in the previous section, there is no difference in syntax between virtual and nonvirtual functions except for the one-time use of **virtual** in a declaration. This is true even though C++ handles them differently. This fact makes it easy to introduce virtual functions into existing C++ projects.

But should you make all your functions virtual just because it's easy to do so? Except for inline functions, you could make almost all your functions virtual simply by putting the keyword everywhere the functions are first declared. But not all functions should be virtual functions.

If there's no chance that a function will ever be overridden by a derived class, then it should not be declared virtual. If you write a class that you never intend to derive other classes from, there is no point in making any function virtual. Every time you call a virtual function, you pay a slight performance penalty. Each virtual function also takes up slightly more space in program memory than its nonvirtual counterpart would. The point is that there's no reason to make a function virtual unless doing so might make a difference.

But if you write a function in a base class and it is clear that the function is intended to be overridden in derived classes, then it is wise to declare the function virtual. You can override a function in a derived class even though it is not virtual, but then in certain situations the wrong function might be called.

In the example at the end of the last chapter, the following code calls the function CStr::cpy (the base-class version) even though it looks as if it should call CPrStr::cpy (the derived-class version).

```
CI.Str prstr;
CStr pStr = &prstr;
pStr->cpy("Initialize me.");
```

But if the cpy function were originally declared as virtual, then this code would call CI.Str::cpy as expected.

```
class CStr {
    ...
    virtual void cpy(char *s);
...
```

Admittedly, this example is not very realistic. There isn't much need to override the cpy implementation except for testing purposes. And because cpy is not likely to be overridden, there isn't much point in its being virtual.

211

The next section presents a couple of member functions that are designed to be overridden and so are perfect candidates to be made virtual.

Menu Command Example

A simple scenario for object-oriented design is a program menuing system. The program displays a series of menus from which the user makes a selection. The program then responds by carrying out the indicated command.

This system is easy enough to implement using traditional, procedure-oriented programming techniques, but object design offers some advantages. If each menu command is coded as a separate object, then the individual menu commands can manage themselves to a certain extent. This arrangement removes the need for the main program to maintain a look-up table or **switch** statement, which would have to be continually revised as new commands were added.

The result is a program that is easier to write, less error-prone, and much more flexible, as we'll see.

Declaring and Defining the Base Class

The base class, CMenu, is a prototype for all the menu commands. The program doesn't instantiate this class. In other words, it doesn't define any object of class CMenu; it defines only classes derived from CMenu.

CMenu is a simple class. It contains only two members, as you can see from the class declaration in **CMENU.H**.

```
// CMENU.H — declaration of the CMenu base class

class CMenu {
```

```
public:
    char title[81];
    virtual void Do_Command(void) = 0;
};
```

This example introduces a new bit of syntax. The characters =0 at the end of the Do_Command declaration indicate that it is a *pure virtual function*. This is the same as any other virtual function except that it has no implementation in the base class; it is implemented only in classes derived from CMenu. The Do_Command function is not defined at all in this class; Do_Command becomes a kind of placeholder for functions to be defined later.

I'll discuss these strange functions further in the section "Functions with No Implementation (Pure Virtual Functions)," later in this chapter.

Each menu-command object implements its own version of Do_Command. Then all the main program does to execute a command is to call Do_Command for the selected object. In effect calling Do_Command in effect, sends a message to the object saying, "Execute your command."

Declaring and Defining the Menu Objects

Each menu command is represented as a CMenu object that implements the CMenu function Do_Command. This example program uses three menu commands. When printed, they appear as follows:

```
1. Sound a bell.
2. Print a wise saying.
3. Add two numbers.
```

The declarations for all the menu commands are identical except for the class name. Each declaration must declare

Do_Command to indicate that it is overriding the definition in the base class.

```
// CMDS.CPP — Defines and initializes menu commands

#include <stdio.h>
#include "menu.h"

class CMenuBell : public CMenu {
    void Do_Command(void);
};

class CMenuSaying : public CMenu {
    void Do_Command(void);
};

class CMenuAdd : public CMenu {
    void Do_Command(void);
};
```

Each of the Do_Command implementations carries out an actual command. These functions can be of any length. Some of them are relatively shorter, and others are longer.

```
CMenuBell::Do_Command(void) {
    putc('\007');
}

CMenuSaying::Do_Command(void) {
    puts("If you know the meaning of the universe,");
    puts("Make the sound of one hand clapping.");
}

CMenuAdd::Do_Command(int n) {
    double    x, y;

    printf("Enter a number: ");
```

```
    scanf("%lf", &x);
    printf("Enter a number: ");
    scanf("%lf", &y);
    printf("The total of the numbers is %f.", x + y);
}
```

Finally, the **CMDS.CPP** file declares an array of pointers to CMenu objects, an integer storing the number of commands, and an initialization function. All these are used by the main program.

```
int num_commands;
CMenu *commands[20];

void Init_Commands(void) {
    commands[0] = new CMenuBell;
    strcpy(commands[0]->title, "Sound a bell.");
    commands[1] = new CMenuSaying;
    strcpy(commands[1]->title, "Print a wise saying.");
    commands[2] = new CMenuAdd;
    strcpy(commands[2]->title, "Add two numbers.");
    num_commands = 3;
}
```

Using the Objects

The main program is now almost trivial to write, because almost all the work is being done by the menu objects. This is consistent with the basic theme of object orientation, which tends to decentralize decision-making and resources in favor of objects rather than the main program loop.

The main program must first gain access to the two pieces of global data—num_commands and the commands array—by declaring them with the **extern** keyword. This keyword is necessary if you want to use variables declared in another module.

```
// MAIN.CPP — Uses the menu objects to manage a menu

#include <stdio.h>
#include "menu.h"

extern int num_commands;
extern CMenu *commands[];
```

The main function first calls Init_Commands to initialize the menu. Then it sets up a loop that displays the menu and responds to commands. One additional command, Exit, enables the loop to end.

```
void main(void) {
    int i, sel;

    Init_Commands();
    do {
        puts("\nMENU:\n");
        for (i = 0; i < num_commands; i++)
            printf("%d. %s", i+1, commands[0]->title);
        printf("\nEnter a selection: ");
        scanf("%d", &sel);
        if (sel >= 0 && sel <= num_commands)
            commands[sel]->Do_Command();
    } while (sel <= num_commands);
}
```

This is the entire program. It shows the effect of the **virtual** keyword clearly. Suppose that the program were the same except that the Do_Command was not declared virtual. In that case, the following line of code would always execute the same command no matter what the user's selection was:

```
commands[sel]->Do_Command();
```

If Do_Command were not virtual, then, during compilation, C++ would resolve the function call based on the class that commands[sel] points to. The variable commands is an array of pointers to CMenu objects. Because Do_Command isn't virtual, the compiler would resolve this as a call to CMenu::Do_Command.

In this case, CMenu doesn't provide any implementation of Do_Command at all, because in CMenu Do_Command is a pure virtual function. But if Do_Command were not virtual, the base class would have to provide some implementation, which we could call the default implementation. Without virtual functions, the main program would always end up executing this default implementation. The actual menu commands would never execute.

The Advantage of Virtual Menu Commands

Given the way this code is written, the use of virtual functions is clearly required. But does it have to be written this way? What was gained by designing a program-menu system based on virtual functions?

Certainly, you can write this menu program using traditional programming techniques. But in the traditional approach, more control must be placed in the main loop. For example, rather than call Do_Command through the current object, code inside the main loop would have to test the value of the selection and then take a different action depending on the value:

```
switch (sel) {
    case 1:
        Bell_Do_Command();
        break;
    case 2:
        Saying_Do_Command();
        break;
    case 3:
        Add_Do_Command();
        break;
};
```

Every time the menu structure of the program changed, this code would have to be revised, as would any place in the program that activated a menu command. The program is easier to maintain using the virtual-function approach, which requires only one statement to activate a selected menu command:

```
commands[sel]->Do_Command();
```

The main point is not that the traditional approach necessarily requires much more coding overall or even that it is less elegant (although it is). The main point is that the traditional approach centralizes all control inside the main loop. With the virtual-function approach, the code in **MAIN.CPP** never needs to be recompiled. Future menu commands can be added without having to rewrite or rebuild the main program.

And there are other advantages to the virtual-function approach. The menu has to be initialized somewhere; in this case, it is initialized in the Init_Commands function. But once the virtual-function framework is in place, you can use any initialization technique. For example, you could initialize the menu from a data file. (In Windows programming, the build process does something like that by using the resource compiler to build menus.)

With the virtual-function approach, the menu can even change during run time. For example, because of a condition determined during running, some menu items may no longer apply, or new ones may be needed. (Look at how the File menu of Microsoft Word and other popular applications change during run time.) The virtual-function approach is much more dynamic; it can revise the menu structure at any time. With the **switch** statement used in the traditional approach, the menu structure is *hard-coded*. In other words, it is firmly fixed in the flow of control of the program and cannot be changed after the program is compiled.

218

Most object-oriented aspects of C++ can be simulated in C, although the C implementation is usually clumsier and requires additional work. This is true in the case of virtual functions. You can simulate the virtual-function capability through the use of callback functions. A callback is a function whose address you pass to the main program or a specialized routine, which can then call the function you have written.

You could use callbacks instead of virtual functions, but you would need to write a callback function for each menu command and then initialize an array of structures specifying menu titles and callback function addresses. The virtual-function approach involves slightly less work and provides a more coherent, easy-to-read structure for this same program mechanism.

The section "How Virtual Functions Are Implemented" further describes the connections between virtual functions and callback functions.

Functions with No Implementation (Pure Virtual Functions)

The Do_Command function is an example of a pure virtual function. The characters =0 indicate that Do_Command has no implementation in this class—that is, there is no function definition for CMenu::Do_Command. However, classes derived from CMenu can implement Do_Command.

```
class CMenu {
public:
    char title[81];
    virtual void Do_Command(void) = 0;
};
```

Any class that has at least one pure virtual function is an *abstract base class*. The CMenu class is an abstract base class, because Do_Command is a pure virtual function. As an abstract base class, CMenu has an important limitation: it cannot be directly used to define (instantiate) an object. You can, however, declare pointers to CMenu.

```
CMenu *pMenu;        // OK
CMenu menu_thing;    // Error! Cannot instantiate
```

If abstract base classes cannot be instantiated, of what use are they? Abstract base classes are useful as general patterns for classes. You can use abstract base classes to create generalized interfaces, which the derived classes then implement. The CMenu class is a good, albeit simple, example of this approach.

The CMenu class could have implemented Do_Command by having it do nothing:

```
// CMENU.H — declaration of the CMenu base class

class CMenu {
public:
    char title[81];
    virtual void Do_Command(void);
};
```

```
// MENU.CPP — implementation of CMenu

CMenu::Do_Command(void) {
}
```

However, this involves needless extra work, because there was never any intention of instantiating CMenu directly or calling CMenu::Do_Command.

How Virtual Functions Are Implemented

For the most part, I'm don't focus on how C++ is implemented in this book. Sometimes there is more than one way for a compiler to implement a specific feature of C++, and you don't usually need to understand underlying compiler implementation to understand object orientation and C++.

However, C programmers do tend to worry about program efficiency and trade-offs between speed and size—and C++ programmers tend to have the same mind-set. The speed and size penalties involved with virtual functions are worth understanding. In the simple case (no multiple inheritance), the implementation of virtual functions is relatively straightforward and standard from one C++ compiler to the next.

As I hinted earlier in a note, virtual functions are closely related to callback functions. Both mechanisms take advantage of the processor's ability to make indirect calls, which are function calls through a pointer. For example, the following code uses C syntax to call the function Hello indirectly.

```
int Hello(int n) {
    printf("Hello, your lucky number is %d.\n", n);
}


int   *pFunction;


pFunction = &Hello;
(*pFunction)(5);     // Call Hello through pFunction
```

The virtual-function capability adds several things to this indirect-call capability: it expresses indirect calls in terms of member functions, it builds tables of function pointers for each class, and it hides the indirect-call syntax so that calls to virtual functions look just like calls to any member function. In some cases, if you are writing a derived class, you may even have forgotten that a particular function is virtual. But with C++, the fact that a function is virtual makes no difference in the way you write it or call it.

All these things are ultimately programming conveniences, but that's not to say they aren't important. By making indirect function calls easier to use, the virtual-function capability encourages you to use them. It also provides a framework (class hierarchies) that gives them meaningful structure and context.

For each class that has any virtual functions, C++ builds a table of function pointers for that class. Each entry in the table contains the address of a virtual function. For example, consider the following class:

```
class CShape {
public:
    virtual int SetPoints(double ptArray[]);
    virtual void DrawMe(void);
    virtual void Move(double x, double y);
};
```

In the CShape class, the three functions SetPoints, DrawMe, and Move are good candidates for being made virtual, because they will probably be overridden in classes derived from CShape.

The C++ compiler constructs a table of function pointers for the CShape class. Notably, it does not construct such a table for each individual CShape object; one table for the entire class is enough, because all objects of the same class share all member functions.

This table is the *virtual function table,* or vtable, for the class. It has a pointer to the definition of each virtual function. If there are any nonvirtual functions in the class declaration, the nonvirtual functions do not appear in this table. There is no reason that they should; nonvirtual functions can be handled as normal function calls.

Figure 9.1 shows what the function table for CShape looks like.

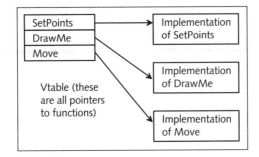

Figure 9.1 Virtual function table for CShape.

Any number of other classes can be derived from CShape, and all these classes implement their own versions of these three functions. (Such classes can also add other virtual functions, but those functions are added to the end of the vtable.) At run time, how does an object "know" that it is an object of type CShape, for example, as opposed to some other class derived from CShape?

The answer is that each individual object has a hidden data member that points to the vtable for the class. (Note that if the object's class has no virtual functions, then the compiler does not need to add this member.) This hidden pointer, which we can name pVtable, is placed at the beginning of the object. In reality, the object doesn't *know* its type and doesn't need to. The program code simply makes an indirect function call through the pointer, and the appropriate function code is called automatically. Each object's pVtable member points to the vtable for its class (CCircle and CSquare, for example, would each have its own vtable), so the object is linked to all the function code for its class.

Figure 9.2 illustrates the structure of a CShape object. You can see how an indirect function call through pVtable results in a call to function implementations for the class.

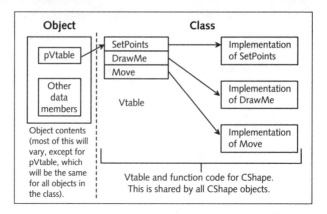

Figure 9.2 A CShape object and the virtual function table (vtable).

Consider a call to a virtual function through an object, myshape:

```
CShape myshape, pShape;
pShape = &myshape;
pShape->DrawMe();
```

The C++ compiler translates the call to DrawMe into the following indirect function call:

```
(*(pShape->pVtable->DrawMe))();
```

This entire virtual-function mechanism can certainly be done in standard C. However, you would have to carry out the following steps:

1. For each class, declare a structure consisting of a function pointer for each virtual function.

2. Initialize each member of this structure so that it points to the appropriate function.

3. Alter the class declaration so that it includes an additional member, pVtable.

4. Initialize pVtable to point to the class virtual function table.

5. Translate all virtual-function calls, as shown in the previous code fragment.

None of this is impossible to do. But, clearly, C++ is much more convenient because it automates all this work for you.

C++ The Language,
An Alphabetical Listing

Definition

An abstract class cannot be used to create objects; it can be used only as a base class for other classes. What makes a class abstract is that it has one or more pure virtual functions.

Surprisingly, such classes are sometimes useful. The abstract class is a protocol or general interface consisting of one or more virtual functions. The abstract class creates a general pattern for derived classes, each of which can implement the virtual functions differently.

Syntax Rules

A class is abstract when it has at least one pure virtual function. Such a function has no implementation (function definition) in this class. The symbols =0 follow the declaration.

```
virtual type return_name(arg_list) = 0;
```

An abstract class cannot be used to define an object, but you can declare pointers to the class.

Example

This example is taken from Chapter 9, "Virtual Functions and Why They're Good." The CMenu class is an abstract class because it contains a pure virtual function, Do_Command. This class forms the general pattern for all specific menu classes, each of which provides an implementation for Do_Command.

```
class CMenu {
public:
    char title[81];
    virtual void Do_Command(void) = 0;
};
```

For example, the CMenuBell class is derived from CMenu. Although CMenu cannot be used to define objects, CMenuBell can.

```
class CMenuBell : public CMenu {
    void Do_Command(void);
};

CMenuBell::Do_Command(void) {
    putc('\007');
}
```

Abstract Data Types

Definition

An abstract data type is a high-level description of a type. This description makes no reference to the type's internal structure but instead describes what you can do with the type.

This term is the source of a certain amount of disagreement and confusion: exactly how much can you describe about a type while still considering it abstract? In its pure form, the concept of abstract data type has little to do with the specifics of any programming language, because once you start to write code, you are dealing with a specific representation.

However, in C++ there are some things you can do to represent a type in a more abstract way than in C. See "Data Abstraction" for more information.

Definition

The address operator (&) helps you initialize pointer variables as well as supply an address for a function such as scanf. At the machine level, processors deal with addresses all the time. The difference between C++ and other high-level languages is that C++ often makes the use of addresses explicit, whereas other languages do many of the same operations under the covers.

Pointer operations involve both the indirection (*) and the address operators, which can be considered inverses of each other. Indirection means "get the contents at," whereas the address operator means "take the address of." Taking the address of a variable and then getting the contents at that address gets you back to the variable you started with, so *(&var) means the same thing as var.

Syntax

The address operator forms an expression from a single operand:

&*expression*

The expression must be a valid l-value (see "L-values"). In general, this means that *expression* must be a variable of primitive type or pointer type, or a structure, array, or union member having primitive type or pointer type. The easiest way to think about this is that you can always take the address of a simple variable. You can also take the address of a pointer variable (which would result in a pointer to a pointer).

 You cannot take the address of a bit field, although in other respects a bit field is a valid l-value.

NOTE

Address Operator (&)

Usage

The address operator occurs only in executable statements
and pointer initialization. The operator produces a constant
address expression. Such an expression is useful for setting a
pointer to point to a simple variable or for passing an
address to a function. For example:

```
int i *ptr = &n;
scanf("%d", &n);
```

When you call scanf, you must supply an address expression. Unlike printf, scanf changes the value of its arguments. The argument must be passed by reference so that
scanf can change its value; passing by reference requires the
use of an address type in C++. (The scanf function gets the
location of n, and not just its value, so that it knows where
to copy the data input by the user.)

Definition

An aggregate is a series of constants treated as a single group. Most often, aggregates are used in initialization. Character strings are the most common aggregates and can be used both for initialization and input to a string function such as printf.

Syntax

Each aggregate has one of the following forms:

```
"string_of_characters"
{ item, item ... }
```

Here the ellipses (...) indicate that *item* is repeated any number of times; each item is a valid constant (and itself may be an aggregate of the appropriate type).

Usage 1: Character Strings

When you use a character string in C++ code, the compiler creates space for the string, including the null-terminating byte, and returns a pointer to the beginning of the string. You can therefore use a pointer to initialize character strings and pointers to strings, and to pass as arguments where the address of a char is expected. For example:

```
char *p = "Here is a string";
char s[] = "Here is another string";
char big_string[20] = "The end";
printf("Hello there, machine.");
```

In each case, the actual string text is placed in program data and its address is assigned or passed as an argument.

Depending on implementation, the last example causes the string to be allocated in memory reserved for constants; the other examples initialize memory reserved for variables. The difference between the first two statements is that p is a variable that may change, whereas s holds a constant address. In the case of big_string, 20 characters are allocated, but only the first eight—including null terminator—are initialized with "The end".

See "String Literals" for more information on character strings.

Usage 2: Set Aggregates

The set-brace syntax ({}) is useful for initializing arrays and structures. If the variable being initialized has a specified size, the number of items in the aggregate may be less than or equal to the size. If no size is specified, the compiler allocates just enough space for the aggregate. For example:

```
// Last three elements not initialized.
short nums[6] = {1, 2, 3};
// ERROR: too many items.
int nums2[3] = (1, 2, 3, 4, 5};
// nums3 is 4 ints in size.
int nums3[] = {99, 7, 28, 58};
```

In the last example, nums3 is exactly four elements long, causing a reference to nums3[6] in an executable statement to result in an error.

As mentioned earlier, a member of an aggregate can itself be an aggregate; this makes sense if you are using it to initialize a complex data type, such as a two-dimensional array or an array of structures. Here, the third member (x) of each structure is left uninitialized, whereas the first two members of each structure are initialized:

```
struct   rectype {
   char *name;
   int age;
   float weight;
};

struct rectype employees[3] = { {"Curly", 30},
   {"Larry", 25}, {"Moe", 35} };
```

Definition

An anonymous union is a union declared without a name; it declares only members. (A better term might be *unnamed union*.) When an anonymous union is declared as part of a structure, the union members can be referred to directly without reference to the name of the union.

Example

Suppose that you want to create a structure consisting of two short integers and one field that can contain either a long integer (lng) or a pointer to a character string (str). Figure A.1 shows the layout in memory.

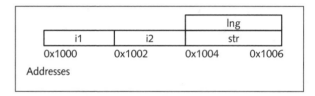

Figure A.1 *Memory layout of a union embedded in a structure.*

In C, the traditional way to declare this structure is as follows:

```
struct mystruct_type {
    int i1, i2;
    union {
        long lng;
        char *str;
    } myunion;
} mystruct;
```

Given this declaration, here's how you would refer to the string (the character pointer inside this structure):

```
mystruct.myunion.str
```

237

In C++, the structure can be rewritten without giving a name to the union:

```
struct mystruct_type {
    int i1, i2;
    union {
        long lng;
        char *str;
    };
} mystruct;
```

Now, you can use a shorter expression to refer to the string:

```
mystruct.str
```

The names declared within the anonymous union must not conflict with other members at the same level of visibility—in this case, the members i1 and i2 in the structure mystruct.

 C supports unions, but standard C does not include support for anonymous unions at this time.

Definition

Arrays provide a marvelous way to represent large areas of memory and to efficiently process such areas in a loop. Chapter 3, "Pointers, Strings, and Things," introduces the topic; this section provides a summary and discusses some fine points.

C++'s treatment of arrays is distinctive in a couple of ways. First, the connection of arrays to pointer variables is very close. Second, multi-dimensional arrays are treated as arrays of arrays.

Syntax

An array reference or declaration has one of the following forms, depending on whether it is one-dimensional (the first case) or multidimensional (the second case):

```
name[index]
name[dim1_index][dim2_index]...
```

Here the ellipses (...) indicate that [dim_index] can be repeated any number of times. The brackets ([]) are intended literally. In declarations, each index specifies the number of elements of the array (or the number in the given dimension of the array). In executable statements, valid indexes run from 0 to one less than the index in the declaration. Thus, for an array declared "int array[10]", the last element is array[9].

In certain circumstances (described at the end of the next section), index can be omitted from the declaration.

239

Case 1: One-Dimensional Arrays

The connection between pointers and arrays is very close. In many cases, an array name can be used interchangeably with a pointer that points to the array.

```
short   x[100]
short   *y = x;
```

Here, x is an array of 100 short integers. The first statement allocates 200 bytes. The second statement allocates room only for y, a pointer; it also intializes y to x, which has the effect of setting y to point to the start of the array. This is because a reference to an array (in this case, x) is translated into the array's starting address.

A reference to y translates into the starting address of the array, as does x. In the following statements, x and y are interchangeable. But bear in mind that x is a constant, whereas y is a variable that can change so that it points to a new address:

```
x[50] = i;
y[k] = j + 5;
*x = 2;
*y = 2;
*(x + 1) = 0;
*(y + 5) = 8
```

The last two statements use pointer arithmetic, which multiplies an integer by the size of the base type (this is called *scaling*) before adding or subtracting to the address. Consequently, the last two statements are equivalent to the following:

```
x[1] = 0;
y[5] = 8;
```

In general, any reference to *name*[*index*] in an executable statement is equivalent to the following:

240

*(*name* + *index*)

Of course, the version that uses brackets ([]) is more convenient.

In a declaration, *index* determines the size of the array; *index* must be a constant. Within an executable statement, *index* can be any valid integer expression—with the caveat that when evaluated it must fall into the range 0 to *size* –1, in which *size* is the index used in the declaration. In the case of x above (100 elements), elements range from a[0] to a[99].

 You can actually use an index outside this range; however using an out-of-range index would result in overwriting or reading data outside the array's area in memory, which is guaranteed to cause errors.

 A frequent mistake in C++ programming is to set initial or terminating conditions of a loop incorrectly. This is an easy mistake in part because the maximum index is not equal to the number of elements in the array; it is one less than this number. A correct loop to initialize an array might look like this—notice the initialization and loop condition:

```
for (i = 0; i < NUMBER_OF_ELEMENTS; i++)
    array[i] = 0;
```

In declarations, *index* can be omitted if the size information is supplied elsewhere. This happens in two cases: with initialization by aggregates (see "Aggregates"), in which the initializer determines the size; and in argument declarations where arrays of variable sizes are accepted. For example, consider the following prototype:

```
void array_function(int a[], int *b);
```

Here, a and b are virtually the same type. In each case, my_function expects the address of an integer; it may be a single integer or the first element of an integer array. The size of the array is up to the calling function. Generally the function called will need some way of knowing the array size. This can be communicated in a variety of ways: there may be a programwide standard size, there may be a nullterminator (as is the case with a character string, which is just an array of **char**), or size information may be passed separately in another argument.

Case 2: More than One Dimension

Everything said about one-dimensional arrays also applies to multidimensional arrays. However, the use of more than one dimension adds a few interesting quirks.

Ultimately, all arrays are one-dimensional, because memory itself is one-dimensional: an array is really just a sequence of base elements laid out contiguously in memory (meaning that the array takes up a solid block of memory with nothing interspersed between elements).

For each individual dimension used in declaring the array, the maximum index is always 1 less than the index used to declare an array. Suppose an array, big_matrix, is declared as follows. The total size is 5 * 10 * 10, or 500 elements.

```
double big_matrix[5][10][10];
```

The first element in the array is:

```
big_matrix[0][0][0]
```

The last element is:

```
big_matrix[4][9][9]
```

This may seem strange, but the reason for it is plain: in declarations, each index specifies the *number of elements* and not the *last element*. Simple math tells you that 0, 1, 2, 3, 4 is five elements.

Although memory is laid out one-dimensionally, arrays can be a convenient way to express matrixes and higher-dimensional arrays called for by program logic. The compiler translates a multidimensional array by multiplying each index by the product of all the dimensions *after* the current dimension.

As a two-dimensional array, name[i][j] is translated into:

```
**(name  +  i * dim2  +  j)
```

You can think of dim2 as the row size; it's equal to the number of columns and is the second dimension in the declaration. So two-dimensional array references are resolved by multiplying the row number (i) by the row size (dim2) and adding the column number (j).

As a three-dimensional array, name[i][j][k] is translated into:

```
***(name  +  i * dim2 * dim3  +  j * dim2  +  k)
```

C++ uses row-major order, which means that the last dimension changes most quickly. Suppose that an array is declared as "int 3d[2][2][2];". This defines a 2 * 2 * 2 (eight-element), in which the elements are laid out in memory in this order:

```
3d[0][0][0]
3d[0][0][1]
3d[0][1][0]
3d[0][1][1]
3d[1][0][0]
3d[1][0][1]
3d[1][1][0]
3d[1][1][1]
```

243

A two-dimensional array is actually an array of arrays, a three-dimensional array is an array of arrays of arrays, and so on. Thus, for a given array definition,

```
int arr[3][5][5];
```

the identifier "arr" is interpreted as an array of three elements (arr[0], arr[1], and arr[2]); each element is itself a 5 * 5 two-dimensional array. Therefore:

- arr is the address of (it *points to*) a two-dimensional array, arr[0].

- arr[0] is the address of a one-dimensional array, arr[0][0].

- arr[0][0] is the address of an integer, arr[0][0][0].

Each expression (arr, arr[0], arr[0][0], and arr[0][0][0]) is at a different level of indirection. This is why even after adjusting the address of arr, you have to apply the indirection operator (*) three times to get an integer. The following two expressions, for example, are equivalent:

```
***arr
arr[0][0][0]
```

Assignments

Definition

In C++, assignments perform the usual role of copying data to a location. However, a C++ assignment has the peculiar quirk of forming an expression itself. This means that you can place assignments inside other assignments or almost any kind of expression.

Syntax

The assignment operator forms an expression from an l-value and a subexpression:

```
l-value = expression
```

The *l-value* is typically a variable but can also be a class-member reference, an indexed array element, or a dereferenced pointer. For more information, see "L-values." The assignment itself evaluates to the value of *expression*—that is, the value assigned.

Examples

The following examples illustrate some simple assignments:

```
a = 1;
a = b * 2;
card[12] = 0;
*p1++ = *p2++;
```

An assignment can be placed inside larger expressions, as in:

```
a = b = c = d = e = 0;
```

For a fuller discussion of how this works, see Chapter 2, "Basic Features of C/C++ Programs."

Definition

The **auto** keyword declares that a variable has automatic storage class—meaning that it is temporary and is allocated on the *stack*, the area of memory reserved for function-call overhead. This means that, in a sense, the variable flashes in and out of existence.

In practice, the **auto** keyword is never necessary, because **auto** is the default for local variables anyway. To be honest, it's included in the language only for the sake of completeness. You will probably go your entire programming career without finding a legitimate need for this keyword.

Syntax

The auto keyword precedes a variable declaration:

```
auto    data_declaration;
```

The data definition must occur at a local level (inside a function definition or inside a block); such variable definitions are always auto unless declared **extern** or **static**.

Definition

A base class is a class you inherit from. From the standpoint of another class, a base class is something like a parent (although, as with single-cell animals, there is typically only one parent!). The child class is called a *derived* class, and it automatically inherits all the members of its base class, including both data members and functions. The derived class can also add members of its own.

Chapter 8, "Inheritance: C++ and Good Genes," introduces the general subject of base classes, derived classes, and inheritance. This section summarizes base-class syntax and introduces some advanced features that Chapter 8 does not cover.

Basic Syntax

The simplest way to inherit from a base class is to use the following syntax. (Note that if you are declaring a **struct** or **union** class, substitute **struct** or **union** for **class** in this syntax.)

```
class derived_class : public base_class {
    declarations
};
```

The *derived_class* inherits all the members declared in *base_class*_name, with the exception of constructorsand assignment-operator functions. The *declarations* specify new members as well as member functions in *base_class* to be overridden.

The **public** keyword specifies that the members of *base_class* are to be inherited without modification in their status. Although you can specify **protected** or **private** instead (as described later in this topic), **public** is generally recommended here. This use of **public** does not cause any members, inherited or otherwise, to become public, as you might think.

Although a derived class does not inherit constructors, a derived-class constructor does call a base-class constructor to initialize the portion of the class inherited from the base class. In other words, the base-class constructor is called even though, technically speaking, it is not inherited.

N O T E

Example

The following simple example specifies that CFurn is a base class of CChair:

```
CChair : public CFurn {
private:
    int number_of_legs;
public:
    CFurn() {}
    CFurn(int legs) {number_of_legs = legs;}
}
```

The CChair class has all the members that the CFurn class has, in addition to number_of_legs. CChair also has its own constructors, because it does not inherit the CFurn constructors.

Advanced Syntax

The following syntax shows a more comprehensive picture of declaring base classes. Again, substitute **struct** or **union** for **class** as appropriate if you are declaring a structure or union:

```
class derived_class : base_decl [, base_decl] ... {
    declarations
};
```

Here, the brackets indicate that there can be any number of occurrences of *base_decl*; if there are more than one, separate them by commas. Each *base_decl* is a base-class declaration, which has the following syntax:

```
[private | protected | public] [virtual] class_name
```

This syntax indicates that, at most, one access specifier—**private**, **protected**, or **public**—can occur. (If none is specified, the default is **private**, which is usually not the access level you want.) The brackets around **virtual** indicate that this keyword is optional.

The "Base-Class Access Specifiers" section describes the purpose of **private**, **protected**, and **public** in this context. The **virtual** keyword is explained in the topic "Virtual Base Classes."

Listing more than one base class is supported in all versions of C++ except the earliest ones. This use of more than one base class is called *multiple inheritance*.

Advanced Syntax: Examples

In the following example, D is the derived class, and B1, B2, and B3 are base classes:

```
class D : public B1, public B2, private B3 {
   ...
};
```

In the next example, D inherits from B1 and B2, but each is a virtual base class:

```
class D : public virtual B1, public virtual B2 {
   ...
};
```

Base-Class Access Specifiers

Access specifiers for base classes are among the most mis-understood features of C++. For the most part, you are safest sticking to the use of **public**. I've come across few situations that justified the use of **protected** or **private** in this context. This is an example of feature overkill in the C++ language.

What's confusing is that in this context, these keywords play a role strongly related to, but not the same as, the member-access levels that appear inside a class declaration. Table B.1 summarizes what these keywords do when they modify a base class declaration.

Table B.1

BASE-CLASS MODIFIER	DESCRIPTION
public	All members inherited from the base class as is.
protected	Same as **public**, but public members inherited from the base class become protected within the derived class.
private	All members from the base class become private within the derived class.

To put the matter simply: if you place the **private** keyword in front of a base class, the members inherited from that class have private access. You might conceivably do this if you want to inherit from a particular class B without expos-ing any of B's members. The B members would then be for internal use only.

Pointers to Base Classes

One of the interesting ways in which base classes are relat-ed to derived class is through pointers: you can declare a pointer to a base class and then make it point to an object of the derived class.

250

For example, the following code declares a pointer, pB, to a base class:

```
class D : public B {...};

B *pB;
```

The pointer pB can now be set to point to an object of the derived class, D:

```
D object;
pB = &object;
```

Note that you cannot go in the opposite direction (assigning a base-class object to a pointer to the derived class).

Although this sort of operation, might not seem useful at first, it has an important role to play in polymorphism and virtual functions. A pointer of base-class type can be assigned to objects of many different derived types at different times during the running of the program. If the classes have virtual functions, this means that the same line of code can execute any of a number of different functions, depending on conditions determined at run time. (This, in turn, is a technique for decentralizing control so that the main loop doesn't have to make all the decisions.) For clarification, see Chapters 8 and 9 for an introduction to inheritance relationships and virtual functions.

Definition

Base-class constructors are an impressive example of C++ flexibility and efficiency; they enable the efficient initializing of inherited members. Be warned, however: you need to have a solid grasp of the concepts of base classes, inheritance, and constructors before tackling this topic.

In a function definition, you can specify which constructors for each base class get called and which arguments get passed to the constructor. This ability extends to ancestor classes so that you can specify a constructor for the base class of a base class. For this idea to make sense, you first need to understand how an object is initialized.

When an object is initialized, a constructor is invoked. But before that, two things happen, in this order:

1. If the object is a member of a class that has a base class, then a certain portion of the object is contributed by the base class. This portion consists of members declared in the base class rather than in the class itself. During object creation, a base-class constructor is called to initialize this base-class portion of the object.

2. Each contained object in the class is created. This action invokes a constructor for each object.

After these things happen, the class's own constructor is invoked. At this point, it is sometimes desirable to initialize inherited members (those contributed by the base class). There are two problems with doing so, however: the members may be private to the base class and therefore not visible in the derived class, and it is often less efficient to initialize members this way than in the base-class constructor. Using the derived class's constructor to initialize may result in the same member being initialized twice.

C++'s solution is to let you specify any valid constructor for a base class. It does not assume that you always want to use the default constructor for the base class.

Syntax

To specify one or more base class constructors in a function definition of a constructor, use this syntax:

```
class::class(args) : base_class(args) {
    statements
}
```

You can include more than one occurrence of *base_class*(*args*). If you ido so, separate each with a comma

Example

Suppose that two classes—CAuto and CSportsCar—are defined as follows (I am deliberately keeping these simple):

```
class CAuto {
private:
    double horses;
    int     passengers;
    CStr    make;
public:
    CAuto() {}
    CAuto(double h, int p, CStr m)
        {horses = h; passengers = p; make = m;}
};

class CSportsCar : public CAuto {
private:
    double accel_0_60;
    int stripes;
```

```
public:
    CSportsCar(double h, CStr m, double a);
};
```

The function definition of the CSportsCar constructor is written with a base-class constructor for CAuto, in which CAuto(double, int, CStr) is specified rather than the default constructor, CAuto().

```
CSportsCar::CSportsCar(double h, CStr m, double a) :
    CAuto(h, 2, m) {

    accel_0_60 = a;
}
```

The CSportsCar constructor calls the base-class constructor CAuto(double, int, CStr), passing the arguments h, 2, and m. The first and third arguments are from the argument list of CSportsCar. These arguments are passed to the base-class constructor. The second argument is a constant. Constant and global-variable expressions are valid in this context, as are parameters from the CSportsCar argument list.

If a base-class constructor were not used here, then CAuto's default constructor would be invoked. In that case, this example would be impossible to write correctly, because the three members—horses, passengers, and make—are private to CAuto and therefore are not visible within CSportsCar. (Note that CSportsCar inherits all members of CAuto, private or not, but these members are not necessarily visible within the scope of CSportsCar.)

Figure B.1 illustrates the role of the base-class constructor, in terms of a CSportsCar object layout. The base-class constructor is responsible for initializing the portion of CSportsCar that was declared in CAuto.

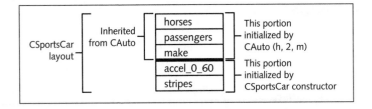

Figure B.1 Initialization in the CSportsCar class.

Definition

Like a skilled surgeon, you can use bit fields—one of the tools that C++ provides to pull apart the insides of a byte and extract individual bits. Of course, such bit surgery is possible with bitwise operators such as & and |. In fact, bit field operations translate directly into bitwise operations when used in programs. The purpose of bit fields is to provide a technique for making bitwise operations easier to understand. Although not all bitwise operations can be expressed with bit fields, those that can be so expressed make for more readable programs.

Syntax

To declare bit fields, declare a class or structure and qualify members with a bit width, as follows:

```
struct [struct_type_name] {
    unsigned  field1 : width1;
    unsigned  field2 : width2;
    . . .
    unsigned  fieldN : widthN;
} [struct_variables];
```

Here, each *width* is a nonzero integer, which is one or larger. This number, which must be a constant expression, specifies size of the field in bits. The corresponding field is used just like any other structure member except that its range is restricted according to its size. For example, a bit field of size 1 can take only two values: 0 or 1.

You cannot take the address of a bit field, although in other respects a bit field is a valid l-value.

NOTE

Bit Fields (continued)

Syntax for Bit Field Access

Bit fields are integer fields and are accessed exactly like other structure members:

```
structure_var.member
```

Examples

Suppose you need to represent several Boolean values in a small amount of space. You could represent each value with a separate **int** or **char** variable, but this would be wasteful of memory. Using bit fields conserves space. The following example uses bit fields to store each Boolean (1 or 0) value in one bit:

```
struct {
    unsigned shift:1;
    unsigned alt:1;
    unsigned ctl:1;
} shift_state;
```

Now you can easily store a single bit value in each field. The following code accesses these fields just like ordinary structure members, but it is setting and testing individual bit positions:

```
shift_state.shift = 1;
shift_state.alt = 0;
if (shift_state.ctl)
    ctl_function();
```

These statements are roughly equivalent to the following lines of code, which use the three least-significant bits to represent the SHIFT, ALT, and CTL states, just as the previous example does. The difference is that this version does it the hard way.

```
#define SHIFT_MASK 0x1
#define ALT_MASK   0x2
#define CTL_MASK   0x4

int shift_state

shift_state |= SHIFT_MASK;      // Set SHIFT bit.
shift_state &= ~ALT_MASK;       // Unset ALT bit.
if (shift_state & CTL_MASK)     // Test CTL bit.
    ctl_function();
```

The bit field version, you'll probably agree, is somewhat more readable than this version.

Bit fields can be wider than one bit and sometimes are. You should always bear in mind, though, that the width of the field strictly limits the range of that field. A single bit can represent one of two values (0 or 1), two bits can represent four values (00, 01, 10, or 11), and so on.

Suppose you wanted to represent a playing card's identity in as small a space as possible. By the way, this obsession with space may strike you as odd, but there are many cases where space is significant, especially when you're using large arrays or file operations. When you write many data records to a file, saving a few bytes per record can add up to a great deal of saved disk space. As a side benefit, cutting down on the amount of file space can have great impact on program speed.

In any event, it's possible to represent the two components of a playing card in a small space because each component—suit and rank—is restricted to a small range. To pick the size of the fields, we have to review how many possible values there are for each component and compare these numbers to powers of two. Two bits is enough to represent as many as four different values. Four bits is enough to represent as many as 16 values (see Table B.2).

Table B.2 Number of bits needed to represent suit and rank.

Field	Number of Values	This is Equal to or Less Than	Third Column Equals this Power of 2
suit	4	4	2
rank	13	16	4

Suits can be represented in two bits, and ranks can be represented in four bits. The bit field declaration looks like this:

```
struct cardtype {
    unsigned suit:2;
    unsigned rank:4;
} my_card;
```

To make the values easier to work with, let's assign enumerated values 0–3 to the symbolic constants CLUBS, DIAMONDS, HEARTS, and SPADES and use the following symbols for rank values: 1 for ACE, 11–13 for J, Q, and K, and face value for the other ranks.

```
enum {CLUBS, DIAMONDS, HEARTS, SPADES};
enum {ACE =1, J = 11, Q, K};
```

The **enum** keyword is just a convenient way to declare constants. See "enum Declarations" for more information on the **enum** syntax.

With the bit field structure and the constants all defined, it's now an easy matter to assign settings to a card. Let's look at a couple of examples. First, the ace of spades:

```
my_card.suit = SPADES;   // SPADES = 3, or 11 binary
my_card.rank = ACE;      // ACE = 1
```

The value of SPADES is equal to 3, or 11 binary. The value of ACES is 0001 binary (the leading zeros reminding us that the rank is stored in a field four bits wide). Figure B.2 shows how these values are placed in the resulting structure.

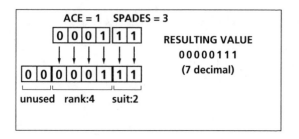

Figure B.2 Assigning ACE of SPADES to rank and suit.

Next, let's assign the king of hearts to a card. The following statements assign this value to the my_card structure variable:

```
my_card.suit = HEARTS;     // HEARTS = 2, or 10 binary
my_card.rank = K;          // K = 13, or 1101 binary
```

The value of HEARTS is 2, or 10 binary. The value of K (king) is 13, or 1101 binary. Figure B.3 shows how these values are placed in the resulting structure.

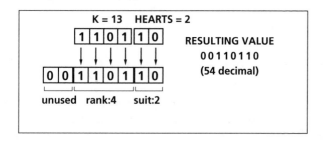

Figure B.3 Assigning KING of HEARTS to rank and suit.

As I mentioned, bit fields are convenient ways of representing bitwise operations. The bit field operations for wider fields are less obvious than the operations for fields of only one bit, but the amount of code is not much greater.

When a value is assigned to the suit field, the two corresponding bit positions must first be set to zero—"ANDed out," as it were. Then the new value can be set with the OR operator (|). The following statements assign HEARTS to the suit field:

```
#define SUIT_MASK  0x3    // 3  = 00000011 binary
#define RANK_MASK  0x2C   // 2C = 00111100 binary

(my_card &= ~SUIT_MASK) |= HEARTS;
```

The case of the rank field is slightly more complicated. Before the bit pattern of K can be combined with the structure, this bit pattern must be shifted to the left two places (two being the size of the preceding field, suit). In other respects, the logic of placing the bits into the proper bit positions in my_card is the same. The following statement executes this bit assignment properly:

```
(my_card &= ~RANK_MASK) |= (K << 2);
```

Clearly, the bit field version is more readable than using bitwise operators directly. Moreover, the bit field version has the virtue of not requiring you to remember how many places to shift a bit value.

Bitwise Operators

Definition

The bitwise operators do just what the word bitwise implies: they work on the individual bits of two values. (These values must be some form integer expression, such as **int**, **short**, **long**, **unsigned**, or **char**.) When you use them, you should be serious about wanting to manipulate individual bits. You can use bitwise AND and OR, for example, to form complex logical expressions, but the logical (non-bitwise) operators are recommended for those situations and are more reliable.

Examples

Bitwise operators are most commonly used when you're creating or testing bit masks. See Chapter 2, "Basic Features of C/C++ Programs" for bit masks used in an example.

Figure B.4 shows how bitwise AND, OR, and XOR (exclusive OR) would operate on sample byte values.

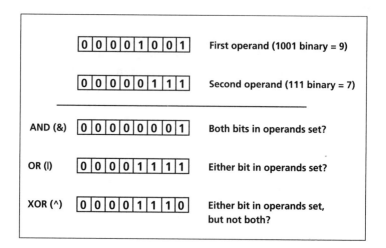

Figure B.4 Bitwise operators.

Boolean Values

Definition

Some programming languages have a special Boolean type—a value that can be either TRUE or FALSE. This is a useful concept, because you want to be able to perform comparisons (for example, testing to see whether x is equal to 0) and have the program do something different depending on the true or false value of the result. You may even want to store the true or false value and use it later as part of a complex decision.

C++ is fully capable of handling true or false values but does not have a special type for them (although you can use the **typedef** keyword to define a special BOOLEAN type if you wish). In any programming language the implementation of a Boolean type is actually an **int**, a **short**, a **char**, or a bit field; C++ lets you choose the storage most appropriate for the program. It's usually easiest to represent a Boolean value as an **int**, unless you need to pack into a compact structure, in which case **char** (a one-byte integer) or bit fields may be most appropriate.

Syntax Rules

Boolean operations in C++ follow two rules:

- Control structures consider any nonzero value to be "true." A condition such as (n) is equivalent to the condition (n != 0).

- All comparison and logical (non-bitwise) operators evaluate to 1 if the result of the operation is "true" and 0 if it is "false."

These two rules work together. If a comparison is true, for example, it evaluates to 1, which in turn is considered "true" by a control structure such as an **if** statement. This means that conditions in a control structure work as you would expect:

```
// The statement is printed if a is greater than b. */

if (a > b)
    printf("a is greater than b.");
```

A strange consequence, is that the numbers 15 and 16 (to take some examples) represent "true" just as the number 1 represents "true." Consequently, a logical expression such as

```
15 && 16   // Combine 15 and 16 with logical AND
```

evaluates to 1, although bitwise AND produces a completely different result.

Definition

The **break** keyword exits out of a loop. It's also used to terminate a series of statements for a case within a **switch** statement. This latter use of **break** is probably the most common.

Syntax

The **break** keyword, followed by a semicolon, forms a complete statement:

```
break;
```

This statement is valid only within a **switch** statement, a **for** loop, a **while** loop, or a **do-while** loop. The statement causes an immediate exit from the nearest loop. (To break out of several loops, use **goto**.)

Example

Within a **switch** statement, **break** causes control to transfer to the end of the **switch** statement block. Without the use of **break**, control would *fall through* to the next case, meaning that execution would continue sequentially. For example:

```
case 1:
    strcpy(strNum, "One");
    break;
case 2:
    strcpy(strNum, "Two");
    break;
    . . .
```

In some cases, it may be convenient to let execution fall through to the next case, so **break** would be omitted. See "switch Keyword" for more information.

C/C++ Compatibility

Definition

This topic provides guidelines for porting code from C to C++.

From a theoretical viewpoint, C++ has its own unique grammar— unlike C, for example, it views structure and class declarations as fundamental type definitions. But for all practical purposes, you can consider C++ to be a superset of C except for a few additional restrictions. Of course, any C++ restrictions can be a major annoyance if you are trying to port large amounts of existing C code to C++ source files.

In porting C code to C++, look for the following areas in which C++ does not compile C code and make appropriate corrections:

- C++ functions that are declared with a return type other than **void** must return a value. Failing to do so might get you off with a warning in C; in C++, this error is a more grievous sin.

- C++ requires that function-definition headings use prototype style rather than old-fashioned C function syntax (the only form supported in the first versions of C). For example, the following heading of a function definition is valid in C:

```
void swap(a, b)
double *a;
double *b;
{...
```

This syntax is invalid in C++ and would have to be rewritten as follows:

```
void swap(double *a, double *b) {...
```

267

- C++ imposes stronger type checking. In particular, you cannot assign an address expression (such as a pointer) to an address expression of a different type, unless you use a type cast or are assigning to a **void*** pointer. Assignment between pointers of different types does not merely generate a warning as in C; instead, it is an out-and-out error. Type casts solve the problem:

```
void *vp;
int *ip;

ip = (int*) vp;  // Data cast required
vp = ip;         // Ok: you can assign to void*
```

- C++ requires that functions be declared before being used. With C, you can get away without declaring the function first; the result is that C assumes an **int** return type and an indeterminate argument list. This is sloppy programming and never recommended, but you can slip it into your C code as long as you're happy with the default **int** return type. C++ is less permissive here.

- It's possible to have name conflicts in C++ that did not arise in C. In C, for example, you can recycle a global name by using it once to name a structure or union type (a "tag name" as opposed to a **typedef**'ed name) and using it again to name a function or variable. You cannot do this in C++, because C++ places all these identifiers in the same name space. Fortunately, this kind of name conflict is rare.

There is another pitfall to watch for if you are mixing C and C++ source modules. Given the same symbol, C++ generates a different name when it generates object code. The C++ naming convention *decorates* each name so that type information is embedded into the object code. Then

268

the linker won't recognize MyVar declared as **int** and MyVar declared as **float** as the same symbol. (This is called *type-safe linkage*.) By the way, the decoration scheme is implementation-specific, so avoid making assumptions about it.

The result is that when linked together, C and C++ modules won't recognize each other's symbols. Fortunately, C++ provides an easy workaround: use **extern "C"** declarations in the C++ module, to import symbols defined in C. An **extern "C"** declaration suppresses the usual name decoration performed by C++.

```
extern "C" {
    long  way_home; // way_home defined in a C module
};
```

Going in the reverse direction—from C++ to C—is potentially much more difficult, because C++ supports so many more features. You will probably never want to go in that direction. If you did, you might need to rewrite a lot of code. Although C++ is stricter when it comes to the use of types, it allows more freedom than C in the following ways:

- You can place variable declarations and other statements (executable statements, if you will) in any order. In C, you have to put all local declarations at the beginning of a function or statement block.

- You can use any valid expression to initialize a variable or object. You are not limited to initializing with constants, as in C.

- When you declare a class (including a structure or union), the class name automatically becomes a fully usable type name. You do not have to qualify the class name with the **class**, **struct**, or **union** keyword in order to make it a type. In C, you would need to qualify a structure named Record as "struct Record" to use it in declarations and casts, or else use **typedef** to create a true type name. For the sake of backward compatibility, C++ supports syntax such as "struct Record" and "class Record," although this is never necessary in C++ code written from scratch.

If you write code to be compiled in both C and C++ (for example, you're writing a source-code library for a variety of customers), you must observe the strongest restrictions of both C and C++.

Definition

The **case** keyword labels a statement used within a **switch** statement block. As a label, it identifies a specific value you are testing for.

Syntax

The **case** keyword turns a statement into a labeled statement:

```
case    constant_value:
            statement
```

This statement is valid only within a **switch** statement block. A labeled statement is itself a statement; this implies that a statement may be immediately preceded by any number of labels (as in the following example).

The *constant_value* is a constant integer expression. Note that this includes character constants, which are really just integer values.

Example

What's tricky about **case** is that it is only a statement label. Labels don't automatically change the flow of control; this is why each case has to be separated by a **break** statement unless you want execution to fall through. In this example, all five vowels label the same statement block, which exits (**break**) before falling through to the default statement block:

```
switch (c) {
    case 'a':
    case 'e':
    case 'i':
    case 'o':
    case 'u':
        printf("Character is a vowel");
        break;
    default:
        printf("Character is a consonant.");
        break;
}
```

Definition

A type cast converts a value from one data type to another; for example, you might convert an integer into floating-point data. There are a number of situations in which C will do this for you automatically; a type cast gives you more control.

See "Explicit Type Conversions" for more information.

char Data Type

Definition

The **char** data type is simply a one-byte integer, but typically it is used to store characters: letters, digits, symbols, and so forth—in other words, text. See Chapter 3, "Pointers, Strings, and Things," for an introduction to the subject.

Examples

One **char** variable or array element holds a single character, and arrays of characters form character strings. In the case of the latter, you can initialize the character string with a string literal. For example:

```
char letter = 'a';
char name[] = "John Q. Public";
char address[80] = "123 Main Street USA";
```

In the first declaration, a single **char** variable, letter, is declared. In practice, this variable should usually be declared as an integer, because functions that get another character (getc, for example), sometimes need to hold integer values.

```
int letter = 'a';
```

In any case, letter is initialized with a character constant. This constant translates to the numeric code for 'a', which is 97: you can look this up in an ACSII table. (Most personal computers use the ASCII format, although assuming support for ASCII values is not always safe if your code is intended to be ported to different architectures.) Character constants are actually integers.

The preceding declarations of name and address are similar except that they initialize arrays by using character string literals. There is an important difference between single character constants (enclosed in single quotes) and string literals (enclosed in double quotes). A string literal allocates space for every character as well as a null-terminating byte. A string literal also evaluates to the address of the first character, which can be assigned to a pointer or used to initialize an array.

A single character constant evaluates to an integer and not a pointer. This means you can place a string literal anywhere you could place a **char*** type.

The **char** data type is a byte value, so it can hold only 256 different values. Two variations of **char** are:

- **unsigned char**, which ranges from −128 to 127
- **signed char**, which ranges from 0 to 255

The **char** data type without the **signed** or **unsigned** modifier may be signed or unsigned depending on your compiler.

Definition

The name "cin" stands for "character-oriented input stream." Instead of using **scanf**, you can read characters from the standard input device—usually the keyboard—by combining cin with the stream-input operator (>>). (This operator is actually the overloaded right-shift operator.) When you read characters into a numeric variable from **cin**, the input is automatically translated into the appropriate numeric format.

cin is an object of the istream class, and both of them are provided by the C++ library. As an object, cin contains its own built-in functions, in addition to support for the >> operator.

For a fuller description of the object's capabilities, see the topic "istream Class."

Syntax

Remember to include the file **IOSTREAM.H** or **FSTREAM.H** before using **cin** in programs.

```
#include <iostream.h>
```

```
cin >> object      \\ Expression produces another
                   \\ reference to cin
```

Here, *object* is a reference to an object of primitive type (such as **int**, **short**, **long**, **double**, or **char**), character string (**char***), or any class that has built-in support for the stream operator >>. See "istream Class" for a description of how to add this support for your own classes.

Examples

You can use **cout** to print a prompt string, and **cin** to get input in response.

```
#include <iostream.h>
...
cout << "Oh lucky man! Enter your lucky number: "
cin >> lucky_num;
```

Because the expression cin >> object evaluates to cin itself (after setting the value of object), you can use cin to get input for several variables at once:

```
cin >> amount >> n >> xpoint;
```

By rules of associativity (the operator always obeys the associativity and precedence rules of the right-shift operator, >>), the preceding statement is equivalent to this one:

```
((cin >> amount) >> n) >> xpoint;
```

But the expression cin >> amount evaluates to cin, as does cin >> n. So this last statement is in turn is equivalent to the following:

```
cin >> amount;
cin >> n;
cin >> xpoint;
```

Definition

The idea of a class is in many respects the central concept in C++. (As Einstein might say, "All the rest is details.") The idea itself is relatively simple: a class is a user-defined type that has both data and behavior. A class is like a structure in C except that a class can have built-in function support. In addition, a class can have some members that are private and cannot be accessed outside the class. This is called *encapsulation*, and it's a useful way to hide details that the rest of the program should not see.

 Don't let the terminology mislead you here. I'm contrasting classes in C++ with structures as they are supported in C. Actually, in C++, a struct class is just another kind of class, so there is little distinction between classes and structures within C++ itself.

Classes are distinct from objects in that a class defines a type. Classes in C++ are comparable to primitive types such as **int**, **char**, and **double**, and a class name (once declared) can appear in any context that **int**, **char**, or **double** can. An object, by contrast, is like an individual integer, character, or floating-point value. An object has a particular state, whereas a class is a general description of the code and data and does not hold state information. For each class there can be many objects. An object is often referred to as an *instance* of a class, and this terminology is apt.

Much of the apparent complexity of C++ stems from its flexibility and elaboration on the basic concept of class. For example, some member functions have special purposes. Operator functions let you overload operators such as +, /, *, and so on, enabling you to define what these operators do when applied to objects of your class. Constructors and destructors are member functions that take care of initialization and termination.

Devotees of object orientation sometimes speak of classes as enabling you to create data types at a higher level of abstraction than you can in C. What this means is that to some extent you can define a class by defining what it *does* (write functions that carry out the behavior of the class), and you can hide the details of *how* the class does what it does.

Syntax

The full syntax for class declarations is fairly complex. This section summarizes that syntax as much as possible.

You can declare a class in C++ by using either **class**, **struct**, or **union**:

```
class | struct | union  name [base_class_declarations]
{
    declarations
} [object_definitions];
```

Here, the syntax indicates that exactly one of three keywords—**class**, **struct**, or **union**—must be used at the beginning of the declaration. The brackets are used here to indicate that *base_class_declarations* and *object_definitions* are optional.

For the format of *base_class_declarations*, see the topic "Base Classes." The *object_definitions* consist of zero of more variable definitions and can include pointers, arrays, and other compound types.

Each of the three keywords—**class**, **struct**, and **union**—creates a class, with these differences:

- The default member-access level is private if **class** is used. The member-access level is public if **struct** or **union** is used.

- The **struct** and **class** keywords create a type similar to a structure in C. A **union** creates a type in which all data members start at the same address in memory. This means that multiple data formats can exist for the same area of memory. See the topic "Unions" for more information.

Most significantly, the *declarations* in a class consist of any variable and object declarations (data members), function prototypes (member functions), or both. Use of member functions is always optional, as are data members. Note that you can declare member functions even if the class is declared with **struct** or **union**.

Member-access keywords (**public**, **private**, and **protected**) can appear before any of the declarations. These keywords affect all declarations until the next member-access keyword or the end of the class declaration is read.

Syntax

The following declaration of the CStr class includes two data members and six member functions, including one constructor and one destructor:

```
class CStr {
private:
    char *pData;
    int  nLength;
public:
    CStr();              // Constructor
    ~CStr();             // Destructor
    char *get(void) {return pData;}
    int  getlength(void) {return nLength;}
    char *cpy(char *s);
    char *cat(char *s);
};
```

Comments

Definition

The purpose of comments is to let you place useful remarks for a human to read in the source file. A comment has no effect on the actual program, and a programmer is free to put any text in a comment. In addition to remarks on how the program works, comments often contain information such as program author, date, and even a copyright notice—unless the programmer is in a silly mood, in which case the comment might contain anything.

Syntax

The preferred style of comment in C++ is line comment, which causes the compiler to consider all text to the end of the physical line to be a comment:

```
// comment_text
```

C++ also supports the traditional C-language style of comment: comments consist of all text appearing between /* and */. This text forms a part of the program listing or source file, but it is ignored during compilation:

```
/* comment_text */
```

The text may optionally span multiple lines:

```
/* some _text
...
more_text   */
```

The comment syntax has the following exceptions: a begin-comment symbol (// or /*) inside a quoted string does not begin a comment. Also, a begin-comment symbol inside a comment does not begin a comment. This last statement, though it sounds trivial, has important implications for nesting of comments, which I'll discuss at the end of this topic.

Examples

You can use both multiple-line and single-line comments in code:

```
// The next two lines of code are data declarations,
//   declaring two ints and two doubles.

int i, j;      // Indexes into 2-D array
double x, y;   // Point coordinates
```

Where you place comments is entirely up to you. Just remember that you have to write the comments yourself. Usually, you're the main person to read the comments as well. You may come back to a program six months from now and want to modify or debug it. At that point you may find yourself scratching your head, wondering: what *was* the purpose of that function? So comments can be helpful, especially if well written.

The Problem of Nested Comments

One of the uses of traditional C-language style comments is to "comment out" a block of code. To some extent, the risks of doing this are reduced if most of your comments use the C++ line comment symbol (//). However, the practice can still produce errors, so be careful. Using of #if and #endif to temporarily remove lines form compilation is recommended.

For example, the following code, which attempts to next two comments inside one larger comment produces errors. The problem is that the compiler reads a comment from the first /* to the first */.

```
/*
int i, j;      /* Indexes into 2-D array */
double x, y;   /* Point coordinates */
*/
```

Definition

A compound statement is a series of C++ statements (data declarations or executable code) enclosed in braces. This concept is truly simple. The reason it's *useful* is mainly that it enables an **if** block, a **while** loop, or a **for** loop to contain any number of statements.

Some people also refer to a compound statement as a multiple statement.

Syntax

Anywhere an executable statement can occur, a compound statement can also appear. In terms of C++ grammar, a compound statement forms a single, unified statement.

```
{
      statements
}
```

The *statements* consist of one or more C++ statements, and data declarations can be included as long as they precede all executable statements within the compound statement. Generally, each statement is terminated with a semicolon, but that would not be the case if one of those statements were itself a compound statement. Note that a semicolon is not used to terminate the statement block. That's because the closing brace (}) is sufficient for the compiler to know that the end of a compound statement has been reached.

The idea that a compound statement is itself a statement shouldn't be at all confusing, because the concept is taken from English grammar. The statement "First I woke, and then I cried," is made up of two grammatically complete subsentences, but the whole statement makes up one unified sentence.

Example

The following **if** statement tests to see whether a value is out of range. If it is, then the two statements within braces ({}) are executed: a statement that prints an error message and a **return** statement. If the value is not out of range, then neither of these statements is executed, and execution skips past the closing brace (}):

```
if (x < 0 || x > 100) {
    printf("x out of range.");
    return -1;
}
```

Definition

The conditional operator is one of those C++ operators that might seem redundant at first. It returns one of two different values depending on the value of a condition; clearly, you can do the same with an **if-else** statement. But the operator is not entirely redundant, and it does add important elements to the language.

You can find at least two practical purposes for the conditional operator: first, it's an effective code-compacting technique, sometimes reducing several lines of **if-else** code to a one-line expression; second, it's the only reliable way to put **if-else** logic into macro functions, because macros are almost always written as expressions and not as complete statements.

Syntax

The conditional operator forms an expression from three smaller expressions:

```
conditional_expr ? expr1 : expr2
```

Because the result is an expression (and not a complete statement), it can be placed inside larger expressions.

To evaluate this expression, the program first evaluates *conditional_expr*. If it is nonzero, the value of the entire expression is *expr1*. If *conditional_expr* is zero, the value of the entire expression is *expr2*. The program evaluates either *expr1* or *expr2*, as appropriate, but never both.

Usage

One of the simplest ways to use the conditional operator is to call one of two functions. For example:

```
a == b ? function1() : function2();
```

285

This is equivalent to the following if statement:

```
if (a == b)
    function1();
else
    function2();
```

It's more typical, though, to use the value of the expression by placing it all inside a larger expression. Here, one of two different strings is given as input to a printf statement:

```
printf("The value of n is %s.", n ? "one" : "zero");
```

Presumably, n has been limited to one of two values in this example—one and zero.

In this example, the expression using the conditional operator is:

```
n ? "one" : "zero"
```

If n is any nonzero value, this expression returns a pointer to the string "one". Otherwise, it returns a pointer to the string "zero". To understand this example, remember that when a string literal such as "one" appears in code, the compiler allocates the string data in memory somewhere and replaces the expression with a pointer to this data. Consequently, the conditional expression evaluates to the address of one of two strings ("one" or "zero"), and this pointer value is passed as an argument to printf.

So the entire printf example is equivalent to:

```
if (n)
    printf("The value of n is %s.", "one");
else
    printf("The value of n is %s.", "two");
```

Clearly, the version that uses the conditional operator is more compact.

Definition

The **const** keyword lets you create a variable or argument while ensuring that its value won't change. This keyword modifies a declaration, informing the compiler that it must watch for and prevent all assignments to the item. Initialization, however, is allowed.

Arguments and pointers are particularly useful contexts for the **const** keyword: you can use a **const** pointer argument to prevent data corruption by a function ("Usage 3," below.)

Syntax

When used at the beginning of a declaration, **const** modifies the *type*:

```
const type items;
```

Any *items* so declared cannot be the target of an assignment. They can, however, be initialized in the declaration and usually are. If an *item* is a pointer, then anything the pointer points to (such as **item*) cannot be the target of an assignment.

The **const** keyword can also be used inside a pointer declaration:

```
type * const pointer
```

With this syntax, the pointer itself cannot be modified (*item*), but what it points to is not necessarily constant (unless *type* itself is preceded by **const**).

Usage 1: const Variables

The use of **const** with a simple variable is, well, simple. Once a variable is defined with **const**, the compiler flags all statements in which the variable is the target of an assignment.

```
const int id = 12345;   // This is valid; id may be
                        //   initialized.
...
id = 10000;    // ERROR! attempt to assign new value.
```

You can also declare compound types, such as arrays and structures, as **const**. All elements or members become **const** items. For example, no member of the **const** array in the following example can be assigned a new value. (You can think of each element as being a **const** integer.)

```
const int magic_nums[] = {10, 27, 4, 53}
...
magic_num[2] = 99;      // ERROR!
```

Usage 2: const Pointers

If you're familiar with pointers, you may have thought up a loophole for changing a **const** variable. Perhaps you could get a pointer to point to the variable and then use the pointer to change it:

```
const int id = 12345;
int *p;

p = &id;      // ????
*p = 10000;
```

But C++ is just too smart to permit this. C++ does not allow the address of a **const** variable to be assigned to just any old pointer, so the statement that it catches you on this:

```
p = &id;      // ????
```

For the address of a **const** variable to be assigned to a pointer, the pointer must itself point to a **const** type (in this case, **const int**). So the following is legal:

288

```
const int id = 12345;
const int *p;

p = &id;   // Valid, because both are "const int"
                 types.
```

But if you then used p to change the value of the variable indirectly, the compiler would flag that as an error:

```
*p = 10000;   // ERROR; *p cannot change.
```

Think of p, declared as **const int***, as "a pointer to a constant integer." So *p cannot change, because *p is the integer that p points to. Now p itself can change as often as you like, being made to point to different **const** integers. It can also point to regular integers. But *p cannot be assigned a new value as long as p is declared as **const int***.

If you want to prevent p *itself* from changing, place **const** to the right of the indirection operator (*):

```
int * const p = &i;            // p cannot change.
```

Here the pointer p cannot change after being declared and initialized. But the item it points to is of type **int**, so *p can be freely assigned new values. To declare a constant pointer for which neither p nor *p can be assigned a value, use **const** twice:

```
const int * const p = &id;
```

Again, p can be initialized in the declaration, but it cannot be assigned a value in any other assignment statement.

Usage 3: const Argument Types

As pointed out in Chapter 3, "Pointers, Strings, and Things," passing by reference is useful for two reasons: first, it efficiently passes a variable by placing just the address on the stack; second, it enables the function to change the value of the variable.

But in some cases, you might want the advantages of the first reason while preventing the second from happening. You might want to pass an address but guarantee that the function won't change anything at the address—or, if the item pointed to is an array, you want to guarantee that nothing in the array will be changed.

The way to provide this guarantee is to declare the argument as a pointer to a **const** type. For example:

```
void fnct(const char str[], const double *px, *py);
```

This is a function prototype declaring that the pointer variables str, px, and py cannot be used, through indirection, to assign new values to any data. This is useful information, even in a prototype, because it means that you can call the function with complete confidence that it won't corrupt your data. (Of course, some functions do need to change some arguments and so should not use **const** declarations for those arguments.)

Within the function definition itself, you could always *read* the value of *str, *px, or *py. But any of the following statements would be flagged as errors:

```
*str = 'a';
str[1] = '2';
str[2] = 'z';
*px = 0.0
*py = 98.6;
```

Although all the argument types are **const** pointers, you can pass any **char** and **double** addresses you want. Their types do not need to be **const**. This is a consequence of the following rules:

- The address of a **const** item cannot be assigned to a regular pointer (a pointer or argument that is not **const**).

290

- However, the address of a regular item can be assigned to a **const** pointer.

So the following is perfectly legal:

```
void fnct(const char str[], const double *px, *py);

char str[] = "Nice kitty";
double  x, y;
...
fnct(str, &x, &y);
```

Usage 4: onst Member Functions and Objects

If you have a **const** object, you can only call **const** member functions of this object. Such member functions agree not to change any member data.

You can declare a member function as **const** by placing the keyword at the end of the declaration, but before the definition, if any. For example:

```
class:CStr {
        int getlength(void) const {return nLength;}
        char *get(void) const {return pData;}
        ...
```

A **const** member function must not change any data member. Note that you can overload a member function so that it has both a **const** version and a version that is not **const**.

See Chapter 6, "Another Look at Constructors," for more information about **const** member functions.

Constants

Definition

Just as programs have variables, they also have constants, which are fixed values in the program: simple examples include numbers such as 5 and 1.002. Virtually any useful program uses constants somewhere.

Constants come in three basic kinds: literals, symbolic constants, and **const** variables. The rest of this topic concerns literal constants. Symbolic constants (see "#define Directive") are translated into literals by the preprocessor. Variables declared with **const**, are, strictly speaking, variables; but the compiler prevents assignments to them. The purest form of a constant is a literal constant, which expresses a constant value directly.

Syntax

The different forms of literal constant include integer, floating-point, and string literals:

digits	// integer constant
0*digits*	// integer constant, octal notation (leading zero)
0X*digits*	// integer constant, hexadecimal notation
digits.digits	// floating-point constant
*digits***E***exp*	// floating-point constant with exponent
"*string_text***"**	// character string constant
'*character***'**	// single character constant

Here, **X** and **E** indicate either an uppercase or a lowercase letter.

Thus, 5 is an integer constant, whereas 5.0 is a floating-point constant. Here are some examples of other floating-point constants:

```
3.1415
12000.5
63e-2
85.66789e12
```

Storage Specification

Constant values are stored in memory in the most efficient way possible, although you can control how they are stored to some extent. On 16-bit systems, an integer is stored as a two-byte signed integer if not outside the two-byte integer range; if outside this range, it must be stored as a long. However, the suffix U forces it to be stored as an unsigned integer regardless of size. An L suffix forces it to be stored as a **long**. (The lowercase versions of these letters can also be used.) The suffix UL forces it to be stored as an **unsigned long**. For example, the following number is stored as a long, even though it is small:

```
7L
```

Floating-point constants are normally stored as double, regardless of value, unless you specify float as the size with an f or F suffix:

```
1.005F
```

Single-character and character-string constants are different, which is why it's important to remember to use only single quotes with character constants. A character constant translates into its ASCII equivalent. For example, '0' is another way of representing the number 48. But its the way a value is used, rather than its numeric value, that determines whether it is a letter or a number. Although you can print the numeric value of a character constant, such constants are usually intended to be used in string operations.

A string constant is an array of type **char**, and has a terminating null byte. See Chapter 3, "Pointers, Strings, and Things," for more information, and the topic "String Literals" for some of the more advanced rules applying to strings representation.

Constructors

Definition

A constructor is a function that is automatically called when an object is created. When you first start using C++, you may view constructors as the source of extra work ("You mean, I have to write a constructor for each of my classes?"), but, they're really a great convenience. Serious C programs often create new data that needs to be initialized. C programmers end up writing initialization functions they have to call explicitly.

By providing constructors, C++ enables you to write initialization functions that are called automatically. This saves time and reduces the possibility of error from forgetting to call the function. Moreover, C++ increases flexibility by letting you write a variety of constructors, each using a different type of data, or combination of data, to initialize an object.

> **When you dynamically create objects, use new and delete rather than the malloc and free functions.**
> N O T E **Otherwise, C++ cannot determine that the constructor and destructor should be called.**

Chapter 6, "Another Look at Constructors," introduces the subject of constructors in detail. As that chapter explains, constructors (as well as destructors) are particularly useful with classes that involve dynamic memory allocation or some other special operation requiring initialization.

This topic summarizes constructor syntax and gives a few short examples. After giving the basic syntax, the topic discusses the two special kinds of constructors: the default constructor and the copy constructor.

Basic Syntax

A constructor has the same name as the class it's a member of. Constructors have no return type (not even **void**). The class itself is the implicit return type.

```
class(arguments)
```

Here, *arguments* is zero or more arguments. Using function overloading, you can create any number of constructors. Constructors are like other member functions in almost every respect, although constructors are not inherited.

Make sure that constructors are declared as public, or else the rest of the program won't have access to them (except inside a friend function). For example:

```
class CPict {
private:
    long cost;
    int  nStars;
    CStr sDirector;

public:
// Constructors
    CPict();
    CPict(long c, int n, CStr dir);
...
};

// Function defintions for constructors
CPict::CPict() {
}

CPict::CPict(long c, int n, CStr dir) {
    cost = c;
    nStars = n;
    sDirector = dir;
}
```

Like most other functions, constructors can be inlined. For example:

```
class CPict {
...
    CPict() {}
```

Default Constructor

The default constructor in each class is the constructor that has no arguments. This constructor is important because C++ automatically invokes it in the following situations: when someone defines an object of the class with no arguments, when an array of objects is declared with uninitialized members, or when the **new** operator is used but no arguments are specified for the new object.

 Technically speaking, a default constructor is one without any nondefault arguments. You can specify one or
NOTE more arguments with default values (see the topic "Default Argument Values"), and the result is still a default constructor. But because of C++ function overloading rules, you will never have more than one default constructor in any case.

Here's the syntax for a default constructor:

```
class()
```

Interestingly enough, C++ provides a compiler-supplied (hidden) default constructor—but only as long as there are no constructors in the source code. This is significant: unless a constructor of the appropriate type exists, C++ will not let you create an object. The fact that such a constructor might "do nothing" (perform no statements in the body of the function) does not matter. C++ still insists that the constructor be there.

The practical significance of all this is that if you rely on the hidden default constructor and then go back and add any other constructor, the hidden default constructor will mysteriously vanish! You won't be able to define objects without specifying arguments. As a bit of defensive programming, you should always supply your own default constructor even if it does nothing.

To save time and space, you can write a simple constructor that does nothing and inline it, as described at the end of the previous section.

Copy Constructor

In some ways, the copy constructor is the most interesting constructor of all, because it's invoked in situations you might not think about: initializing an object by using another of the same class, passing an object by value, and using an object as a return value from a function. The following code provides examples of all three situations:

```
// Call copy constructor to create paul_revere

CHorse  harry_the_horse;  // Default constr.
CHorse  paul_revere(harry_the_horse); // Copy constr.

// Call copy constructor to pass an argument

Bet_On(paul_revere);

// Call copy constructor for CHorse return value

return harry_the_horse;
```

The second and third examples assume that the CHorse object is not passed or returned as a reference, because in that case the copy constructor is not invoked. (See the topic "Reference Operator (&).")

Whenever you do not explicitly write a copy constructor for your classes, the C++ compiler provides a hidden copy constructor for you. This constructor does not mysteriously vanish as the default constructor can (see the discussion in the previous section). The compiler provides a default behavior: a simple member-by-member copy operation. This copying in turn invokes the copy constructor of each individual member.

In many cases, this member-by-member copying is sufficient. However, if objects of the class require any special initialization—if, for example, they have one or more pointers to dynamically allocated memory—relying on this default copying behavior can cause errors. Worse, the errors are likely to crop up when you might not expect it (for example, you innocently pass the object as a value argument to a function). Therefore, whenever any dynamic memory or pointers are involved, write your own copy constructor.

The syntax for a copy constructor is as follows:

```
class(class& src)
```

The constructor may include other arguments as long as they have default values. (This variation on the syntax is relatively rare, however.)

Note that the argument (*src*) must be passed as a reference. This is required not only for reasons of efficiency, but also because otherwise the passing of *src* would involve another call to the copy constructor—leading in turn to an infinite regress.

The following example is taken from Chapter 6, "Another Look at Constructors." Note the use of the strcpy function, which implements a so-called deep copy operation—as opposed to simply copying pointer values.

```
class CStr {
...
public:
    CStr(CStr &str);
...

CStr::CStr(CStr &str) {
    char* s = str.get();
    int n = str.getlength();
    pData = (char *) malloc(n);
    strcpy(pData, s);
    nLength = n;
}
```

Context Operator (::)

Definition

The context operator (::) clarifies what symbol you're referring to. For example, this operator can turn a function name into a reference to a member function of a particular class (*class::function_name*). The context operator can also be used to refer to a global symbol—that is, one not defined in the class.

When code appears inside a member function, it has class scope. By default, such code refers to class members rather than global variables whenever there is a name conflict. Therefore, specifying global context (*::symbol*) is sometimes the only way to refer to a global function or variable.

This operator is most often used in member-function definitions, as described in Chapter 5, "A Touch of Class."

Syntax

The context operator is used in one of two ways:

```
class::symbol
::symbol
```

The first syntax specifies that the symbol referred to is the one declared in the *class*. The second syntax specifies that the symbol referred to is the one not declared in any class.

Usage

By far the most common use of the context operator is in definitions of member functions, in which the function is defined outside the class. Here, the context operator is necessary because any number of different classes can have a member function of the same name. Even if you don't currently use the function name in more than one class, C++ still requires the *class::* prefix.

```
class CStr {
    char *get(void);
    int getlength(void);
...
char *CStr::get(void) {  // CStr:: prefix used here
    return pData;
}
int CStr::getlength(void) { // CStr:: prefix used here
    return nLength;
}
```

Another common use is inside a derived class to refer to a base-class version of a member function. For example, in the following code, CStr::cpy refers to the version of the cpy function defined in CStr, the base class. The name cpy, appearing without a prefix, would refer to the version defined in CIoStr (CIoStr::cpy). This makes a difference if CIoStr overrides the cpy function in CStr by providing a different definition.

```
void CIoStr::input(void) {
    char buffer[256];

    gets(buffer);
    CStr::cpy(buffer);   // Call base-class version
                         //  of cpy.
}
```

300

Definition

The **continue** keyword jumps to the end of a loop but (unlike **break**) doesn't exit the loop. This is a reasonably simple idea; it's like someone saying, "Go onto the next page, please."

Syntax

The **continue** keyword, followed by a semicolon, forms a complete state306
ment:

```
continue;
```

This statement is valid only within a **for** loop, a **while** loop, or a **do-while** loop. The effect is to jump to the bottom of the loop (executing the *increment* expression, if in a **for** loop) and then continue to the next iteration.

Examples

Ultimately, the **continue** statement isn't a necessity but is merely a convenience. You could accomplish the same results by putting a label at the bottom of the loop and then using a **goto** statement. For example, the following code

```
while (expression) {
    statements
    continue;
    statements
    }
```

is equivalent to the code shown in Figure C.1.

301

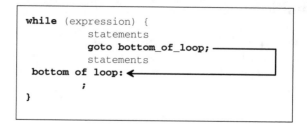

```
while (expression) {
        statements
        goto bottom_of_loop;
        statements
  bottom of loop:
        ;
}
```

Figure C.1 Effect of a continue statement.

In Figure C.1, I've added an empty statement—a lone semicolon (;)—for syntactical correctness. At least one statement must follow a label. An empty statement is completely legal and is useful in this situation.

There is one respect in which Figure C.1 is an oversimplification: you wouldn't put a naked **continue** or **goto** inside the loop like this. A **continue** or **goto** is almost always enclosed within an **if** statement. Otherwise, the second set of statements would never be executed, and it would have been pointless to have written them in the first place.

In any event, the purpose of the **continue** keyword is get out of the statement block early, without getting out of the loop. For example, the following code prints all the prime numbers between 1 and n. The body of the loop first tests i to see whether it is a prime number and then advances directly to the next value of i if it is not a prime. Otherwise, it prints the results before advancing to the next value of i.

```
for(i = 1, num_of_primes++; i <= n; i++) {
    if (! is_a_prime(i))
        continue;
    printf("%d\n", i);
    num_of_primes++;
}
```

In this example, is_a_prime is a function defined in the program. This function could be defined as follows:

```
#include <math.h>

int is_a_prime (int n) {
    int i, test_val;

    test_val = int(sqrt(n));
    for (i = 2; i <= test_val; i++) {
        if ((n % i) == 0)
                return 0;
    }
    return 1;
}
```

**It's certainly possible to write nested loops in C++
(loops inside other loops). The continue statement
always applies to the nearest (most tightly enclosing)
for, while, or do loop.**

Definition

A conversion function does what you'd expect; it's a member function that tells C++ how to convert from an object to another type. Notably, a conversion function handles an outgoing conversion (converting from objects of the class to another type); incoming conversions are handled by constructors. This distinction is discussed in Chapter 8, "Class Operations."

For a given class C, with a member function to convert to type T, the conversion function is invoked when any of the following occurs:

- An explicit type cast, (T), is applied to an object of class C.

- An object of class C is specified as an argument in a function call, where type T is expected (and for which C would not otherwise be accepted).

- An object of class C is assigned to a destination of type T.

The last two cases are examples of C++ implicit type casting. C++ supports this conversion only to one level. For example, if class C has a conversion function to T and if T itself is a class with a conversion function to T2, this does not necessarily imply that there is a conversion from C to T2.

Syntax

To enable conversions from a class to a specified *type*, declare a member function within the class as follows:

```
operator type ()
```

The function must return a value of the indicated *type*.

Example

The following example declares a hypothetical class, CFix, which has a member function to convert to long. The CFix class supports a fixed-point number, which is scaled by a factor of 1,000. Thus, 7.5 is represented as 7500, and 11.003 is represented as 11003. The conversion function uses the modulus operator (%) to get the remainder from dividing by 1,000, which can be used to round up or down by one.

```
class CFix {
private:
    long amount;

public:
    operator long ();   // Convert CFix to long
...
};

CFix::operator long () {
    int round = ((amount % 1000) >= 500);
    return amount / 1000 + round;
}
```

Definition

The name "cout" stands for "character-oriented output stream." Instead of using **printf**, you can print characters to the standard output device—usually the monitor—by combining cout with the stream-output operator (<<). (This operator is actually the overloaded left-shift operator.) When you print numeric values using **cout**, the output is automatically translated into ASCII form (or whatever character-coding convention is used on your computer).

cout is an object of the ostream class, and both of them are provided by the C++ library. As an object, it contains its own built-in functions in addition to support for the << operator.

For a fuller description of the object's capabilities, see the topic "ostream class."

Syntax

Remember to include the file **IOSTREAM.H** or **FSTREAM.H** before using cout in programs.

```
#include <iostream.h>
```

```
cout << value  // Expression produces another
               // reference to cout
```

Here, *value* is an expression of the following type: primitive type (such as **int**, **short**, **long**, **double**, or **char**), character string (**char***), or any class that has built-in support for the stream operator <<. See "ostream Class" for a description of how to add this support for your own classes.

Examples

You can use **cout** to print a prompt string, and **cin to** get input in response.

```
#include <iostream.h>
...
cout << "Oh lucky man! Enter your lucky number: "
cin >> lucky_num;
```

Because the expression cout << value evaluates to cout itself (after printing the value), you can use **cout** to print several expressions at once:

```
cout << "You made " << d << " dollars.\n";
```

By rules of associativity (the operator always obeys the associativity and precedence rules of the left-shift operator, <<), the preceding statement is equivalent to this one:

```
((cout << "You made ") << d) << " dollars.\n";
```

But the expression cout << "You made " evaluates to cout, as does cout << d. So this last statement is in turn is equivalent to the following:

```
cout << "You made ";
cout << d;
cout << "dollars.\n";
```

Data Abstraction

Definition

The meaning of *abstraction* is a source of endless arguments among C++ devotees, but the term does have some meaning. In ordinary language, *abstract* means "transcending the details." We might apply the concept to programming languages by rephrasing it as *"freedom* from details."

Data abstraction attempts to define a data type in terms of how it is used, while at the same time hiding the details of implementation. To some extent, the concepts of "integer" and "floating point" can be viewed as abstract types. But it is important to know about ranges, which in turn involves knowledge of the size of the type.

A file pointer (a pointer to a FILE structure, defined in **STDIO.H**) comes closer to realizing the goal of data abstraction. You can use a file pointer without ever seeing or caring about the actual layout of the FILE structure. The general notion of file pointer is the abstract type, and code that uses it should work regardless of the brand of compiler or machine. The declaration of FILE for a particular compiler is the implementation.

Although data abstraction is almost more a state of mind than anything else, C++ provides several tools that can be used to further the goals of data abstraction:

- Use of private members (encapsulation) helps hide a data type's implementation.

- You can declare as private some or all the data members in a class and provide access only through member functions. This means that the class is defined in terms of what it *does* rather than how it's built.

- In the case of collection classes, you can use templates to define a general type. (See the topic "Templates.")

Data Types

Definition

C++ supports a variety of data types. The two major categories are primitive data types and compound data types. Primitive data types are ones directly supported by keywords such as **int** and **double**. Compound data types can be created through complex declarations that involve the **class**, **struct**, or **union** keywords, pointers, or arrays. You can optionally use the **typedef** keyword to provide an alias for a complex type and then use this alias to declare variables just as you would use primitive-data-type keywords.

The rest of this section summarizes the standard data types in C++ and their minimum ranges. Some implementations of C++ support extended types, such as 64-bit integers. For more precise information on range and precision, see topics for individual keywords.

C++ has no primitive string type unless you define one. Text strings are represented as arrays of **char**.

Table D.1 Data types in C.++

Type	Description	Range and Precision
signed char	One byte integer	−128 to 127
unsigned char	One byte integer, unsigned	0 to 255
char	Same as **char** or **unsigned char**, depending on the implementation	
short	Two-byte integer	−32,768 to 32,767
unsigned short	Two-byte integer, unsigned	0 to 65,535
long	Four-byte integer	Approx. −2.147 billion to 2.147 billion
unsigned long	Four-byte integer, unsigned	0 to approx. 4.292 billion
int	Same as **short** or **long**, depending on implementation	
unsigned int, or unsigned	Same as unsigned **short** or **unsigned long**, depending on implementation	
float	Four-byte floating point	Approx. plus or minus 3.4 times 10 to the 38th. Seven digits of precision
double	Eight-byte floating point	Approx. plus or minus 1.7 times 10 to the 308th. π15 digits of precision

Declarations

Defintion

True to their name, declarations are like declarative sentences in English. They don't exactly tell the processor to do something; they give information about how a variable or function is to be used. Executable statements, in contrast, are more nearly like imperative sentences, commanding an action such as adding numbers or printing a result.

In C++, a declaration has one of two purposes: to define a variable or to provide type information to the compiler about something defined elsewhere in the program. The latter category includes **extern** declarations and function prototypes.

Syntax

A declaration forms a complete statement. The possible syntax for declarations is potentially complicated, but it can be basically summarized as below:

[storage] [cv] type item [, item]... ;

Here the brackets indicate that something is optional. The ellipses indicate that *item* can be repreated any number of times. The *storage* can be **extern**, **static**, **auto**, or **register**. The *cv* syntax represents **const** or **volatile**.

The critical part of this syntax is *item*, which itself can be simple or frighteningly complex. Each *item* has the following syntax:

decl_specifier [= initializer]

The initializer can be any valid constant, including an aggregate in the case of compound types. (See "Aggregates.") The *decl_specifier* is frequently just a variable name, but it may also involve pointer indirection (*), a function call (parentheses), and array brackets ([]), to any level of complexity. In general, the *decl_specifier* can be any of the following:

identifier
decl_specifier[index]
*decl_specifier
decl_specifier(argument_list)

In decl_specifier[index], the brackets are intended literally." The *index* is optional; it need not be fixed if the dimension size is supplied elsewhere (by the calling function or by an aggregate). If it is supplied, *index* must be a positive, constant integer.

Examples

By applying this syntax recursively, you can make declarations as complex as needed. Some examples should help clarify. The simplest declaration just declares a variable (in this case, a variable called "count"):

```
int count;
```

On one line, you can declare as many variables—all of the same type—as you need. Unless preceded by the **extern** keyword, these declarations are definitions—that is, they actually create the variables.

```
int     count, a, b, c;
double  x, y, z;
```

When defining variables, you can selectively initialize any variables in the list that you wish. This is a particularly good idea with local variables, which otherwise are intialized to random values (global variables are initialized to zero or NULL).

```
int     count = 0, a, b, c = 15, d;
```

Any of the items declared can be an array, a pointer, a function, or compound types made up of these elements:

```
double    a, b, *ptr, c, fn(), arr[50], x, y;
double    matrix[5][5];
long      (*fn1)(), *f2(), *array_of_ptrs[10];
```

Parentheses can be used to determine precedence in interpreting the operators. For example, in the last declaration above, fn1 is a pointer to a function returning type **double**; f2 is a function returning a pointer to type **double**.

Prototypes and Pointers to Functions

In the last line of the preceding example, *f2() is a function prototype and (*fn1)() is a pointer declaration. The way to distinguish these correctly is to consider that if (*fn1)() appears in executable code, the indirection operator (*) is resolved before a function call is launched. Therefore, f1 must be a pointer to a function, whereas *f2() is a function returning a pointer to a **long**.

```
long      (*f1)(), *f2();
```

Let's look carefully at how the operators resolve. First, suppose that f1 is declared along with a function, fnct, that simply returns a **long**:

```
long      (*f1)(), fnct();
```

Because f1 is a pointer, it needs to be initialized to the address of a function:

```
// After this assignment, f1 points to fnct(), so that
// *f1 refers to fnct().

f1 = &fnct;
```

Now if the expression (*f1)() appears in an executable statement, it is resolved as shown in Figure D.1.

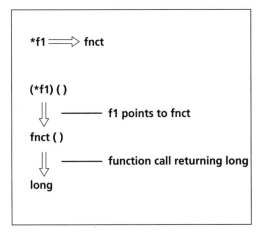

Figure D.1 Calling a function through a pointer.

Figure D.1 shows how f1, used in code, is evaluated as a *pointer to a function.* A declaration reflects how something is used in code; therefore, f1's status as a pointer to a function is determined by its declaration. Similarly, if *f2() appears in executable code, it must be resolved as a function returning a pointer, as shown in Figure D.2.

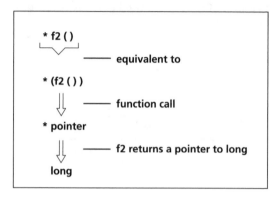

Figure D.2 A function that returns a pointer.

So f2 must be an actual function—regardless of its return type—and it must have a function definition somewhere in the program. So far, it has only been declared as a prototype.

To improve type checking, an argument list should be added to the prototype. The argument names (a and b) are optional.

```
long    *f2(int a, int b);
```

Even if the function is intended to be called with no arguments, it should have an argument list: **void**.

```
long    *f2(void);
```

If f2 is an actual function, what is f1? Because f1 is only a pointer, it would be an error to provide a function definition for f1. Instead, f1 must be set to point to something that *is* a real function (a_real_function in the following example). At that point, indirect calls can be made through f1.

```
long  johns = 0;
long  a_real_function(int a, int b);
```

```
long  (*f1)(int a, int b);

f1 = & a_real_function; // f1 -> a_real_function
johns = (*f1)(3, 5);  // Call function f1 points to.
...
long  a_real_function(int a, int b) {
    return (a * b);
}
```

Pointers to functions may seem strange, but they definitely have their uses. See "Pointers to Functions" for further discussion.

Storage Class and Other Modifiers

Each declaration may have one of the following storage class modifiers:

extern
static
auto
register

And one of the following modifiers:

const
volatile

The use of these keywords can affect the overall meaning of the declaration. If a variable declaration includes the **extern** modifier and does not have an initializer, it is an external variable declaration only; it does not *define* the variable (it does not actually allocate space for this variable in program memory). The variable must be defined somewhere in the program—either in the current source file or in another module to be linked to the program.

```
extern int  cents_less;  // cents_less defined somewhere
```

315

With **extern**, declarations do not define the variable. Be careful here, because a variable of global scope must be defined in only one place. For this reason, **extern** declarations should be placed in header files, and variable definitions should never be placed there. (If you're not using multiple modules, by the way, **extern** is not particularly useful and even header files are not terribly necessary.)

Class Declaration

Class declarations are another major kind of declaration in C++. See "Classes" for more information.

Default Argument Values

Definition

C++ lets you specify parameters (formal arguments) that take on a default values when omitted from a function call. Parameters with default values must come at the end of the argument list, so C++ can to figure out which parameters should get argument values and which should get their default values.

Syntax

An argument with a default value has the following declaration, which follows the same rules as initialization in a variable definition:

declaration = value

Argument declarations with default values must come at the end of an argument list. All nondefault argument declarations, if any, must precede all declarations with default values, if any. Beyond that there are no restrictions on number: you can have zero or more of each kind. So a function declaration that had multiples of each kind (nondefault arguments and default arguments) has the following form:

type funct(type1 arg1, type2 arg2, ...
typeN argN=val1, typeM argM=val2, ...);

Examples

The simplest case is a function with a single argument having a default value:

```
short SetFlag(short bVal=1);
```

Given this declaration, the following calls are equivalent:

```
SetFlag();
SetFlag(1);
```

A more complex example uses multiple arguments:

```
void SetVars(int count, double a = 0.0; double b = 0.0);
```

This function must be called with at least one argument (because count does not have a default value) and, at most, three arguments. So the following function calls are equivalent:

```
SetVars(5);
SetVars(5, 0.0, 0.0);
```

C++ assigns argument values to parameters in left-to-right order. The first argument, for example, gets assigned to the leftmost parameter. The second argument, if any, gets assigned to the next parameter. This is why default arguments must come at the end of the list.

Consider this function call:

```
SetVars(5, 3.5);
```

This function call passes 5, 3.5, and 0.0 to the parameters count, a, and b, respectively. Assigning values to the leftmost arguments first, C++ does not assign either of the two arguments to b in this case. Therefore, b gets the default value.

Comments

Some additional comments about default argument values may be of interest, especially if you use this feature often.

There's nothing magic about this feature. It is implemented at compile time as a convenience to the programmer. The C++ compiler itself recognizes that a call to

```
SetVars(3);
```

is the same as

```
SetVars(3, 0.0, 0.0);
```

So the compiler implements the call by generating code to place three arguments on the stack. This is different from the variable-argument-list feature of C and C++, in which a different number of arguments may actually be placed on the stack at run time. Here, the function always expects exactly three arguments.

The use of default arguments has an effect on function overloading. To recognize that two functions sharing the same name are actually separate functions, function overloading depends on the types of two arguments differing. But the arguments must differ in at least one *nondefault argument*. This makes perfect sense if you think about it. Suppose overloaded functions were declared as follows:

```
void MyFunc(int i=1);
void MyFunc(double x=0.01);
```

How would the compiler know which function to call, given the following statement?

```
MyFunc(); // Call MyFunc(int) or MyFunc(double)???
```

Definition

The **#define** directive has three broad purposes: first, to provide an easy, efficient way to create readable constants (called *symbolic constants*); second, to enable you to write macro functions, which are similar to functions but supported through text replacement at compile time rather than through a run-time call. Finally, the directive can be used to define a symbol for the sake of controlling a condition during compilation (in conjunction with statements such as **#ifdef**).

Syntax

The **#define** statement can be used in any of the following ways:

#define   *identifier replacement*
#define   *identifier(arg1 [,arg2...]) replacement*
#define   *identifier*

Here, the brackets indicate an optional item that can be repeated any number of times. The *replacement* is a series of nonspace characters; however, *replacement* can include embedded spaces if delimited by parentheses or quotation marks. You can use line-continuation (\) to continue beyond one physical line.

Usage 1: Symbolic Constants

Many programs deal with arbitrary or difficult-to-remember numbers. For example, you might have a program that does a lot of trig calculations, and you need to use pi (an important quantity in math equal to approximately 3.14159265). You can define a constant to represent pi as follows:

```
#define PI   3.14159265
```

By convention, symbolic constants are always uppercase. (This distinguishes them from variables.) Of course, the compiler will let you use any name you want.

Given this **#define** directive, wherever the word "PI" appears in your program, the compiler replaces PI with the numeral 3.14159265. This happens from the point at which PI is defined to end of the current source file. If you ever change the value of PI—perhaps you decide to use a more precise approximation—you need only change it in one place: the **#define** directive.

 The symbol is not replaced if it appears in a comment, a quoted string, or as part of a larger word (PI inside PIG is not replaced).

A symbolic constant is different from a variable that merely has a constant value, although the two things may at first seem the same. For example, you could define PI as a variable set to this value:

```
double pi = 3.14159265;
```

This data definition allocates a double-precision floating-point number (eight bytes), taking valuable space in the data area used for program variables. Using a **#define** here would have taken no variable space; instead, the compiler's preprocessor replaces each occurrence of "PI" in the program text with "3.14159265." The change is not permanent; it does not overwrite your copy of the program source code. But the effect is the same as if you had typed "3.14159265" everywhere instead of "PI".

An important aspect of symbolic constants is that you can use them for variable initialization. For example, you couldn't do the following if PI itself were a global variable:

```
double angle1 = PI / 2;
```

Symbolic constants are most frequently used for representing arbitrary numbers, such as the maximum string size or size of an array. Typically, you define all such numbers as symbolic constants at the beginning of the program—or in a header file if using multiple modules (because constants have to be defined in each individual module, and a header file ensures that every module gets them). Then, if you ever need to change a definition, you need change it only in one place. For example:

```
#define   ROWSIZE   30
#define   COLSIZE   20
...
int matrix[ROWSIZE][COLSIZE];
int matrix2[ROWSIZE][COLSIZE];
```

The **#define** directive need give no replacment value; in that case, if the symbol is found anywhere, it is replaced with an empty string (no characters); in other words, the occurrence of the symbol is simply removed without replacement, before compilation.

Usage 2: Macro Functions

Macro functions are similar to standard functions but are implemented by the C++ preprocessor rather than through a run-time call. For example, given the definition

```
#define max(A, B)   ((A)>(B)?(A):(B))
```

the preprocessor replaces the expression "max(i, j)" with the following just before compiling:

```
((i)>(j)?(i):(y))
```

The effect is roughly the same as if you wrote a function named max that returned the larger of two values passed to it.

There are few things possible with standard functions that are not possible with macros. The main limitation of macro functions is that they provide absolutely no type checking.

The use of parentheses around each argument in the replacement pattern (as shown in the previous example) is a good idea because it forces evaluation of each argument before the surrounding operators are resolved. Otherwise, if the arguments themselves contain operators, the effect of a macro function can be difficult to predict.

Usage 3: Controlling Compilation

If you use the **#ifdef** or **#ifndef** directive anywhere in the code, then the compiler either reads or ignores certain blocks of code, depending on which symbols are defined. See "#ifdef Directive" for a fuller explanation.

The **#ifdef** and **#ifndef** directives don't care where a symbol is defined, merely that it is defined. You can define a symbol without giving it a replacement value; in that case, if it does appear anywhere, it is replaced with an empty string. However, it is still a valid symbol for the purposes of directives such as **#ifdef**:

```
#define USE_8086
...
#ifdef USE_8086
// Optimize for Intel
...
#endif
```

Most often, symbols that control compilation are specified on the command line; see your compiler documentation for more information.

Definitions vs. Declarations

Definition

The terms *definition* and *declaration* are closely related in C++:

- Every definition is a declaration.

- But not every declaration is a definition.

The difference is important. A definition creates a variable—meaning that it actually causes the compiler to allocate space in program memory. Each variable must have a unique definition that occurs once and only once in the program. Other kinds of declarations—**extern** declarations and function prototypes—are not unique and can be included in every module.

The following example is a variable definition. Because the definition creates the variable and allocates space for it, it can also initialize it.

```
int i = 5;
```

Declarations that are not definitions exist only to give scope and type information to the compiler. The two most common examples are extern variable declarations and function prototypes. Declarations can also create structures, unions, and types. All kinds of declarations can be profitably placed in a header file, especially when you are working with more than one module.

Examples

Here are some examples of declarations that are not definitions:

```
extern int i; // Integer i defined somewhere, possibly in
              // another module

void fnct(double x); // Prototype
```

324

NOTE A #define directive is neither a data definition nor a declaration but is merely an instruction to the preprocessor. Despite the name, a #define directive is much more like a declaration than a definition, because it can safely be placed in a header file.

Definition

The **delete** operator destroys an object that has been dynamically allocated with the **new** operator. Statically created objects, which are created by defining them at the local or global level, are automatically destroyed when they go out of scope or when the program terminates. But when you create an object with the **new** operator, it is never destroyed and the memory it occupies is never released unless you use **delete**. Letting a program end without destroying all your dynamically created objects is a source of memory leaks; these leaks in turn can cause your system to mysteriously run out of memory over time.

In many respects, **delete** is the counterpart of the **free** function, which is used with **malloc**. But there is an important difference: the **new** and **delete** operators call the new object's constructors and destructors. When you allocate and free memory used for primitive types, it is safe to use **malloc** and **free**. But when the memory is to be used to hold more sophisticated objects, you should always use **new** and **delete**.

Syntax

To destroy an object previously created with **new**, use one of the following:

```
delete  pointer;    // Points to an object
delete [] pointer;   // Points to an array of objects
```

Here, *pointer* holds the value returned by a previous use of **new**. If this use of **new** involved either a one-dimensional or multidimensional array, then use the second syntax; otherwise, use the first syntax.

Example

The following short example illustrates the use of **delete**:

```
CStr *pStr = new CStr("Hello there.");
...
delete pStr;
```

Definition

A derived class is a class with one or more base classes. This generally means that one or more members of the class are not declared in the class itself; instead, they are declared in a base class. This is the C++ facility known as *inheritance*, which is frequently a convenient technique for reusing code. A derived class is typically a more specialized variation of its base class. For example, the CMammal class, derived from CAnimal, has all the characteristics of CAnimal but adds specialized characteristics of its own.

The term *derived* is relative, because a derived class can be a base class for another class. For example, from CMammal you could derive CPrimate.

For more information on the syntax of derived classes, see Chapter 8, "Inheritance: C++ and Good Genes," or the topics "Base Classes" and "Inheritance."

Definition

A destructor is a function that is automatically called when an object is destroyed. (Yes, this sounds harsh. See the note on terminology.) Destruction can happen when an object goes out of scope, when the program ends, or when the **delete** operator is used on a pointer to the object. When you declare a class, the C++ compiler creates a default destructor for you if you don't write one yourself. Therefore, there is always a destructor present even if you don't see one in the code.

When an object is destroyed, the default behavior is to destroy each member of the object (except for static members). In many cases, this behavior is perfectly adequate. But it's important to write your own destructor when there is additional cleanup to be done: The most common example is an object that has pointers to dynamically allocated memory or to open files.

N O T E The use of "destroyed" here, as in "...when the object is destroyed," may seem unnecessarily violent. But there is good reason to use the term. Freeing memory is not necessarily the same as destroying it, although freeing memory might be sufficient in plain, ordinary C. When an object is destroyed in C++, it means that its destructor is called and not merely that its memory is freed. Destruction is actually benevolent. It implies that each object terminates by first calling destructors, if any, for each of its member objects, thus politely giving every object the chance to tie up any loose ends. This process happens recursively, so all the destructors that need to get called do get called.

Syntax

A class destructor has the same name as the class except that the name is preceded by a tilde (~):

~class()

A destructor has no return type (not even **void**) and no arguments. Destructors cannot be declared **static**, **const**, or **volatile**, but they can be declared **virtual**.

Example

In this example, the CHorse class dynamically allocates memory for a name when a CHorse object is created. The destructor, ~CHorse(), frees this memory.

```
#include <malloc.h>
#include <string.h>

class CHorse {
private:
    char *pName;
public:
    CHorse(char *name);
    ~CHorse();
...

CHorse::CHorse(char *name) {
    int n = strlen(name);
    pName = (char*) malloc(n);
    strcpy(pName, name);
}

CHorse::~CHorse() {
    free pName;
}
```

do Statement

Definition

In working with loops, sometimes you want to ensure that the body of the loop is executed at least once. This is what a **do-while** loop is for. In virtually all other respects, it is the same as a **while** loop—executing as long as a specified condition is true.

Syntax

A **do-while** statement forms one unified statement in C++:

do
    loop_body_statement
while (*expression*);

The *loop_body_statement* is frequently a compound statement (see "Example"). Because the entire **do-while** loop forms one statement, it can be nested inside other control structures. The loop continues execution as long as *expression* evaluates to a nonzero (true) value.

Example

The following statements output characters from a file until the end of the file is reached. At least one character is read. In the case of an empty file, this character is an end-of-file character (EOF), which is defined in the file STDIO.H.

```
#include <stdio.h>
...
do {
    c = getc(fp);
    putchar(c);
} while (c != EOF);
```

Definition

The **double** data type is a double-precision floating-point number, stored in eight bytes. The related, but smaller, type is **float** (although one would expect it to be "single" so as to correspond better to **double**).

Range and Precision

Approximately plus or minus 1.8 times 10 to the 308th power, with 14 places of precision after the decimal point. Tiny nonzero values can get as close to zero as approximately plus or minus 4.9 times 10 to the –324th power. The type can also hold the value zero precisely.

Syntax

You can declare any number of double-precision floating-point numbers by placing **double** at the beginning of the declaration statement:

[*storage*] [*cv*] **double** *items*;

Here the brackets indicate optional prefixes: *storage* is a storage-class specifier (**auto, extern, register, static**) and *cv* is **const, volatile**, or both. The *items* are one or more simple or complex variable declarations.

Example

The following statement defines a simple variable (temperature), an array (daily_temps), and a pointer (ptr_to_float):

```
double   temperature, daily_temps[200], *ptr_to_float;
```

Usage

The **double** floating-point format is generally preferable to **float**, except where storage space is at a premium (such as files, structures, and arrays of structures). It's difficult to compare efficiency of **float** calculations against those using **double**, because different systems implement floating-point operations in different ways. However, math coprocessors typically operate directly on eight-byte floating-point numbers, making **double** at least as fast to operate on as **float**. The recent trend in microprocessors is to support on-board math-coprocessor instructions, having the effect of giving every system a coprocessor.

#elif Directive

Definition

The **#elif** directive is useful in conditional compilation when you want to specify a series of alternatives, similar to an **else if** statement. An **#elif** directive specifies a compile-time condition just as an **#if** directive does.

Syntax

The directive specifies a condition that is a constant integer expression:

#elif *constant_expression*

As with the **#if** directive, the *constant_expression* may not include the **sizeof** operator, type casts, or **enum** constants. The expression may include the special **define**(*symbol*) operator, which evaluates to 1 if *symbol* is previously defined and 0 otherwise.

See "#if Directive" for a discussion of conditional compilation as well as complete syntax.

Definition

The **else** keyword is needed to provide an alternative. The **if** keyword executes a statement—or statement block—conditionally; **else** lets you specify what to execute when the condition is not met.

What's useful to know about **else** is that by combining it with a nested **if** statement, you can, in effect, create any number of **else if** clauses, even though there is no "elseif" keyword.

Syntax

The **else** keyword appears in the following syntax:

if (*expression*)
　　　statement1
[**else**
　　　statement2]

Here the braces indicate that the **else** clause is optional. Note that either *statement1*, or both, can be a compound statement. If *statement2* is itself an **if-else** statement, you can create multiple alternatives, and are not limited to two.

See "if Keyword" for more information and examples.

Definition

An empty statement (also called a null statement) consists of a lone semicolon:

```
;
```

The statement doesn't do anything, and it certainly doesn't seem to have much purpose. However, it's useful in a few cases—mainly when you need to jump to the very end of a function or loop. Because *some* statement must follow every label, you can't place a label at the very end of a statement block —there must be some statement, and an empty statement is perfectly legal. See "continue Keyword" for an example.

As a consequence of an empty statement being legal, the C++ syntax is fairly forgiving when you type too many semicolons. For example, the following function definition does not cause an error:

```
double pythagorus(double a, double b) {
    return sqrt(a*a + b*b);;;;;;
}
```

The function consists of one useful statement followed by five empty statements—none of them serves a useful purpose, but at least they don't cause an error.

Definition

Encapsulation means to protect the insides of something. In C++, you protect the insides of a class by making some of its members private. Like the contents of a capsule taken as medicine, the private members of a class can be neither changed nor seen. Private members can influence the behavior of the class a great deal, but the influence is indirect and behind the scenes. (These members are much like the behind-the-scenes personnel of a film who, unlike the actors, are never visible to the public.) The point of contact between a class and the outside world is the class interface, which is the collection of all the public members.

The advantage of encapsulation is that reducing the points of contact between objects reduces the possibilities for error. In traditional approaches to programming, one part of a program can refer to any data structure in any other part of the program (at least within the same source file). As soon as one part of the program is altered, the rest of the program may become invalid as a result, because it was written with assumptions about what all the data structures look like.

In a way, the private members are not really being protected from the outside world. The situation is more the reverse: the outside world is protected from the members! As long as a class interface does not change, code that uses that class is relatively safe. The internals can change any number of times without breaking other code—precisely because this other code can never see the internals and cannot be affected by them.

Example

Suppose the first version of a class CSwitch is written this way, with two private members—fon and foff:

```
class CSwitch {
```

```
public:
    void set(BOOL on_off) {fon = on_off;
                            foff != on_off;}
private:
    BOOL fon;
    BOOL foff;
};
```

This is far from the most efficient way to write this class. The on/off condition can be better represented by a single piece of data. Moreover, it's possible to represent an on/off flag in a single bit. This is a particularly good idea if there's a chance that more flags may be added later. Here's the revised version of the class:

```
class CSwitch {
public:
// Represent the on/off condition by setting the
//  rightmost bit of flags to 1 or 0.

    void set(BOOL on_off) {flags = 0xFFFE |
                            (on_off != 0);}
private:
    short flags;
};
```

The point of this example is that any code that was using CSwitch before will still work perfectly well, despite the substantial revision of the class. For example, the following statement will work just as well in the program after CSwitch is revised as it did before. (In fact, it will work better, because the new class is more efficient.)

```
CSwitch switch1, switch2;
switch1.set(TRUE);
```

This code can refer only to the interface of CSwitch, which consists of the type information for the public member: the set function. The private members—as well as the definition of the set function—are not visible outside the class. The outside code is therefore protected from breaking. This would not be true if the code could refer to internals of CSwtich such as the variables flags, fon, or foff.

Definition

The **endif** directive is a necessary part of conditional compilation syntax. Anytime you use the **#if** directive or any of its variations (**#ifdef** and **#ifndef**) you have to use **#endif** to end the section of the program that is conditionally compiled.

Curiously enough, the **#if-#elif-#endif** syntax is much closer to the syntax of the IF statement in Visual Basic than it is to anything else in C++.

Syntax

The **#endif** directive appears on a line by itself:

```
#endif
```

This terminates the syntax that begins with an **#if** directive. See "#if Directive" for a discussion of conditional compilation as well as complete syntax.

Definition

In English, *enumeration* is a fancy word for list—especially a list in which items are counted in a particular order. Similarly, in C++, an enumeration is a sequence of items in which each item is assigned an identifying number: 0, 1, 2, 3....

Suppose you want to record whether a card is a club, a diamond, a heart, or a spade. It's inefficient to copy a string every time you want to record this information. It's much easier to assign each suit an arbitrary number (0, 1, 2, or 3) and then consistently use that numbering scheme to represent a suit.

Syntax

An **enum** declaration declares a series of constants and can optionally declare a type and variables:

```
enum [enum_type_name] {
    name_1 [= init_1],
    name_2 [= init_2],
    ...
    name_n [= init_n],
} [variable_declarations];
```

Here the braces indicate optional items.

The effect is to define *name_1* through *name_n* as symbolic constants. Any item in *variable_declarations* is an unsigned integer that is restricted to one of these values. The default value of *name_1* (if not initialized) is 0. The default value of any other name is the value of the preceding item plus 1.

Usage 1: Simple Lists

In general, the use of **enum** is a good alternative to a series of **#define** directives like this:

```
#define  CLUBS     0
#define  DIAMONDS  1
#define  HEARTS    2
#define  SPADES    3
```

The actual values may be irrelevant. In this example, all that matters is the ability to test the constant.

```
card_suit = CLUBS;
...
if (card_suit == CLUBS) {
    // Get bitmap for clubs
}
```

Or (as in the game of bridge) the values may be meaningful, but only in terms of the relative ordering (CLUBS is less than SPADES).

In any case, an **enum** declaration creates the same symbol constants with less work:

```
enum {
    CLUBS,
    DIAMONDS,
    HEARTS,
    SPADES
};
```

You can sav3e even more space by putting everything on the same line:

```
enum { CLUBS, DIAMONDS, HEARTS, SPADES };
```

The effect is the same as in the series of **#define** directives. CLUBS is 0, DIAMONDS is 1, HEARTS is 2, and SPADES is 3. But the **enum** version is more convenient. As with the **#define** directives, each of these names is a symbolic constant and not a variable.

Often, a simple list of values starting with 0 is sufficient. Sometimes, however, you might want to start the enumeration at a certain integer value. The following code declares constants for certain number words, assigning to each the value you would expect:

```
enum my_numbers {
    TWELVE = 12,
    THIRTEEN,
    FOURTEEN,
    FIFTEEN,
    TWENTY = 20,
    TWENTY_ONE,
    TWENTY_TWO,
    HUNDRED = 100
};
```

Remember that3 each constant, if uninitialized, is set to 1 plus the value of the constant before it.

Usage 2: Complex Lists

The simplest applications of **enum** define a series of constants with the values 0, 1, 2, 3..., or possibly 1, 2, 3.... You can create more-sophisticated series of values. One interesting use is in bit masks.

Once a constant is defined, it can immediately be used to specify other values. For example, here the left-shift operator

is used so that the first constant sets the rightmost bit and
each subsequent constant moves this bit one place to the left.

```
enum file_attr {
    SYS_FILE = 0x01,
    HIDDEN_FILE = SYS_FILE << 1;
    ARCHIVE_FILE = HIDDEN_FILE << 1;
    READONLY_FILE = ARCHIVE_FILE << 1;
};
```

Defining Variables of Enumerated Type

You can give an enumeration a type name and use the type
to define variables. For example:

```
enum card_suit {
    CLUBS,
    DIAMONDS,
    HEARTS,
    SPADES
} card1;

enum card_suit card2, pack[52];
```

Here, card1 and card2 are variables of type enum card_suit,
and pack is an array of 52 elements of type enum card_suit.

As variables of this type, they can be assigned only the
constants CLUBS, DIAMONDS, HEARTS, or SPADES. No
other assignment is legal:

```
card1 = CLUBS;
pack[5] = card2 = DIAMONDS;
card2 = 100;   /* ERROR! */
```

Only a few operations are possible with variables of an enumerated type. They can be assigned one of the constants in

344

the **enum** series, they can be assigned values from other expressions of the same type, and they can be compared to other expressions of the same type.

Although an **enum** variable cannot be assigned a regular integer expression (except via an explicit type cast), an integer can always be assigned an enumerated constant:

```
int i = SPADES;
```

Definition

C++ exception handling is a flexible technique for detecting and responding to exceptions. An *exception* is almost always a run-time error, such as running out of memory or failure to open a file, although it's possible to design exception processing for other purposes. Error handling is not important when you're first learning the language and writing programs only for your own use. But it's a requirement of professional-quality software. So if you're serious about programming, you need to learn about exception handling.

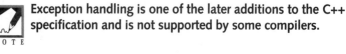

Exception handling is one of the later additions to the C++ specification and is not supported by some compilers.

N O T E

The traditional approach to exception handling is awkward and unreliable. If you detect a run-time error in C, for example, your best response is to immediately return an error code indicating the condition. The code that handles the error—possibly by closing down open resources and printing a diagnostic message—may be several layers up in the function-call stack, as illustrated in Figure E.1. The error must be propagated through the layers, a process that breaks down if any function in the chain fails to cooperate.

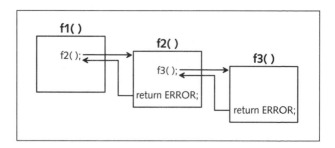

Figure E.1 Error propagation in C.

But in C++ exception handling, control passes directly from error reporting to the error handler, as illustrated in Figure E.2.

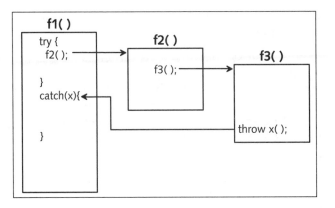

Figure E.2 C++ exception handling.

Not only is the C++ version easier to write and maintain, but it also has another advantage specific to C++: it is the only way to report an error from inside a constructor, which does not return a value.

Syntax: Reporting an Exception

In C++, reporting an exception is called *throwing* an exception. The term suggests the image of tossing a ball in the air and hoping someone catches it. In many ballgames, more than one player may be eligible to catch the ball. So it is with exceptions; you throw the exception, knowing that some block of code will respond to it.

In any case, throwing an exception uses a simple syntax:

throw *value*;

The value's type is important. The exception will be caught—that is, handled—by the first exception handler that accepts a value of this type. For example, you can throw an integer:

347

```
if (fp == NULL)
    throw 1;
```

This exception is caught by the first exception handler that accepts an integer argument.

In this context, the "first" exception handler is the one closest in scope or on the function-call stack. If there are multiple exception handlers, then the exception travels the shortest possible distance on the stack before it is caught. (Figure E.2 illustrates this sense of distance: in this case, the exception in the example travels two levels.)

Incidentally, the meaning of the value thrown, as well as its type, is entirely programmatic. In other words, it's up to your program to determine the difference between "throw 1" and "throw 2."

Syntax: Handling Exceptions

In its simplest form, the C++ exception-handling syntax consists of two blocks: one block is the protected area of code, and the second block is the exception handler.

```
try {
    statements
}
catch (argument_decl) {
    statements
}
```

The *statements* inside the **try** block are executed unconditionally. This block, unlike the **catch** block, is part of the normal flow of program execution. The statements in the **try** block constitute a protected area of code: if any exception is thrown during exececution of the *statements*, that exception can be caught by the exception handler.

The exception handler consists of the **catch** keyword and the statements that follow it. Unlike the **try** block, the **catch** block is executed only under special circumstances.

The *argument_decl* is an argument declaration. It can consist of a type, a type followed by an argument name, or a special syntax:

```
catch(type)                 // - OR -
catch(type argument_name)   // - OR -
catch(...)
```

Each of the first two statements creates an exception handler that looks for matching types. As with overloaded functions, the exception handler is activated only if the argument that is passed (or rather, thrown) matches the argument declaration.

The third statement is a special syntax meaning "any exception." You can use this syntax to write default exception handlers that catch all exceptions not already caught. Here the ellipses (...) are intended literally.

The full syntax for **try** and **catch** enables you to write any number of exception handlers at the same level:

```
try {
    statements
}
catch (argument_decl1) {
    statements
}
catch (argument_decl2) {
    statements
}
...
```

Here, as in most of this book, the ellipses (...) are not intended literally but simply mean that you can have any number of **catch** blocks following a **try** block.

When an exception is thrown during execution of the **try** block, the program checks each **catch** block in turn until it finds an *argument_decl* matching the type of the exception thrown. (This is why the type of the value in the **throw** statement is important.) As soon as a match is found, the statements in the **catch** block are executed. Assuming the program has not terminated, execution then resumes normally after the end of all the **catch** blocks in the current function.

Note that the exception is caught here only if it has not been caught by a more deeply nested function. As noted earlier, the handler closest to the source of the exception (as measured by distance on the function-call stack) gets the first chance to catch it.

Syntax: Passing the Buck

An exception handler may decline to handle an exception. In that case, it throws the exception back in the air using this variation on the **throw** syntax:

```
throw;
```

When this statement is executed, the program continues to look for the next **catch** block in the chain of exception handlers until it finds another match. Here, **throw** means, "I can't handle this after all; go look for someone who can."

In those cases in which no block of code catches and handles the exception, the exception is ultimately caught by the C++ default exception handler. This handler terminates the program and prints a generic error message.

Examples

Exception handling is hard to understand without examples, so I provide two here. In both cases, the code defines one or more special classes specifically for the purpose of returning an exception. In the first example, only one class is used, and its members contain information that is useful in error reporting.

The start of the program declares an exception-handling class, file_err. An object of this class is what gets thrown.

```c
#include <stdio.h>
#include <string.h>
#include "prog.h"

// file_err class: contains information to be
//   passed during reporting of a file-open error.

class file_err {
public:
    char file[256];
    char mode[10];
    file_err(char *f, char *m)
        {strcpy(file, f); strcpy(mode, m);}
};
```

The **main** function calls three functions—open_files, init_vars, and run_prog—which essentially run the entire program. Because they are inside a **try** block, these function calls are executed unconditionally. The **catch** block catches any exception of type file_err that is thrown during execution of the **try** block.

```c
// main function - note open_file, init_vars,
//   run_prog, and close_existing_file all declared
//   in PROG.H and defined later in the code.

void main() {
    try {
        open_file();
        init_vars();
        run_prog();
    }
    catch (file_err ferr) {
```

```
            close_existing_files();
            printf("File error opening %s in %s mode.",
                   ferr.file, ferr.mode);
            exit(1); // exit is a library function
    }
}
```

The function definition of the open_files function contains code that throws an exception in case of an error. The **throw** statement passes a value of type file_err.

```
// Open files function:
//   If fopen is unsuccessful, it returns NULL,
//   indicating exception should be thrown.

void open_files(void) {
    FILE fp;
    file_err ferr;
    char *fname = "MYFILE.DAT";

    fp = fopen(fname, "r");
    if (fp == NULL)
        throw file_err(fname, "r");
    ...
```

The **throw** statement here uses a relatively uncommon C++ syntax: it calls the file_err constructor directly. The implicit return type of a constructor is an object, so the effect of this statement is to create a file_err object on the fly and then immediately pass it to the exception handler by throwing it:

```
        throw file_err(fname, "r");
```

The drawback to calling a constructor this way is that the created object is unnamed. However, because the only point of creating a file_err object is to throw it, the lack of a name does not matter in this case.

The handler in **main** catches the exception because it is looking for an object of type file_err to be thrown. This han-

352

dler uses the information placed in this object to report information to the user. The name ferr is similar to a function-argument name.

```
catch (file_err ferr) {
    close_existing_files();
    printf("File error opening %s in %s mode.",
        ferr.file, ferr.mode);
    exit(1); // exit is a library function
}
```

The next example uses special error-handling classes but doesn't use them to pass information. In this case, the only thing that matters is the type of the object thrown and not any content placed in this object. Therefore, the various error classes are declared without members.

```
#include <stdio.h>
#include "prog2.h"

// file_err class: contains information to be
//   passed during reporting of a file-open error.

class file_err {};
class fopen_err : public file_err {};
class fread_err : public file_err {};
class fwrite_err : public file_err {};
class fsize_err : public file_err {};

void main() {
    try {
        open_file();
        init_vars();
        run_prog();
    }
    catch (fopen_err) {
        puts("Could not open all files.");
        exit(1);
    }
```

```
    catch (file_err) {
        puts("Misc. file error.");
        exit(1);
    }
    catch (...) {
        puts("Misc. error.");
        exit(1);
    }
}
```

This example takes advantage of inheritance relationships. If a file-open error is detected, then an error of type fopen_err is thrown and caught by the first **catch** block.

```
throw fopen_err();  // Signal fopen error.
```

Note how the constructor is called explicitly to create an object of type fopen_err, which is then thrown.

Because of inheritance, if any other type of file-error exception is thrown, it is caught by the second **catch** block. For example:

```
throw fwrite_err();    // Signal file-write error.
```

Here, an exception of type fwrite_err is thrown. (Again, the constructor is called.) There is no exact match for this type. However, the second **catch** block accepts the general type file_err. The type fwrite_err is a derived class of file_err; therefore, wherever file_err (the base class) is a valid argument type, so is fwrite_err (the derived class). For this reason, the second **catch** block catches all errors of classes derived from the general type, file_err, that have not been caught by the first **catch** block.

The third **catch** block, using the special syntax (...), catches all remaining errors not caught by the first or second block.

Definition

An explicit type conversion, or *cast*, gives you complete control over how data is treated. The word *cast* suggests a mold used to reform a substance, changing its form in some way.

(Years ago I used to spell this incorrectly, as *caste*. I was thinking of a rigid social hierarchy in which each data type occupied a special slot. In my imagination, converting data was like moving it to a new caste in society. This may be a colorful metaphor, but the idea of casting, as in molding an object's form, is more accurate.)

Why would you ever want to change thee type of a variable or expression? The truth is, the majority of simple programs have little use for casts. But as you start to work with more-sophisticated types—especially pointers—they become vital.

Syntax

A type cast applied to an expression (often a variable, an argument, or a function return value) forms a larger expression:

(*type*) *expression*

The resulting expression has the same numeric value as *expression* but is converted to the indicated type. Variables and constants in the original expression are not affected.

Usage

The compiler handles most of the obvious cases in which data needs to be converted. For example, when an integer is added to a floating-point value, the compiler automatically converts the data type of the integer to double-precision floating-point:

```
double  x, y;
int i;
...
x = y + i;  // i promoted to type double.
```

You can usually rely on the fact that i would be converted to a **double** in this situation. However, if you wanted to make absolutely sure that this happened (and not rely on the compiler's behavior), you could specify the data conversion this way:

```
x = y + (double) i;
```

But most situations that require type casts involve pointers. Casts are particularly common when you're working with **void** pointers.

Certain library functions (such as malloc) return a **void** pointer. Such a pointer can be used to hold an address; but because its type is **void**, it can't actually be used to access anything. Consider how little sense the following statement would make—if the C++ language let you do it (which it doesn't):

```
void *p;
short thing;

p = malloc(500);
...
thing = *p;  // Error! p is void*
```

What data does *p refer to? You might think that because thing is a short (two-byte) integer, the statement automatically transfers two bytes of data. But it doesn't work that way, because p is **void***. Even though the destination of the assignment is an integer (thing), the program has no idea how you're using the chunk of memory pointed to by p. The expression *p means "the thing p points to." Because p is a pointer to **void**, it doesn't yet point to anything—it's just an address that needs to be recast before being used.

This is easy to remedy. You can use the (**short***) data cast to tell the program to treat p as a pointer to short—that is, a two-byte integer:

```
thing = *(short*)p;
```

The data cast (**short***) changes a **void*** expression to a **short*** expression—a pointer to a **short**. The indirection operator (*) gets the contents at this address. The expression

```
*(short*)p
```

is a little misleading the first time you look at it, because the indirection operator seems to be applied twice. Don't be fooled by this; indirection is applied only once. The use of the asterisk (*) inside the parentheses is used only to help specify the type, that's all.

In plain English, what the expression means is, "Use the address in p as a pointer to a short integer; then get that integer." Or more succinctly, "the short integer pointed to by p." (See Figure E.3.)

As this figure shows, the data copying is direct (there is no conversion), because thing has the same type as the expression "*(short*)p"

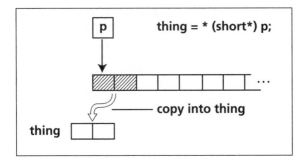

*Figure E.3 Direct copy using (short *).*

Now imagine that the chunk of memory is being used to hold single-precision floating-point data (**float**). In this case, a different data cast is called for:.

```
thing = *(float*)p;
```

This statement says, "Use the address in p as a pointer to a floating-point number; then get that number." The data is assigned to thing.

The program gets four bytes of data rather than two. But that's not all. Because the data is floating-point, its format (sign, mantissa, exponent) is radically different from integer format. The program calls a special helper function under the covers, to pull apart the floating-point data and convert it to integer. Any fractional part is dropped in the process. How this magic occurs is not important—it's enough to know it works—but remember that you need to be very clear about what is floating-point and what is not.

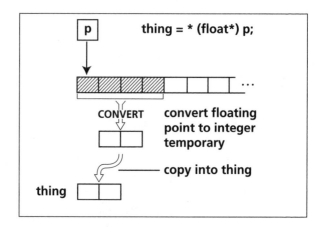

*Figure E.4 Copy using (float *) type.*

As this figure shows, the program converts from floating-point to integer before placing the data in thing. The compiler knows that this conversion must take place because it knows that thing is integer.

You can make the conversion explicit by adding yet another type cast. This other cast isn't required, but it helps document what is going on:

```
thing = (int) *(float *)p;
```

To review, here's how this works:

- p is a nondescript pointer to an address. There's no indication yet of what kind of data it points to.

- The expression (float *)p points to a four-byte floating-point number at this address (changing a **void*** expression to a **float*** expression).

- The expression *(float *)p is the floating-point number itself.

- The expression (int) *(float *)p is the integer equivalent of this floating-point value, after conversion.

As I pointed out in Chapter 3, "Pointers, Strings, and Things," the best way to dynamically allocate memory is to cast the pointer as soon as you get it back from malloc. For example:

```
int *p, i = 10;

p = (int *) malloc (1000 * sizeof(int));
*p = i;
```

The virtue of this approach is that because p is declared as **int***, it contains its own type information so that no further casts are required when doing integer operations.

Expressions

Definition

In general, an expression is any valid combination of variables, constants, and operators. All of the following are statements, but none forms a complete statement, because none is terminated by a semicolon (;).

```
5
x
x + y
f(12.05, a, "Joe Smchoe")
(10 + fnct()) / 25
n++
a = 3 + i
```

You can turn any of these expressions into a statement by terminating with a semicolon:

expression;

The first three examples, however, would not form useful statements unless used in part of a larger expression (such as an assignment or function call).

With few exceptions, an expression evaluates to a single value, which can be used in a larger expression. One exception is a **void** function call, which does not have a return value.

One of the unique aspects of C++ is that an assignment is an expression like any other and does not automatically form a complete statement unless terminated by a semicolon (;). An assignment evaluates to the value assigned (thus, "a = 5" evaluates to 5), and this value can be reused within the larger expression.

See Chapter 2, "Basic Features of C/C++ Programs" for more explanation of assignments, expressions, and statements.

extern "C" Declarations

Definition

An **extern "C"** declaration has the same purpose as an ordinary **extern** declaration except that it has the additional effect of suppressing the C++ name-decoration scheme. This arrangement enables you to import function and variable names from C-language source files.

Syntax

To suppress C++ name decoration for a given symbol, place its declaration inside brackets following **extern "C"**. These brackets can enclose one or more declarations:

```
extern "C" {
    declarations
};
```

Examples

The most typical use for **extern "C"** declarations is to enable a C++ source file to refer to symbols declared in a C-language source file. For example, the following declaration enables you to call a function CLangFunc and refer to a variable Kount, each of which is defined in a C module somewhere:

```
extern "C" {
    long CLangFunct(char *, double, double);
    int Kount;
};
```

As with the use of **extern** by itself, if a variable declared in an **extern "C"** block is initialized, it is a definition—meaning that it creates the variable. The C++ name decoration is still suppressed when the compiler generates object code:

```
extern "C" { long Johns = 0; } // Johns not decorated
```

Definition

Complex programs are nearly always split into several different program files (*source files* or *modules*). Doing so allows several different programmers to work at the same time. Even if you're working alone, you might use modules just to make your life easier.

With multiple modules, variables have scope limited to one module unless given an **extern** declaration. This isn't necessary with functions, which are automatically visible to the entire program.

Syntax

The **extern** keyword modifies a data declaration and is placed at the beginning of the statement:

extern *data_declaration;*

What an **extern** declaration says, in effect, is, "The variable or variables are declared somewhere in the program, either in this module or in another."

Usage

To make a variable global to the entire program, define the variable in exactly one module. Then place an **extern** declaration in every module. The following code makes an integer variable, amount, global to the entire program even though it is defined only in the first module:

```
// MODULE1.CPP
extern int  amount;
int  amount = 0;
```

```
// MODULE2.CPP
extern int  amount;

// MODULE3.CPP
extern int  amount;
```

The **extern** declaration is not really necessary in MOD-ULE1.CPP but does not cause an error. The best way to use **extern** declarations is to place them in a header file and then include the header file in every module by using the **#include** directive. This technique ensures that every module picks up the **extern** declaration.

Any module that does not include the **extern** declaration can have its own variable named amount (although such a confusing practice is not recommended). Such a variable would not be visible to the rest of the program. In fact, it would really be a different variable from the one referred to by other modules.

Example

If no module used an **extern** declaration, then each module would have its own local copy of amount. Changes to amount in one module would have no effect on the variable defined by the other module:

```
// MODULE1.CPP
int  amount;

// MODULE2.CPP
int  amount;
```

363

float Data Type

Definition

The **float** data type is a single-precision floating-point number, stored in four bytes. Oddly, the longer floating-point type is **double**, even though the shorter, four-byte type is called **float** rather than "single."

Range and Precision

Approximately plus or minus 3.4 times 10 to the 38th power, with six places of precision after the decimal point. Tiny nonzero values can get as close to zero as approximately plus or minus 1.4 times 10 to the power of –45. The type can also hold the value zero precisely.

Syntax

You can declare any number of single-precision floating-point numbers by placing **float** at the beginning of the declaration statement:

```
[storage] [cv] float  items;
```

Here the brackets indicate optional prefixes: *storage* is a storage-class specifier (**auto**, **extern**, **register**, **static**), and *cv* is **const**, **volatile**, or both. The *items* are one or more simple or complex variable declarations.

Example

The following statement defines a simple variable (temperature), an array (daily_temps), and a pointer (ptr_to_float):

```
float  temperature, daily_temps[200], *ptr_to_float;
```

Usage

The **double** floating-point format is generally preferable to **float**, except where storage space is at a premium (such as files, structures, and arrays of structures). It's difficult to compare efficiency of **float** calculations against those using **double**, because different systems implement floating-point operations in different ways. However, math coprocessors typically operate directly on eight-byte floating-point numbers, making **double** at least as fast to operate on as **float**. The recent trend in microprocessors is to support on-board math-coprocessor instructions, having the effect of giving every system a coprocessor.

Definition

A **for** loop is a convenient way to execute a statement block a fixed number of times—for example, when you count to a number or process each element of an array. Like FOR and DO loops in other languages, a C++ **for** loop can be used in this obvious way. However, the C++ **for** loop is much more flexible and has many applications.

Syntax

A **for** statement forms one unified statement in C++:

```
for (initializer; condition; increment)
    for_loop_statement
```

The *initializer, condition,* and *increment* are all valid C++ expressions. The *loop_body_statement* is frequently a compound statement (see "Example"). Because the entire **for** loop forms one statement, it can be nested inside other control structures.

The *initializer* expression is evaluated exactly once: before the loop begins execution. The loop then proceeds just like a **while** statement in which *condition* is the loop condition. The *increment* expression is evaluated at the bottom of the loop. So a **for** statement is almost exactly equivalent to the following syntax:

```
initializer;
while (condition) {
    for_loop_statement
    increment;
}
```

Note, however, that a **continue** statement, if used, transfers execution to *increment*, and not to the very end of the loop.

Aside from this difference, the two loops are identical in their effect.

 Don't forget that multiple expressions can be crammed into a single expression by using the comma (,) operator. The initializer expression, for example, can initialize two variables and increment can update two variables:

```
for ( i = 0, k = 1; i < ARRAY_SIZE; i++, j++) {
    . . .
```

Example

The following code initializes the first 100 members of two arrays, a and b, so that the first array holds numbers from 0 to 99 and the second array holds even numbers from 0 to 198:

```
for (i = 0; i < 100; i++) {
    a[i] = i;
    b[i] = i * 2;
}
```

Definition

A friend of a class has access to all the members of that class. No secrets are kept from a friend. When a function F, a friend of class C, uses an object of class C, it's as if all the members of C were declared public. The most common type of friend to a class is a function. Classes can also be friends of other classes. (In my opinion, this last feature is a bit of overkill in language design.)

The term *friend* helps make C++ sound more warm and appealing, helping to offset some of the bad PR associated with terms such as *destructor*. In actuality, though, the concept of friend functions has practical purpose. Its main reason for existence is to help overload binary operators, as I'll show in the example of this topic.

Syntax

To declare a function as a friend of a class, include a prototype of the function inside the class declaration, preceded by the **friend** keyword:

class *name* {

   ...

    friend *function_prototype*;

It does not matter which member-access level (public, private, or protected) is given to this declaration. The access level is ignored in this case. No other adjustment needs to be made to the source code. The **friend** keyword should not appear in front of the function definition.

To declare another class as a friend, use the following syntax. (Substitute **struct** or **union** for **class**, as appropriate, if the friend class is declared with **struct** or **union**.)

class *name* {

...

    friend class *class_name*;

Example

In C++, friendship is to be avoided except where really needed, because by its nature friendship weakens encapsulation.
Friend functions were invented for one practical purpose: to
help write operator functions for a class, in which objects of
the class appears on the right side of an operator. See
Chapter 7, "Class Operations," for a more comprehensive
discussion of this dilemma.

In any case, friend functions solve the problem. A global
operator function can put into any class on either side of the
operator. By being made a friend of a class, the operator
function can then gain access to all the members of the
class. The following example defines addition between long
integers and objects of class CFix (a fixed-point real number,
biased by three decimal places). The function must be written as global, because otherwise CFix objects can never
appear on the right side of the operator (+). Moreover, the
function must be made a friend; otherwise it cannot access
the private member amount.

```
class CFix {
private:
    long amount;
    friend CFix operator+(long lng, CFix cf);
...

// Operator function for long + CFix.
//  Because this function is a friend of CFix,
//  it can access amount, a private member of CFix.
```

```
CFix operator+(long lng, CFix cf) {
    CFix result;
    result.amount = (lng * 1000) + cf.amount;
    return result;
}
```

Additional Rules Regarding Friends

Friendship has two rules of non-transitivity. These rules are not surprising, given the limited scope of use that friends are designed for. Don't fret too much about these rules, because they would matter only in rare situations.

- If class C2 is a friend of C1, then a friend F of class C2 is not a friend of class C1 unless it is declared so separately. The friend of my friend is not necessarily my friend.

- If class C2 is a friend of C1, then a derived class D of class C2 is not necessarily a friend of C1. The child of my friend is not necessarily my friend.

Definition

A function is an independent block of code that typically takes care of a specific task. Once a function is defined, you can execute it any number of times from anywhere in the program. (Executing a function is done through a *function call*.) This fact makes functions far and away one of the most essential tools in a programmer's kit.

What's different about functions in C++ is that the same syntax is used whether or not the function returns a value. Thus, C++ functions replace all the following in BASIC: functions, procedures, and GOSUB routines. (Functions that do not return a value have the **void** return type.) Another distinctive aspect of C++ is that all executable statements must be placed inside a function—although **main** (the "main program") is itself a function.

For an introduction to functions in C++, see Chapter 2, "Basic Features of C/C++ Programs." The rest of this topic summarizes the syntax.

Syntax 1: Function Definition

A function definition forms an independent statement block in a program and is *not* terminated by a semicolon(;).

```
return_type  name(argument_list) {
        statements
}
```

The *argument_list* includes a series of argument declarations, including both type and name (similar to a prototype, except that the names are not optional). Arguments are separated by commas if there are more than one. The *argument_list* should contain **void** if there are no arguments.

The *return_type* can be a valid type or can be **void**. If the return type is not **void**, then *statements* can include any number of **return** statements to return a value:

return *expression*;

Syntax 2: Prototypes

A function declaration prototype is an item in a declaration:

name(*argument_list*)

A prototype can also be declared alone in its own declaration:

return_type name(*argument_list*);

The *argument_list* is a series of argument declarations, separated by commas if there is more than one:

type item1, type item2 ...

In a prototype, the argument names are optional and exist principally for documentation purposes. The following prototypes are considered equivalent by the compiler:

```
long fnct(int a, float x, char string[]);
long fnct(int, float, char[]);
```

Syntax 3: Function Calls

A function call forms an expression:

name(*argument_list*)

Here, *argument_list* is a list of actual values to be passed to the function. If the function's return type is not **void**, then the function call can be used as part of a larger expression:

```
a = abs(b) + 3;
```

goto Statement

Definition

C++ includes a standard goto statement, as virtually all other programming languages do. The danger of using **goto** with wild abandon is that you'll create spaghetti code—programs famous for complex, intertwined connections that are next to impossible to follow (unless you're the computer). Still, goto is included because it provides a C++ programmer with complete control over jumps when needed.

Syntax

The **goto** keyword, along with a target label, forms a complete statement:

goto *label*;

The statement unconditionally transfers control to the target labeled statement, which must be in the same function as the **goto** statement. See "Labels" for more information.

A **goto** statement is occasionally useful as a way of breaking out directly from several levels of enclosed loops. In most cases, the use of **for**, **do**, and **while** loops makes **goto** statements unnecessary.

Definition

Header files contain declarations that are useful to one or more source modules. As a rule, header files come in two basic varieties:

- Header files for standard library functions. For example, you should include STDIO.H if doing any kind of input or output, and you should include MATH.H if using one of the math functions from the standard C++ library. These files provide all the necessary prototypes for using the library functions, and this saves you from having to declare them yourself. It's much easier just to include the file. For example:

  ```
  #include <stdio.h>
  ```

- Header files for your own declarations. If you work with multiple modules, you should throw in prototypes for all your functions, extern declarations for all global variables to be shared programwide, and declarations for other types (typedef, struct, union, enum, class) that you want to share between modules. This is a much easier approach than having to declare these for every single module. For example:

  ```
  #include "myprog.h"
  ```

This second use is convenient because declarations are not automatically shared between multiple modules. In C++, function definitions are the only entities that are automatically visible to the rest of the program. But even functions need a declaration (a prototype) to be included in each individual module.

A particularly helpful aspect of header files is that if you declare things once in a header file and then use the #include directive to include this file in each module, you are guaranteeing that things are declared the same way everywhere. This practice prevents the problem of potential errors due to inconsistent declarations in different files.

Some of the items to place in header files include:

- Prototypes for all functions except those that you do not want to share. (These functions should be qualified with the **static** keyword to make them private to their modules.)

- **extern** declarations for all global variables to be shared between modules. Note, however, that in addition to the extern declarations, each individual variable must be defined in one, and only one, module. A good approach is to define all your global variables in the main module.

- **#define** statements for symbolic constants that are used throughout the program as well as for macros.

- **enum**, **struct**, **union**, and **typedef** declarations.

You should never place data definitions or function definitions in header files. These definitions (not to be confused with uses of the **#define** directive, which is completely different) create a variable or a function, and they must be unique. A header file is normally intended to be included by more than one module. Therefore, placing a data definition or function definition in a header file would cause an error because the variable or function would be defined more than once, which C++ in its wisdom does not allow.

See "#include Directive" for exact syntax rules governing **#include**.

Definition

An identifier is a name you create: this includes not only variable names but also namesof funcitons, structures, symbolic constants, **enum** constants, and user-defined stypes. For example, in the following structure definition, the names data_record, **x**, **y**, and title are all identifiers, whereas **struct**, **int,** and **char** are keywords:

```
struct data_record {
    int x, y;
    char title[30];
};
```

The difference is that keywords have built-in meanings universal to all C++ programs, but identifiers have meanings that you (or another programmer) create within a given program.

Syntax

C++ has three basic rules for forming a valid identifier:

1. An identifier cannot be the same as any C++ keyword.

2. An identifier must be composed from the following character set:

   - Digits 0 through 9

   - Uppercase and lowercase letters A through Z

   - The underscore (_)

3. The first character must not be a digit.

So the following are all valid identifiers:

```
a
x04
count
xx1
thing27
do_your_own_thing
The_End
BYTE
```

 Although identifiers can begin with an underscore (_), you should avoid that practice. The C++ compiler N O T E **defines a number of special symbols (normally hidden from you) that use leading underscores. These are implementation-specific, so they are difficult to antici- pate and "program around." But if you simply avoid leading underscores in your own identifiers, you avoid conflicts with these implementation-defined symbols.**

Case Sensitivity

All identifiers (as well as keywords) are case-sensitive in C++, so bigfoot and BigFoot, for example, are two distinct names. You could use both in a program, although it is not advisable.

Linker behavior can sometimes cause problems. The C++ compiler is always case-sensitive even though case sen- sitivity can be switched off by the linker (as is true in Windows programming, for example). This creates a pitfall: bigfoot and BigFoot are considered two different variables by the compiler, but the linker thinks they're the same sym- bol. The result is that either your program will be wrong or the linker will make a mistake. The solution is to avoid using two names that differ only in case.

Definition

Despite its apparent similarity to the **if** statement, the purpose of the **#if** directive is entirely different from that of the **if** statement. There are two principal uses of the **#if** directive: conditional compilation and temporarily "commenting out" lines. Conditional compilation is useful as a way of maintaining different versions of your program without having to duplicate the parts common to all versions.

An **#if** directive marks the beginning of a conditional-compilation block. If the expression specified by the **#if** directive is nonzero (true), the C++ preprocessor compiles the statements that follow it, up to the next **#elif**, **#else**, or **#endif** directive.

Syntax

The **#if**, **#elif**, **#else**, and **#endif** directives can appear as follows. Any kind of statement, declaration, or other directive can appear in each *statement_block*:

```
#if constant_expression
statement_block_1
[ #elif constant_expression
statement_block_2 ]
[ #elif constant_expression
statement_block_3 ]
...
[ #else
statement_block_n ]
#endif
```

Here, the brackets indicate optional items; the only mandatory parts of this syntax are the **#if** and **#endif** directives. You can use any number of **#elif** directives but, at most, one **#else** directive, which must follow all **#if** and **#elif** directives.

The C++ preprocessor evaluates each *constant_expression* until one of the expressions evaluates to a nonzero value. Then the preprocessor compiles the corresponding *statement_block*. If all the expressions evaluate to zero and if there is an **#else** directive, the preprocessor compiles the statements between **#else** and **#endif** (*statement_block_n*).

Each *statement_block* can contain any kind of C++ code, including declarations and directives as well as executable statements.

Each *constant_expression* is a C++ expression made up of constants and operators, but it cannot include the **sizeof** operator, type casts, or **enum** constants. In practice, such constant expressions almost always involve symbols previously defined with **#define** directives. A simple test for equality (==) may be involved. These constant expressions can also use the **define**(symbol) operator, which evaluates to 1 if a symbol is defined, and 0 otherwise.

Usage 1: Conditional Compilation

Conditional compilation allows you to create multiple versions of your program. There are several reasons you might want to do this. You might be writing a program for multiple platforms and find that certain sections of code are not portable—they simply have to be rewritten. You also might want to build both a debug version, which is larger and slower but easier to debug, and a release version, which is more compact. For the debug version, you might want a data dump in the middle of program execution.

Maintaining multiple versions creates a dilemma. If you periodically create new versions of your program by rewriting it, you lose the previous version. You'd have to constantly add and erase the same statements. But if you keep multiple versions of your program around, you eat up extra disk space. Worse, you may encounter change-control problems as the new features added to one version aren't necessarily reflected in the other verions.

The answer to these problems is conditional compilation. For example, my program may have to deal with a variety of coordinate systems for different target computers. Instead of having to rewrite many lines of my program every time I compile for a different target, I need only change one line. First, I define a series of meaningful constants:

```
#define UNSIGNED_INT 0
#define INTEGER      1
#define REAL         2
```

To recompile for a different coordinate system, I need only change one line—the line the defines the value of the symbol COORDSYS. Many compilers support a command-line option that even allows you to specify this define on the command line:

```
#define COORDSYS REAL
```

The rest of the program checks the value of COORDSYS, as needed, to decide what to compile:

```
#if COORDSYS == UNSIGNED_INT
unsigned x, y;
#elif COORDSYS == INTEGER
int x, y;
#elif COORDSYS == REAL
double x, y;
#endif
```

Notice how the use of the **#if** directive is different from that of an **if** statement, despite the similarity. The **if** statement evaluates a condition (which incidentally does not have to be a constant), at run time and takes a different action depending on this condition. The **#if** directive evaluates a condition at *compilation time*— this means that the condition is evaluated before the program ever runs. Based on the condition, different lines of code are compiled, in effect creating a different version of the program.

Usage 2: Commenting Out Lines

Occasionally, you might need to "comment out" lines: remove them temporarily from the program in such a way that it is easy to put them back. One obvious way to do this is to place begin-comment (/*) and end-comment (*/) symbols around the block of code. As I explain in the topic "Comments," however, this approach causes errors if any of these lines themselves have comments. This is the problem of nested comments.

The solution is to use **#if 0** and **#endif** to comment out lines. When the condition for an **#if** directive is the constant 0, the lines are simply never compiled. Whether or not the lines contain comments makes no difference. For example:

```
#if 0
int i, j;      /* Indexes into 2-D array */
double x, y;   /* Point coordinates */
#endif
```

The **#if** directive can be nested to any level. The **#endif** directive associates with the nearest **#if** directive.

if Statement

Definition

One of the more essential parts of any programming language is an **if** keyword or conditional jump of some kind. C++ is no exception. The C++ **if** statement is similar to what you may have seen in other languages, with minor syntax differences.

What's different about C++ **if** statements is that the conditional expression can perform many operations, including assignments. Don't forget, however, that test for equality (==) is different from assignment (=). The former is more common within conditional expressions. If you use assignment in a conditional expression, consider the effect carefully.

Syntax

An **if** statement forms one unified statement in C++:

```
if (expression)
        statement1
[ else
        statement2 ]
```

Here the brackets indicate that the entire **else** clause is optional. The statement blocks—*statement1* and *statement2*—are frequently compound statements, using opening and closing braces ({}). Because the entire **if-else** block is itself one statement, it can be nested inside other control structures.

If *expression* is nonzero (true), then *statement1* is executed. Otherwise, *statement2* is executed, assuming that there is an **else** clause. The expression can be any valid C expression of integer type. All comparison and logical operators (==, <, >, <=, >=, &&, !!, !, and so on) return either a 1 (true) or 0 (false).

Examples

The following example tests to see whether a number x is in the range 0.0 to 100.0. Note the use of the logical OR operator (||).

```
if (x < 0.0 || x > 100.0)
    printf("x is out of range.\n");
else {
    printf("x is in range.\n");
    return -1;
}
```

In this example, the statements following the **else** are enclosed in braces because they are executed as a compound statement. This is necessary whenever the **if** clause or **else** clause involves more than one statement.

By nesting an **if** statement inside an **else** clause, you can create a virtual "elseif" keyword:

```
if (a < b)
    return -1;
else if (a == b)
    return 0;
else
    return 1;
```

This statement is equivalent to:

```
if (a < b)
    return -1;
else {
    if (a == b)
        return 0;
    else
        return 1;
}
```

In this case, the braces are used for clarification of meaning but aren't required. See "switch Keyword" for another way to test for a series of alternatives.

Occassionally, braces are required—not only where compound statements are used but also where the association of **if** and **else** isn't clear. By default, an **else** clause always applies to the nearest **if** statement. Suppose a program follows this logic:

If x equals 0, then
*   If y equals 0,*
*   print "x and y are zero"*
Else
*   print "x is non-zero"*

The *Else* is intended to apply to the first *If* and not to the second. Thus, "x is non-zero" is printed whenever x equals 0—the value of y doesn't matter. In this case, braces are required to clarify the association of the **else** clause with the first **if**.

```
if (x == 0) {
    if (a == b)
        printf("x and y are zero");
} else
        printf("x is non-zero");
```

#ifdef Directive

Definition

The **#ifdef** directive is possibly the most commonly used directive for conditional compilation. Consider the following syntax:

#ifdef *symbol*

This means exactly the same as:

#if defined(*symbol***)**

So the lines immediately following the **#ifdef**—up to but not including the next **#elif**, **#else**, or **#endif**—are compiled if the *symbol* has been previously defined. The value of the symbol is irrelevant; only the fact that it has been defined is significant. It can even be defined as an empty string, as in the following definition of 32_BIT_SUPPORT:

```
#define 32_BIT_SUPPORT
```

Many compilers support a command-line option for defining such symbols, a practice that allows you to control conditions from inside batch files and make files.

The use of **#ifdef** is appropriate when you want to conditionally compile based on a simple on/off condition. You turn the condition on by defining the symbol.

For a general description of conditional compilation as well as complete syntax, see "#if Directive."

#ifndef Directive

Definition

The **#ifndef** directive is occasionally used in conditional compilation. Consider the following syntax:

```
#ifndef symbol
```

This means exactly the same as:

```
#if ! defined(symbol)
```

So the lines immediately following the **#ifdef**—up to but not including the next **#elif**, **#else**, or **#endif**—are compiled if the *symbol* has not been previously defined.

The use of **#ifdef** and **#ifndef** is appropriate when you want to conditionally compile based a simple on/off condition. You turn the condition on by simply not defining the symbol.

For a general description of conditional compilation as well as complete syntax, see "#if Directive." See also "#ifdef Directive."

Implicit Type Casts

Definition

Not all data types are the same. And because they're different, adjustments have to be made when you combine them. Integer data and floating-point data, in particular, have radically different formats. They can't just be added or multiplied together. In the following example, the value of i, an integer, must first be converted to floating-point (**double**) format:

```
int i;
double x, y = 27.555;
x = y + i;    // Value of i must be converted to
              //double, to match y's format.
```

What happens is that C++ applies an implicit type cast, which is equivalent to the following explicit cast:

```
x = y + (double) i;
```

Usage

You can blithely program for a long time, ignoring the fact that C++ does this—after all, it is automatic. (Other programming languages also do this, by the way.) However, sometimes it's useful to know exactly what the program is doing to your data and how it's stored. The following list is a guide to how and when C++ implicitly casts data types of expressions. Whenever an expression combines two operands—not involving pointers—the compiler compares them to determine which operand has the type of the lowest rank. The expression of the lower rank is cast to that of the higher rank:

> **double**
> **float**
> **unsigned long**

long
unsigned int
int
other integer types (**short, unsigned short, char, unsigned char**)

For example, if an **unsigned int** and an **unsigned long** expression are added together, the **unsigned int** expression is first promoted to type **unsigned long**. Note that the type cast is only applied to the value of the **unsigned int** expression; it doesn't permanently change the type of any variables.

 One consequence of this rule is that all the smaller types (char, for example) are converted to int before being used in any expression. Depending on implementation, the actual size of an int may be two or four bytes.

Pointers have special rules of their own. Assignment of any pointer to a nonpointer type, and vice versa, requires a cast. (Integer expressions, however, can be added to pointers. See "Pointer Arithmetic.")

#include Directive

Definition

The **#include** directive causes the C++ preprocessor to read another file into the current source file during the compilation process. In other words, if you use the directive #include <stdio.h>, the effect is the same as if you had typed the entire contents of STDIO.H into your program.

Although any file can be specified with **#include**, the directive is best used with header files—files containing declarations needed by more than one module.

Syntax

An **#include** directive uses one of the following two forms:

```
#include "filename"      // Project include file
#include <filename>      // Standard lib include file
```

Upon encountering **#include**, the compiler suspends execution of the current file, reads the file specified by *filename*, and continues. All the files read in this manner are compiled as if they were part of one continuous source. So symbols declared in an included file can be referred to in the main source file.

The difference between the two versions of **#include** is that in the *"filename"* version, the C++ preprocessor searches for the file first in the current directory. Both versions look for the file in the standard include-file directory; on most systems, this directory is indicated by the value of the INCLUDE environment variable or a configuration file that stores such settings. In any case, this should be part of your environment configuration before you run the C++ compiler.

The general rule is to use the **#include** *"filename"* version for your own header files, which are typically kept in the same directory as the rest of your program files. Use **#include** *<file-name>* for standard header files such as STDIO.H.

Included files can be nested to any level. This means that a file read with **#include** can itself have **#include** directives.

Example

The following statement includes the header file STDIO.H:

```
#include <stdio.h>
```

See "Header Files" for more discussion of how **#include** is used.

Indirection Operator

Definition

The indirection operator (*) is central to pointer operations and is therefore important in C++. Basically, the operator means "get the contents at" or "the thing pointed to." So if ptr contains the numeric value 0x2000, *ptr refers to the contents at the address 0x2000 in memory.

When you're first learning C++, possibly the most confusing aspect of the indirection operator is that it uses the same symbol as multiplication. But the two operators have nothing to do with each other. Syntactically, you tell them apart by the fact that indirection is a unary operator: it applies to exactly one operand at a time.

Syntax

The indirection operator forms an expression from a single operand:

*addr_expression

Here, *addr_expression* is any valid expression with an address type. This is typically, but not necessarily, a pointer variable. It might also be an array name.

When used in an executable statement, the type of the resulting expression is one level of indirection less than the *addr_expression*. For example, if *addr_expression* has type **int*** (pointer to **int**), then *addr_expression* has type **int**. If *addr_expression* has type **float**** (pointer to pointer to **float**), then *addr_expression* has type **float*** (pointer to **float**).

Usage

In declarations, the indirection operator creates a pointer variable. The operator must be applied to each individual item declared. Consider the following declarations:

```
double   *a, b, *c, (*f)(), *e[50];
```

This statement declares b as a simple variable of type **double**, a and c as pointers to **double**, f as a pointer to a function returning a value of type **double**, and c as an array of 50 pointers to **double**.

In an executable statement, the indirection operator means "the thing pointed to," and it can be applied to any valid address expression. Figure I.1 expresses the relationship between p (a pointer) and *p.

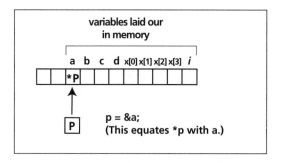

*Figure I.1   Relationship of pointer to *p.*

Although indirection can be applied to any address expression, including any pointer, the value of the address should be meaningful. Applying indirection to an uninitialized or null pointer can cause serious errors at run time. So make sure that you initialize pointers before using them. For example:

```
int *p, i;
*p = 5; // ERROR: p uninitialized!
p = &i; // p now initialized to point to i
*p = 5; // This operation copies 5 to i
```

393

Inheritance

Definition

Inheritance is a technique for giving all the members of one class to another class, without having to retype the declarations of those members. The class contributing the members is the base class. The class getting the members (for free, as it were) is the derived class. Sometimes the classes are identified as parent class and child class, respectively.

In C++, inheritance is also the basis for polymorphism and virtual functions, so it is more than just a convenience. For two classes to implement the same virtual function, they must have a common base class.

Many C++ devotees swear by inheritance and insist that it is one of the principal strengths of C++ as well as of object orientation in general. Inheritance is no doubt a convenient tool for reusing existing code, because you can copy all the declarations from another class without having to re-enter any of them. The typical situation in which you would use inheritance (demonstrated in the example) is when you want to use something similar to an existing class but need to add or alter a member or two.

Some proponents of more recent object-oriented models downplay the importance of inheritance and suggest that aggregation—wrapping one object inside another—is a superior technique for creating reusable code. In reality, aggregation doesn't give you anything that inheritance doesn't give you. Regardless of what you call them, both techniques ultimately boil down to putting one class inside another.

For more information on the syntax of inheritance relationships, see "Base Classes."

Example

Suppose you have an existing CFruitDish class, which describes the number of different kinds of fruit in a gift basket:

```
class CFruitDish {
public:
    int apples;
    int oranges;
    int pears;
    int strawberries;
};
```

This is well and good, but suppose you need a class that has all this data plus another member: a string that records the name of the lucky recipient of the fruit basket. If CFruitDish is already declared, then an easy way to create the class you need is to inherit most of it from the CFruitDish class:

```
class CFruitDest : public CFruitDish {
public:
    char name[30];
};
```

The new class inherits all the members of CFruitDish. The effect is the same as if you had typed all the individual members as follows:

```
class CFruitDest {
public:
// Same as CFruitDish
    int apples;
    int oranges;
    int pears;
    int strawberries;

// New member
    char name[30];
};
```

Definition

To inline a function means to place the function code into the body of routines that call it. This technique saves execution time at the possible expense of added program size.

Normally, a function call is implemented by code that places arguments on the stack and then transfers execution to a different part of the program. If a function is inlined, however, then control does not transfer to another part of the program. Instead, the code for that function is placed right into the body of the current function (the caller).

In its ultimate effect on program behavior, an inline function is similar to a macro call. In both cases, a function call is expanded into the statements in the macro or function definition.

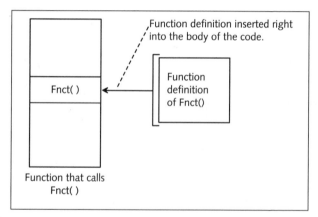

Figure I.2 Inline and macro expansion.

Syntax

In C++, there are two standard ways to create an inline function:

- If it is a member function, you can inline it by placing the function definition inside the class declaration. Note that no semicolon (;) follows the closing brace.

```
class CHorse {
    CStr name;
public:
    CHorse (CStr nm) {name = nm;}
    ...
```

- You can inline any function by placing the **inline** keyword at the beginning of the function definition and all declarations.

```
inline double cube_it(double x) {
    return x * x * x;
}
```

In addition, some compilers (notably Microsoft Visual C++) have command-line options and directives that enable automatic inlining. In any case, the compiler has ultimate control over which functions are inlined. With an advanced optimizing compiler, the **inline** keyword is just a suggestion that can be overridden. Yet the program must behave as though all functions you wrote with the **inline** keyword are inline; none of the syntax rules change, regardless of what the compiler does to optimize the program.

Inline functions obey the following rules in addition to those normally observed by C++ functions:

- An inline function must be fully declared and defined before being used.

- The scope of an inline function is within the current module only. Inline functions cannot be given external linkage.

In general, the impact of these two rules is to make inline functions act very much like macro functions in their scope and declaration. As with macro functions, you should place inline function definitions in header files, because inline functions need to be defined separately for each module and because they need to be defined before any code calls them.

Efficiency Trade-Offs

Inline functions clearly optimize for speed, because they eliminate all the instructions that prepare for function execution by placing arguments on the stack and transferring control. Against this, an inline function does have the potential to increase program size, as is apparent from looking at Figure I.1.

But short functions (such as the two functions given as examples in the previous section) are likely not to increase program size at all. For this reason, short functions are ideal candidates for inlining. It is even possible that inlining a function can decrease program size, because once a function is inlined, a good optimizing compiler can take advantage of the fact that more work is done inside the same routine.

Inlining was developed in part to encourage encapsulation. Because of inlining, C++ can create efficient code for wrapper functions. For example:

```
class CStr {
    char *pData;
...
public:
    char *get(void) {return pData;}
```

Definition

Use of the istream and ostream classes provides an alternative to printf and scanf as well as their file-based equivalents, fscanf, fscanf, and related functions. If you want to do things "the C++ way," you'll probably want to use istream and ostream right away.

The biggest advantage of the stream classes is that they are extensible; you can define how any new type is assigned a value from an input stream. Another advantage is that stream classes support much better type checking. In contrast, the scanf function can read garbage into a random memory location when you forget the address operator (&).

The most common input stream is cin, which is defined for you. You can also create an ifstream object, which represents a file and inherits the properties of the istream class:

```
// Including FSTREAM.H includes IOSTREAM.H with it,
//  and adds file support.
//
include <fstream.h>

ifstream  inf("MYFILE.TXT");
```

Syntax

The most common way to use an object of the istream class is to combine it with the stream input operator (actually the overloaded right-shift operator):

#include <iostream.h>   - or -
#include <fstream.h>

istream >> object

When evaluated, this expression reads in a value of type *object*, converting characters to the type of object as appropriate. The *object* must be an l-value, such as a variable or dereferenced point. This technique is similar to the use of scanf to read characters. (For example, cin >> i, where i is an integer, reads up to the next numeric field and then continues reading characters as long they contribute to forming a single integer field.) Supported object types include all the primitive types as well as **char***, which reads a string up to the first white space.

You can also manipulate a stream by calling one of the member functions of istream objects shown in Table I.1.

Table I.1

FUNCTION	DESCRIPTION
get()	Gets next byte of data, returned as a **char**.
getline(*s, n, ch=*'\n'**)**	Reads a string into **char*** string *s*, for at most *n* characters, until character *ch* is read. The third argument has a default value of **'\n'** (newline).
peek()	Returns next character as in **int**, without advancing through input stream.
putchar(*ch***)**	Puts character *ch* back into the input stream.
read(*s, n***)**	Reads a string into **char*** string *s*, of exactly *n* characters.

Formatting Input

By combining the stream with an I/O manipulator, you can modify the format of data being read from the stream. You can think of these I/O manipulators as input filters. For example:

```
cin >> hex >> n; // Read integer in hexadecimal
                 //Format.
```

The I/O manipulators include hex, oct, dec, and setw. For more information on how these I/O manipulators work, see the topic "ostream Class."

Overloading the >> Operator

To extend istream support for a class, write the following operator function, given here in terms of general syntax. The function is global, but you may need to make it a friend of your own class.

```
istream& operator>>(istream& is, yourclass& obj) {
    statements
    return is;
}
```

A couple of notes on syntax: you can supply any argument names you want, but the rest of the syntax should be entered as shown. The reference operator (&) is used for efficient passing and returning by reference. Returning the istream object enables the stream to be used repeatedly in statements, as in the following:

```
cin >> a >> b >> c;    // Input three numbers.
```

The following simple example implements the >> operator for the CStr class—developed in Chapters 5, 6, and 7—by setting pData from the input stream. pData is a **char*** type, for which the >> operator is already supported.

```
istream& operator>>(istream& is, CStr& obj) {
    is >> obj.pData;
    return is;
}
```

If you followed the development of the CStr class, you may recall that pData is private and cannot be accessed except within the object itself. An easy solution is to make the operator function a friend. Now the reference to pData is legal.

```
class CStr {
private:
    char *pData;
    int nLength;
    friend istream& operator>>(istream&, CStr&);
```

int Data Type

Definition

The **int** data type is an integer that uses the natural integer size of the computer's architecture. This size is usually the processor's register width. For example, in 32-bit architectures, the **int** data type is four bytes in size.

Range

Range varies, depending on whether the size is two or four bytes. When you're using **int** variables, I recommend that you observe the same range as short integers: –32,768 to 32,767.

Syntax

You can declare any number of integer variables by placing **int** at the beginning of the declaration statement:

[storage] [cv] **int** items;

Here the brackets indicate optional prefixes: *storage* is a storage-class specifier (**auto**, **extern**, **register**, **static**) and *cv* is **const**, **volatile**, or both. The *items* are one or more simple or complex variable declarations.

Example

The following statement defines two simple variables (i and j), an array (id_nums), and a pointer (ptr_to_int):

```
int   i, j, id_nums[10], *ptr_to_int;
```

Usage

The **int** data type presents a paradox: if you want to write portable code, you should assume that an **int** type is no more than two bytes wide. This in effect restricts the range of an **int** to that of a **short**: –32,768 to 32,767. But if you're going to observe this restriction, why not just use **short** all the time instead of **int**? The answer is that on 32-bit systems, operations on four-byte integers are faster than those on two-byte integers.

The general principle is that it's best to select **int** for a type whenever you declare a simple variable used for calculation—assuming it won't go out of the range for a **short**. Reserve **short** for compound data types (such as structures and arrays) where space is at a premium.

Definition

Keywords are a special set of words in C++ that have universal, preassigned meanings. You cannot give any of your own functions or variables names that conflict with these words.

There isn't alot to say about keywords other than the fact that when you program in C++, there's a small chance you might accidentally pick a name conflicting with a keyword. In general, it isn't worth trying to memorize the list of keywords to avoid this problem. If it does happen, you'll get a strange syntax error message about a word you thought was a valid name; at that point, you might consider whether you accidentally picked a keyword for a variable name.

The number of keywords in C++ is relatively small, but there are some additional keywords not present in C. In Table K.1, keywords introduced by C++ are marked with an asterisk(*).

Table K.1 C++ Keywords.

auto	dynamic_cast*	new*	switch	while
break	else	operator*	template*	
case	enum	private*	this*	
catch*	extern	protected*	try*	
char	float	public*	typedef	
class*	for	register	typeid*	
const	friend*	return	union	
continue	goto	short	unsigned	
default	if	signed	using*	
delete*	int	sizeof	virtual*	
do	long	static	void	
double	namespace*	struct	volatile	

l-values

Definition

An l-value is something you can assign a value to. The *l* in the name refers to the fact that the item can appear on the *left* side of an assignment.

 It isn't necessary that you master the nuances of this topic unless you're really interested. The bottom line is this: C++ compilers, depending on the implementation, often talk of l-values in the error messages they report. In such cases, you probably mistyped something on the left side of an assignment.

Usage

This concept, which tends to be a little more cut-and-dried in other programming languages, takes on interesting subtleties in C++, largely because of pointers. The simple cases, though, are just like those in other languages. Clearly, the following sort of statement makes sense. It says to put the name 5 into the variable named amount:

```
amount = 5;
```

But the next statement makes no sense, because you cannot put 5 into another constant:

```
27 = 5;   // ERROR! Can't do this.
```

Because 27 is a constant, it cannot appear on the left side. It is not an l-value.

Examples

So what is an l-value? The most common example is a simple variable of primitive type—for example, "amount" in the first example, which is a simple variable of type **int**— Another case is an individual element of an array:

```
double rates[100];
rates[10] = 7.8;
```

Here, rates[10] is an l-value. Broadly speaking, an l-value is any expression that corresponds to a specific location in program memory reserved for variables. This includes the following:

- Simple variables of primitive type (**int**, **char**, **long**, **double**, and so on).

- Members of structures, unions, and arrays, or any compound type, in which a path is fully specified to data of primitive type. For example, rates[10] in the preceding example is an l-value because it refers to a particular integer.

- A pointer variable. In terms of how they are stored and manipulated, pointers are very nearly integers, although they have some special attributes.

- Dereferenced pointers or address expressions, resulting in an expression of primitive type or a pointer type.

The last two categories are the interesting ones, because they are what makes C++ different. Using pointers, casts, the address operator (&), and pointer arithemetic, an address expression can be arbitrarily complex. If this expression is then dereferenced, resulting in an expression of primitive type, it can be used as an l-value.

That's a lot to digest, although the idea is simple enough once you understand it. The most trivial case is a single, dereferenced pointer variable:

```
int i, *ip;

ip = &i;
*ip = 7;
```

There are two assignments here, and each has a legitimite l-value. In the first assignment, ip is a pointer variable, so it may be assigned an address or pointer of the same base type (**int**). The expression &i is the address of an integer and so matches in type.

In the second assignment, a pointer to an integer is specified (ip) and then dereferenced (*ip). It is therefore an l-value. This is a simple case of a dereferenced pointer as l-value:

```
*ip = 7;
```

L-values become interesting when you use a complex expression and then dereference it. Suppose an integer and an array are defined as follows:

```
int my_array[20], i;
```

The following is a valid address expression. The program takes the address of my_array, adds i, and adds the constant 3, doing the appropriate scaling for each addition (see "Pointer Arithmetic").

```
my_array + i + 3
```

You cannot place this expression on the left side of an assignment even though it is a valid address:

```
(my_array + i + 3) = new_val;   // ERROR!
```

But you can use the indirection operator to instruct the computer to place a new value *at* this address:

```
*(my_array + i + 3) = new_val;
```

Array names (my_array, for example) evaluate to the address of the first element and are almost equivalent to pointer variables. One basic difference is that pointer variables can be assigned new values any time, but array names are constants. The following assignment is not valid, because a constant is on the left side:

```
my_array = 1000;
```

This statement, if allowed, would attempt to change the address that my_array represents. It would say that the array is at the location 1000 in memory. That's not a valid operation, because it would be a direct contradiction of fact, just as the assignment "27 = 5" is a contradiction of fact. You can, however, use indirection (*) to assign a new value *at* the address that my_array represents (the address of the first element):

```
*my_array = 1000;
```

This statement puts 1,000 into the first element of my_array.

Incidentally, "my_array = 1000" is a contradiction in fact because my_array has already been allocated in program memory and its address is fixed. But as I've mentioned, pointer variables can hold different addresses at different times and so are legitimate l-values (even when not dereferenced).

Definition

A statement label serves the same purpose in C++ as it does in other languages. A label is like a line number, giving **goto** statements specific locations to jump to. But unlike line numbers, statement labels can have meaningful names, making them easy to use.

Labels also work with a **switch** statement. This aspect of C grammar throws most people at first, because it means you usually need to put **break** between each case.

Syntax

A labeled statement forms a statement in C++ and has one of three forms:

identifier: *statement*
case *constant_expression*: *statement*
default: *statement*

Note that a statement must follow the label, even if it is an empty statement (a lone semicolon).

Because a labeled statement in C++ forms a single, unified statement, you can apply the syntax recursively to precede a statement with any number of labels. However, this is rarely done except with **case** labels, where it can be useful.

Usage 1: Target of goto Statements

The most familiar use of labels is in the first syntax, which gives a statement a meaningful name:

```
start_calculations_here:
    a = x + y / 2;
```

It's irrelevant to the C++ compiler whether the label itself and the rest of the statement are on the same physical line. This fact gives you leeway in spacing.

A statement labeled this way can be the target of a **goto** as long as the **goto** and the statement are in the same function. For obvious reasons, no two statements in the same function can be labeled with the same *identifier*.

Blocks of code that use **goto** statements are usually better written as **if-else** blocks, **while** loops, **do** loops, or **for** loops.

Usage 2: Case and Default Labels

Within a **switch** statement block, you can label statements with **case** and **default** to serve as targets for execution:

```
case 5:
    strcpy(num_str, "five");
    break;
...
default:
    strcpy(num_str, "unknown");
    break;
```

A **switch** statement tests an expression and jumps to the case that matches the expression (or **default**, if no cases match).

The **break** statement is necessary because **case** and **default** are just labels. A label does not change the flow of control, but only serves as a target. Execution starts at the appropriate **case** or **default** statement and continues until one of two things happens: the end of the statement block is reached or a **break** statement is executed.

See the topics "case Keyword," "break Keyword," and "switch Statement" for examples.

Definition

The **long** data type is a four-byte integer. The ANSI C++ standard requires only that a **long** be at least four bytes, but **long** is exactly four bytes wide in the vast majority of implementations.

Range

Approximately plus or minus two billion: –2,147,483,647 to 2,147,483,647, to be exact.

Syntax

You can declare any number of long integers by placing **long** at the beginning of the declaration statement:

[*storage*] [*cv*] **long** *items*;

Here the brackets indicate optional prefixes: *storage* is a storage-class specifier (**auto**, **extern**, **register**, **static**) and *cv* is **const**, **volatile**, or both. The *items* are one or more simple or complex variable declarations.

Example

The following statement defines a simple variable (population), an array (pops), and a pointer (ptr_to_long):

```
long   population, pops[200], *ptr_to_long;
```

Usage

On 32-bit operating systems, a **long** is equivalent to an **int**. However, if you're writing programs that might be ported to different systems, you can't assume that an **int** will be as large as a **long**. Therefore, if there is any chance that a variable will fall outside the range of a **short** (–32,768 to 32,767), declare it as a **long**.

Loops

Definition

C++ has three loop structures: **while**, **for**, and **do-while**.

Loops are at the heart of programming. Computers would not be one millionth as useful without loops in some form. The idea behind loops is simple: it's just the idea of saying go back to step one (or step two, or three, or whatever).

Example

A trivial example is printing all the numbers between 1 and 1,000, a tedious and boring task. If you have to tell the computer to print each individual number, "Print 1, then print 2, then print 3...," you might as well do the job yourself.

Programming starts to become most useful when you realize that you don't have to direct every individual move but can instead set a general pattern of action in motion by writing a loop. The beauty of this is that it's five steps rather than 1,000:

1. Set i to 1.

2. Is i greater than 1,000? If so, exit.

3. Print i.

4. Add 1 to i.

5. Go back to step 2.

In C, this program logic could be equally well expressed as either a **while** loop or a **for** loop. First, the **while** loop:

```
i = 1;
while (i <= 1000) {
    printf("%d\n", i);
    i++;
}
```

The **for** loop does the same thing but is more concise:

```
for (i = 1; i <= 1000; i++)
    printf("%d\n", i);
```

For more explanation of loop syntax, see the topics "do Keyword," "for Keyword," and "while Statement."

Mistakes in Loop Writing

Despite the simplicity and elegance of the idea of loops, they offer one of the most common areas for programmer error. Often, loops go wrong because you didn't correctly set initial or terminating conditions.

This is particularly likely when arrays are involved. Array indexes in C++ run from 0 to size −1, where size is the number of elements. Therefore, when you write a loop that accesses each member of the array in turn, initialize the index to 0 (not 1, as you would in most other languages). The loop should continue as long as the index is *less than* the number of elements. Once the index is equal to the number of elements, the loop should terminate, because the highest index is one less than this number.

The following is an example of a correctly written loop that initializes every element to 10:

```
#define ARRAY_SIZE  1000

int i, numbers[ARRAY_SIZE];

for (i = 0, i < ARRAY_SIZE; i++)
    numbers[i] = 10;
```

Definition

With few exceptions (such as Windows programming and writing code for libraries), every program must have a **main** function—the function that's always executed first. Although **main** is restricted in terms of its arguments and return type, it behaves in almost every respect like a standard function and must observe the same rules.

Syntax

The function definition for **main** can take either of the forms shown in Figure M.1.

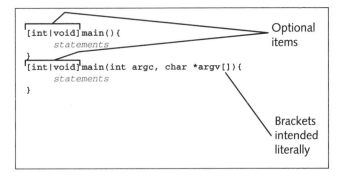

Figure M.1 The function definition for |
main can take either of these forms.

Here, the expression [**int** | **void**] indicates that **main** can be qualified by the **int** or **void** return type, but not both. (By default, **main** has a return type of **int**, which means that **main** should return a value.) However, in the case of *argv[], the brackets are intended literally.

Note that, as with other functions, the function definition of **main** is not terminated by a semicolon (;), which would cause a syntax error.

Main Function (continued)

Case 1: main with No Arguments

Writing a **main** function with no arguments is simple. A **main** function can have local variables and complex statements just like other functions, but in many programs all the **main** function does is to call the other principal functions in the program and let them do all the work.

In the following example, **main** is defined with a void return type, so no return value is expected (a return value would require use of the **return** statement):

```
void main () {
    init_vars();
    prompt_for_input();
    print_results();
}
```

Case 2: main with Arguments

If you're expecting command-line input entered on the command line, you can use the special *argc* and *argv* arguments to get at this input from within the program. In many programs, in fact, the principal work of **main** is to access these arguments and then call other functions.

For example, suppose you wrote a DOS or console application called SORT.EXE, which accepts two command-line arguments: the name of an input file and the name of an output file:

```
sort  datafile.txt  results.txt
```

The *argc* argument contains the total number of items on the command line (in this case, 3). The *argv* argument is an array of pointers. In this case, it would be an array in which the first three elements point to one of the strings—"sort", "datafile.txt", and "results.txt"—and in that order.

In the following example code, the program prints an error message and exits if two command-line arguments were not entered:

```
int main(int argc, char *argv[])) {
    if (argc != 3) {
        printf("Bad number of arguments.\n");
        printf("Syntax: sort inputfile outputfile.\n");
        return -1;
    }
    ...
```

Definition

Modulus operator is the name that many C++ manuals use for what I call the remainder operator. Whatever name it goes by, the function of this operator is to divide one integer by another and return the remainder of the division. A typical use is determining whether a number is even or odd, or whether it's exactly divisible by four.

See "Remainder Operator" for more information.

Definition

Namespaces are a C++ technique for avoiding name conflicts. Defining a namespace is most useful when you're combining libraries and header files supplied by different sources. In general, the term *namespace* refers to a group of names within which conflicts are possible. Names in different namespaces do not conflict and so can duplicate one another.

Classes and structures can be considered special cases of namespaces. The same name may appear in different classes without conflict. You can also use the **namespace** keyword to create namespaces.

 The namespace keyword is a recent addition to the C++ language and is not supported in all versions of the language.
N O T E

Syntax

To create a namespace, use the following syntax:

```
namespace name {
    declarations_and_function_definitions
}
```

Each of the *declarations_and_function_definitions* is placed in a separate namespace, which means that none of them will conflict with your own variable and function names. Within the namespace, a function definition can refer to any other symbol declared in the namespace without qualification. Names within the namespace must not conflict.

Outside the namespace, you have to take special action to refer to anything declared inside it. You can either qualify the use of a name, or you can employ the **using** keyword to make names inside the namespace directly available.

Namespaces (continued)

To qualify the use of a name declared inside a namespace, use the context operator (::) as you would to refer to a member function:

namespace_name::symbol

A **using** definition causes the compiler to recognize all further use of a name without qualification:

using *namespace_name::symbol*;

A **using namespace** declaration causes the compiler to recognize all names within the namespace without qualification:

using namespace *namespace_name*;

Example

A common way to use the **namespace** keyword is to create a namespace around a header file. Doing so enables you to include the file without fear of conflicts with your own global symbols or with symbols declared in other include files.

```
namespace grants {
#include <grant.h>
}
```

As you need to refer to a particular symbol within the namespace, you can selectively enable it with a **using** definition. For example, if you want to refer to the Cary variable declared in **GRANT.H**, use this definition:

```
using grants::Cary;
```

Now the name Cary can be used in subsequent statements without qualification. For example:

```
Cary = 0;   // Set grants::Cary to 0.
```

Alternatively, you can make all the names in **GRANT.H** available, although doing so negates much of the reason for defining a namespace in the first place:

```
using namespace grants;
```

Definition

The **new** operator creates one or more objects dynamically and returns a pointer to the object (or first object, if you create an array). In this context, *dynamically* means that the number of objects needed can be determined at run time. For example, if you start to exceed the size of an array, you could use **new** to allocate an array of larger size.

Unlike the malloc function, **new** calls the constructor (if any) for each object it creates. To this extent, **new** is consistent with other C++ techniques for creating objects.

 The malloc and free functions are supported by the C++ library and are safe to use with types that don't require initialization via constructors. This includes primitive types. So the use of malloc in code ported from C does not pose a problem.

Syntax

To use the **new** operator, place **new** in front of a type name. You can optionally specify arguments to the constructor .

```
new type              // - OR -
new type(args)
```

The expression creates a new object of the specified *type* and returns a pointer to that object. You can also use **new** to create arrays of objects. All dimension sizes except the last one must be constants:

```
new type[var]              // - OR -
new type[d1][d2]...[var]
```

Here, *var* is an integer that need not be a constant. The values *d1*, *d2*, and so on are integer values that must be constants. In this syntax, the brackets are intended literally.

Usage

The **new** operator returns a pointer to an object; in some cases, an object is primarily accessed through a pointer, so the use of **new** is convenient. Another advantage of **new** is that after creating an object, you can destroy it at any time by using the **delete** operator, thus helping you conserve memory. If you create an object by simply declaring it as a local variable, it is not destroyed until it goes out of scope.

Examples

The simplest way to use **new** is to create a single object and assign the result to a pointer.

```
CStr *p;
p = new CStr;
```

A more compact version of this code combines the pointer declaration with object creation:

```
CStr *p = new CStr;
```

Optionally, you can provide arguments to the constructor.

```
CStr *p = new CStr("A string ");
```

Once the object is created, you can manipulate it through the pointer. Remember to free the memory by using the **delete** operator.

```
CStr *p = new CStr("A string ");
...
p->cat("is born.");
puts(p->get());
...
delete p;
```

The final example creates an array of objects of size n, in which n does not need to be a constant but can be a variable whose value is calculated at run time. Note the special syntax required for **delete** when used with arrays.

```
CStr *p = new CStr[n];
...
puts(p[k].get());      // Print element k.
...
delete [] p;
```

Definition

An object is a packet of data that can have functions associated with it. The functions define the object's behavior, so the object can act as an autonomous unit, something like an integrated circuit or brain cell. This may sound like magic, but remember that objects are an extension of the idea of structures in C. See Chapter 5, "A Touch of Class," for an introduction to member functions, classes, and objects.

When you first learn object-oriented programming, one of the major sources of confusion is the distinction between classes and objects. A class is a user-defined type and is created through a declaration. (The keywords **class**, **struct**, and **union** all declare classes in C++.) As a type, a class does not contain any actual data; instead, it contains all the type information necessary to generate objects. The individual objects of that class contain actual data values. The relationship between classes and objects is the same as the relationship between the data type **int** and a specific integer value, such as 55.

Another source of confusion is the distinction between variables and objects. Strictly speaking, all variables are really objects—remember that an object is a packet of data in memory and may or may not have functions associated with it. However, not all objects are variables, because a variable must have both a name and a memory location. Occasionally, C++ creates temporary, unnamed objects as it evaluates expressions. In general, though, the concepts of variable and object overlap a great deal.

Example

The following class declaration creates a type, CPnt, that has two member functions. These functions are CPnt constructors:

```
class CPnt {
public:
    double x, y;
    CPnt() {x=0.0; y=0.0;}
    CPnt(double newx, newy) {x=newx; y=newy;}
};
```

The class does not contain actual data values, but it can be used to create objects. Once declared, a class name can be used just as a type name, such as **int**, **double**, **char**, **short**, **long**, and so on, is used.

```
CPnt    a, b, c;
CPnt    pnt1(1.0, -3), pnt2(65.5, 27);
```

Definition

Operators are symbols (and occasionally keywords) used to build expressions. C++ operators include the C operators, plus a few more. Table O.1 summarizes precdence and associativity.

Table O.1 Concise Summary of C Operators.

OPERATORS	ASSOCIATIVITY
:: *class*::	:: is right to left, class:: is left to right
() [] . ->	left to right
++ -- ! ~ **sizeof** (*type*) + (unary) - (unary) **&** (unary) * (unary) **new delete** **typeid dynamic_cast**	right to left
* / %	left to right
+ -	left to right
<< >>	left to right
< <= > >=	left to right
== !=	left to right
&	left to right
^	left to right
|	left to right
&&	left to right
||	left to right
?:	right to left
= += *= /= %= <<= >>= &= ^= |=	right to left
,	left to right

Table O.2 gives a brief description of each operator. Operators not separated by a solid line are at the same level of precedence.

428

Table O.2 *Descriptive Summary of C++ Operators.*

OPERATOR	DESCRIPTION	ASSOCIATIVITY
::	Global scope: *::symbol*	right to left
class::	Class or namespace scope: *class::symbol*	left to right
()	Function call, as in *fnct(args)*	left to right
[]	Array indexing, as in *array[index]*	
.	Structure-member reference: *struct.member*	
->	Pointer-member reference: *structptr.member*	
++	Prefix increment	right to left
--	Postfix decrement	
!	Logical NOT	
~	Bitwise NOT (one's complement)	
sizeof	Width of type or expression, in bytes	
(type)	Explicit type cast	
+	Unary plus, specifies positive number	
-	Unary minus, specifies negative number	
&	Address-of operators	
*	Pointer dereference	
new	Dynamic object creation	
delete	Dynamic object destruction	
typeid	Returns type of operand	
dynamic_cast	Attempts explicit cast **dynamic_cast**(*type*) at run time	

429

Table O.2 Descriptive Summary of C++ Operators. (continued)

OPERATOR	DESCRIPTION	ASSOCIATIVITY
* / %	Multiplication and division Remainder operator	left to right
+ -	Addition and subtraction	left to right
<< >>	Left and right bitwise shift	left to right
< <= > >=	Tests for less than, less than or equal to, etc.	left to right
== =!	Test for equality Not-equal-to test	left to right
&	Bitwise AND	left to right
^	Bitwise exclusive OR (XOR)	left to right
l	Bitwise OR	left to right
&&	Logical AND (uses short-circuit testing)	left to right
ll	Logical OR (uses short-circuit testing)	left to right
?:	Conditional operator: *exp1* **?** *exp2* : *exp3*	right to left
= += -= *= /= %= >>= <<= &= ^= l=	Assignment Addition/subtraction assignment Multiplication/division assignment Remainder operator and assignment Left/right shift and assignment Bitwise AND, XOR, OR assignment	right to left
,	Comma operator: evaluate both *expr1* , *expr2*; evaluates to *exprl*	right to left

430

Definition

Use of the istream and ostream classes provides an alternative to printf and scanf as well as their file-based equivalents, fscanf, fscanf, and related functions. If you want to do things "the C++ way," you'll probably want to use stream classes right away.

The biggest advantage of the stream classes is that they are extensible; you can define how any new type is printed when sent to an output stream. Another advantage is that stream classes support much better type checking. A value is always printed according to its type. In contrast, the printf function will print any type of data in an integer field if asked to even if it makes no sense.

The most common output stream is cout, which is defined for you. You can also create an ofstream object, which represents a file and inherits the properties of the ostream class:

```
// Including FSTREAM.H includes IOSTREAM.H with it,
//  and adds file support.
//
include <fstream.h>

ofstream  outf("MYFILE.TXT");
```

Syntax

The most common way to use an object of the ostream class is to combine it with the stream output operator (actually the overloaded left-shift operator):

```
#include <iostream.h>      //or -
#include <fstream.h>

ostream << object
```

431

When evaluated, this expression prints a value of type *object*, converting from the object's type to a character-string representation of the object's value. Supported object types include all the primitive types as well as **char***.

You can also manipulate a stream by calling one of the member functions of ostream objects shown in Table O.3.

Table O.3

FUNCTION	DESCRIPTION
put(*c*)	Write one byte of data, *c*.
write(*s*, *n*)	Write exactly *n* bytes, pointed to by **char*** pointer *s*.

Formatting Input

By combining the stream with an I/O manipulator, you can modify the format of data being written to a stream. You can think of these I/O manipulators as output filters. For example:

```
cout << hex << n; // Write integer in hexadecimal
                  //format.
```

The way to understand I/O manipulators is to think of them as objects that, when combined with a stream, alter some aspect of the state of that stream. For example, hex can be combined with cin by using the right-shift operator (>>) or combined with cout by using the left-shift operator. In either case, the result is that the integer format changes to hexadecimal.

The code in the previous example is equivalent to the following:

```
(cout << hex) << n;
```

432

This code in turn produces the same behavior as the following code:

```
cout << hex;
cout << n;
```

Remember that the statement is interpreted this way because of left-to-right associativity and because cout << hex evaluates to cout.

Both input and output streams support the I/O manipulators shown in Table O.4.

Table O.4

I/O MANIPULATOR	DESCRIPTION
hex	Set integer I/O format to hexadecimal.
oct	Set integer I/O format to octal.
dec	Set integer I/O format to decimal.
setw(*n***)** next	Set width of next input field to *n*. (Applies to object input or output only.)

Overloading the << Operator

To extend ostream support for a class, write the following operator function, given here in terms of general syntax. The function is global, but you may need to make it a friend of your own class.

```
ostream& operator<<(ostream& os, yourclass& obj) {
    statements
    return os;
}
```

A couple of notes on syntax: you can supply any argument names you want, but the rest of the syntax should be entered as shown. The reference operator (&) is used for efficient passing and returning by reference. Returning the

433

ostream object enables the stream to be used repeatedly in statements, as in the following:

```
cout << a << b << c;    // Print three numbers.
```

The following simple example implements the << operator for the CStr class (developed in Chapters 5, 6, and 7) by sending pData to the output stream. pData is a **char*** type, for which the << operator is already supported.

```
ostream& operator<<(ostream& os, CStr& obj) {
    os << obj.pData;
    return os;
}
```

If you followed the development of the CStr class, you may recall that pData is private and cannot be accessed except within the object itself. An easy solution is to make the operator function a friend. Now the reference to pData is legal.

```
class CStr {
private:
    char *pData;
    int nLength;
    friend ostream& operator<<(ostream&, CStr&);
```

Definition

Function overloading reflects the strong emphasis on types in C++. Unlike C, C++ lets you write two or more functions that share the same name and scope, but have different argument lists. There are two syntax rules that determine when overloading is valid.

- The two functions must differ in number and/or type of arguments. Two functions that have the same name and argument list but different return types is illegal.

- The argument lists must be at least one *non-default* argument. (See "Default Argument Values" for more information.)

Example

The following prototypes declare three distinct functions. For each of these functions, the program must supply (or link in) a separate function definition.

```
PrintStr(int);
PrintStr(CStr);
PrintStr(char *, int);
```

Each of the following statements calls a different version of the function:

```
PrintStr(23);               // Call PrStr (int)
PrintStr(CStr("cat"));      // Call PrStr (CStr)
PrintStr("dog", 3);         // Call PrStr (char *, int)
```

Definition

Operator overloading provides some of the most fun you can with have C++. You can use operator overloading to help create classes that look like Basic strings or the FOR-TRAN COMPLEX number type. Or you can create entirely new extensions to your types, making them use operators in new ways. The general meaning of an operator should not, as a rule, significantly change when applied to your class. (Though note that the stream operators, << and >>, are really shift operators and are an exception to this principle.)

In essence, the term *operator overloading* refers to the fact that you can define operator functions for your classes. These functions tell the compiler how to interpret the specified operators. For example, the compiler evaluates an expression such as

```
"Leslie " + CStr("Hope");
```

by calling the function declared as:

```
CStr operator+(char *, CStr);
```

The compiler calls this function because the argument return types (**char*** and CStr) match the arguments given. CStr is the return type, but you could specify a different return type if you chose.

The rest of this topic summarizes operator-overloading syntax rules, especially for operators that constitute special cases. For a general introduction to the subject, see Chapter 7, "Class Operations."

General Syntax Rules

The following principles apply to all operator functions generally:

436

- No matter which classes they are applied to, operators retain their fundamental language characteristics including associativity and precedence. (However, operators are not automatically commutative unless you define them that way.)

- You cannot use new symbols; you can use only the operator symbols used in the C++ character set.

- All operator functions are inherited, except for the assignment operator (=).

- Each operator must be defined separately. For example, the addition-assignment operator (+=) must be given its own operator; it is not automatically defined because you wrote a function for assignment (=) and a function for addition (+).

- You cannot use default argument values in an operator function.

- You cannot implement any operator as a static member function, except for **new** and **delete**, which are implicitly static. (See "static Keyword.")

Unary Operator Functions

You can write a unary-operator function for an operator (such as + or -) that C++ already accepts as a unary operator. Given an expression of the form

@operand

in which @ represents an operator, the compiler evaluates the expression by calling one of the following functions, depending on which is defined:

return_type type::**operator@**()
return_type **operator@**(*type*)

in which *type* is the operand's. The type declaration may be given other attributes, such as being a reference or being declared **const**.

Depending on the operator itself, the expression that uses a unary operator may be of the form

operator@

As indicated earlier, the syntax of operators is always consistent with the current syntax of the operator.

Binary Operator Functions

You can write a binary-operator function for an operator (such as +, -, *, or /) that C++ already accepts as a binary operator. Given an expression of the form

operand1@operand2

in which @ represents an operator, the compiler evaluates the expression by calling one of the following functions, depending on which is defined:

return_type type1::operator@(type2)
return_type operator@(type1, type2)

in which *type1* and *type2* are the types of the *operand1* and *operand2*, respectively. Each argument type declaration may be given other attributes, such as being a reference or being declared **const**.

Assignment Operator Functions

Although the assignment operator (=) is a binary operator, it has special restrictions beyond those mentioned in the previous section. The function must be a member function of a class, it must take an object of this class as its sole argu-

ment, and it must return this class as its return value. Both
the argument and the return type must be references. (See
the topic "Reference Operator (&)" for more information.)

The declaration of such a function is:

class& *class*::**operator=(const** *class*&)

For example, the following code illustrates what an assignment operator function might look for with a simple class,
CPoint:

```
class CPoint {
private:
        double x, y;
public:
        CPoint operator=(const CPoint& point);
        ...
};

CPoint& CPoint::operator=(const CPoint& point) {
        x = point.x;
        y = point.y;
        return *this;
}
```

**The compiler supplies a default assignment function for each
class. This default function performs a straight member-by-
N O T E member copying, which in this case would be sufficient.**

Increment and Decrement Operators

Although increment (++) and decrement (++) operators are
unary operators and follow most of the rules for unary operators, they can be either prefix and postfix. If you want to
implement these operators, you'll need to write separate
functions for the prefix and postfix versions.

- The prefix version alters the operand and then returns its value. You should return a reference to the class, because the value of the object (after incrementing or decrementing) and the value of the expression is the same.

- The postfix version returns the value of the operand before altering its value, and therefore does not return a reference. This version requires a dummy argument of type **int**, which is passed the value 0 during a call. The only purpose of this argument is to differentiate the function definitions.

The following example illustrates postfix and prefix versions for the increment operator (++).

```
class CPoint {
private:
        double x, y;
public:
        CPoint& operator++();      // prefix
        CPoint  operator++(int); // postfix
};


// Prefix ++. For efficiency's sake, returns
//  a reference (&).


CPoint& operator++() { // Prefix version
        x++;
        y++;
        return *this;
}


// Postfix ++. Must include dummy arg.
//
CPoint operator++(int dummy) {
        CPoint point(*this);  // Make a copy.
```

440

```
x++;                    // Change original.
y++;
return point;           // Return the copy.
}
```

Other Operator Functions

There are several operators that you will want to implement only under unusual conditions. These operators have a normal, compiler-supplied implementation that works perfectly well for most classes.

The Subscript Operator ([])

You would implement this operator if writing your own array collection class. The **operator[]** function takes one integer argument giving a zero-based array position. You should return a reference, enabling subscript expressions to appear on either side of an assignment.

new and delete Operators

You can implement these operators to control the way a class manages memory. (Note that earlier versions of C++ do not support these operator functions.) To write the operator functions, include the file STDDEF.H and use the following declarations, replacing "myclass" by your own class name.

```
#include <stddef.h>

class myclass {
...
        void* operator new(size_t);
        void  operator delete(void*, size_t);
```

Interestingly enough, the compiler adjusts the pointer returned by **new** or passed to **delete**, automatically casting the pointer to **void***. Your function definitions must treat the pointers as **void***.

The **new** operator function can be overloaded with additional arguments.

The Function Call Operator ()

The purpose of this operator is to enable objects of your class to be used like function names. You can overload this operator with multiple definitions. In the following example, the object Print_it can be used as if it were a function.

```
class Print_class {
        public:
                int operator()(long a);
                int operator()(char *s, int n);
        . . .
};


Print_class Print_it;

// This next statement calls
// Print_class::operator()(char*, int)
Print_it("cat", 3);
```

Definition

Under the covers, pointers are nearly the same as integers, and you can add or subtract them. For lack of a better word, such operations are called *pointer arithmetic*. It's an important subject in C++ because it is the basis for array indexing. Pointer arithmetic has some quirks of its own, which make perfect sense when you consider how pointers are used.

Syntax

The following operations are valid for *addr*, an address expression (such as a pointer, array name, or &variable), and *integer*, an integer expression .

```
addr + integer    // address-expression result
addr - integer    // address-expression result
addr - addr       // integer result
```

The result of the first two operations is an address expression; the result of the third is an integer.

These operations are scaled, meaning that *integer* is multiplied by the size of the base type of *addr* before being added or subtracted. In the *addr - addr* syntax, the pointers must be of the same base type. The difference in the addresses is divided by size of the base type.

 Addition assignment (+=), subtraction assignment (-=), and increment and decrement operators are all supported in a similar fashion, so that addr += integer, for example is valid.

N O T E

Examples

Suppose that my_array and ptr are declared as follows:

```
long  my_array[20];
long  *ptr = my_array;
```

Both my_array and ptr are address expressions, and each has the base type **long** (long integer), which is four bytes in size. So the scaling factor is four. The expression

```
ptr
```

points to the first element of my_array; let's say that this is the address 0x1000 (addresses are usually represented in hexadecimal notation). The following expression evaluates to the address 0x1004, because the integer, 1, is first multiplied by four and then added to ptr:

```
ptr + 1 = (numeric value of ptr) + 1 * sizeof(long)
        = 0x1000 + 1 * 4
        = 0x1004
```

So this expression points to the second element of the array.

Similarly, the next expression evaluates to the address 0x1008, because the integer, 2, is multiplied by four:

```
ptr + 2 = (numeric value of ptr) + 2 * sizeof(long)
        = 0x1000 + 2 * 4
        = 0x1008
```

And this expression, in turn, points to the third element of the array. Figure P.1 illustrates how this works.

This process of scaling—multiplying the integer by the size of the pointer's base type—makes sense because ptr, in this case, points to items of type **long**, and not just to individual bytes. In these expressions, the integer is scaled by whatever the size of the base type is—eight bytes for **double**, for example; possibly more for structures. Only **char*** and **void***—pointer types do not involve scaling (because **char** is one byte in size).

444

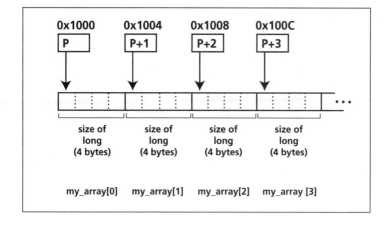

Figure P.1 Pointer addition.

Incrementing ptr is the same as adding 1:

```
// Equivalent expressions: each increases the
   address stored in p by 4.

ptr = ptr + 1;
ptr++;
```

In either case, the number 1 is multiplied by four (assuming that the base type has a width of four) and then added to the numeric value stored in ptr. If ptr points to a position in an array, adding four is the same as saying, "Point to the next element of the array."

Indexing and pointer arithmetic are closely linked. When the expression my_array[10] appears in executable code, it is equivalent to:

```
*(my_array + 10)
```

In fact, the compiler translates the expression my_array[10] into this expression.

Pointers

Definition

Most C++ programs make heavy use of pointers (a pointer is a variable containing an address). The importance of pointers in C++ is that they provide the only ways to do the following: pass by reference, manipulate strings, or use dynamically allocated memory. Moreover, once you've been around pointers for awhile and learn to use them cleverly, they open up new possibilities for writing fast, compact programs and manipulating data. Pointers combined with the right type casts allow you to do almost anything.

For a general introduction to the subject, see Chapter 3, "Pointers, Strings, and Things." This section summarizes some of the finer points of pointer syntax and use. You might also look at the topics "Pointer Arithmetic" and "Pointers to Functions" for specific information about those areas.

Syntax

The pointer indirection operator (*)—not to be confused with multiplication, which is a binary, not a unary, operator—means "the thing that *ptr* points to":

```
*ptr
```

If this expression appears in an executable statement, it refers to the contents of the address stored in *ptr*. So if **ptr* is an integer, *ptr* is a pointer to an integer, and vice versa. The rest of this topic explores the implications of this syntax.

Pointers and Address Expressions

Numeric values can be used to represent many things: the number of cents in your checking account, the population of your state, a position within an array. Some special kinds of expressions represent addresses—that is, numerically indexed locations within the computer's own memory. These *address expressions* look a lot like integers; they are usually stored in either two or four bytes, depending on system architecture. But address expressions have a number of special restrictions and uses.

Suppose that the following variables are declared, and one of them (ptr) is initialized to point to the start of the array:

```
int *ptr, my_array[100], i;

ptr = my_array;
```

All the following are valid address expressions. The variable my_array, when it appears without an index, is interpreted as the address of the first element.

```
ptr          my_array          &i
```

These expressions hold the address of an integer, and all have type **int***. There is an important difference between these expressions: ptr is a variable, whereas the other two expressions are constants. So only ptr can be assigned a new value. For example:

```
ptr = &i;       // Assign address of i to ptr.
ptr = my_array; // Assign address of start of array to
                // ptr.
```

Pointer arithmetic allows you to add or subtract integer values to address expressions: the result is another address expression. (See "Pointer Arithmetic.") Both of the following represent addresses:

```
ptr + 1
array + 7
```

Only a restricted set of operations is permitted with address expressions. You can add integers to them, as done here. You can assign them to a pointer variable. You can also apply the indirection operator (*) to access the contents at the location. The result is an expression of the base type. In this case, because the expressions ptr, array, and &i all have the type **int***, the resulting type is **int** (integer).

```
*ptr
*array
*(array + 7)
*(&i)          // This is the same as i itself.
```

These expressions, which are integers, can be used wherever an integer variable can be used. For example:

```
*ptr = 5;               // Put 5 into the int pointed to
i = *ptr + 10;          // Put 15 into i.
*(&i) = 1;              // Put 1 into i.
*(array + 7) = 100;     // Put 100 into array[7].
(*ptr)++;               // Increment the int pointed to
                        // by ptr;
                        // parens necessary because ++ has
                        // higher precedence than *.
```

The variable ptr has another interesting twist. Because it is a variable and not a constant, it has its own address in memory. Consequently, you can take the address of ptr itself:

```
&ptr
```

The result is a constant expression of type **int****, a pointer to a pointer to an integer.

Pointer Initialization

In addition to the differences noted above, there is one other crucial difference between ptr, a pointer variable, and a constant address expression such as my_array and &i: ptr must be either initialized or assigned an address before being used:

448

```
ptr = my_array;
```

If ptr is not explicitly given a value, its use represents a potential danger to the program. (This is one of the things that gives C++ a bad name among some people; but you just have to learn how to handle your pointers!) Specifically, consider this innocent-looking couple of statements:

```
int p;
```

```
*p = 5;
```

The second statement copies the value 5 to the location pointed to by p. The problem is, what does p point to? If p is global, it is initialized to 0 (NULL). If it is local, it contains some random address. In either case, the statement moves data to an invalid address in your computer's memory. If you're not running on a system with protected memory, then your statement could overwrite basic operating system code! This is why C++ programs that misuse pointers often cause the whole system to come crashing to a halt. You'll have to reboot, and any unsaved data from other running programs is lost.

 Many compilers have a "check for null pointer" feature, which puts in code to check for an error at run time N O T E whenever a pointer with a value of 0 (NULL) is used to read or write data. This is useful, especially when you're first using C++, and it stops the program before it does real damage. For this check to be effective, though, you must initialize all pointers to 0, except those initialized to a valid address. Pointers that contain random values escape detection until it's too late.

Another thing that can save you from having to reboot is an operating system that uses protected memory. Your program will be abruptly terminated and will not be allowed to infect the rest of the system with its random memory operations. Of course, you shouldn't rely on the system to police you like this.

So it's important to initialize pointers. Often, a pointer is declared that is to be assigned an address later. You may want to indicate that, for whatever reason, the pointer is not valid yet and not to be used. In any case, the way to initialize a pointer with no current address is to initialize it to NULL:

```
#include <stdio.h>

int *p = NULL;
```

NULL, in turn, is a symbolic constant defined in the file STDIO.H. NULL is defined as follows:

```
#define  NULL  ((void*)0);
```

As you can see, NULL is just the value zero, cast to a pointer type. C++ programmers frequently make good use of NULL as an indicator that the pointer is not yet assigned a value. Because NULL is equivalent to zero (false), you can test for it in expressions such as the following:

```
if (p)                  // If pointer NOT null,
    *p = new_total;     //   use pointer.
else
    // Pointer not valid; go initialize it.
```

This kind of "fail-safe" logic uses a test to ensure that the pointer p points somewhere before using it. You don't need to do this if you've just assigned a value to p or have reason to be certain p is initialized to a valid address. However, many programs use NULL as a possible value for pointers, indicating that the pointer is not yet ready to use.

Global variables are automatically initialized to zero (NULL) values by default. This applies to pointers as well. Local, nonstatic variables are more troublesome because they can contain random values if not initialized, so take care to initialize local pointers.

Initialization and Aggregates

A pointer can be initialized to any constant address expression. Note that the name of an array is a constant expression that translates into the address of the first element.

```
int n, ages[10];

int *ptr1 = &n;    // Point to n
int *ptr2 = ages;  // Point to 1st element of ages
int *ptr3 = NULL;  // Init to (void*)0
```

One of the differences between pointers and arrays is that an array definition allocates many bytes of storage, whereas a pointer definition allocates only enough room for one pointer—usually two bytes wide on 16-bit systems and four bytes wide on 32-bit systems (or longer, depending on special considerations such as memory model or use of a **far** pointer).

Consider the following definitions:

```
char s[] = "Hello!!";
char *p = s;
```

Here, the definition of s[] allocates eight bytes: one for each character and one for a terminating null byte. The definition of p allocates space for just one pointer (this is four bytes on a 32-bit system).

However, the following definition intializes a pointer through the use of an aggregate. You can do this with string literals, as done here, or with other kinds of aggregates. In either case, the declaration allocates space for the aggregate data and then returns the address of this data. That address is then assigned to the pointer.

```
char *p = "Goodbye";
```

In this case, the definition allocates eight bytes for the string data, plus four for the pointer, for a total of eight bytes.

451

Figure P.2 illustrates how these definitions allocate data.

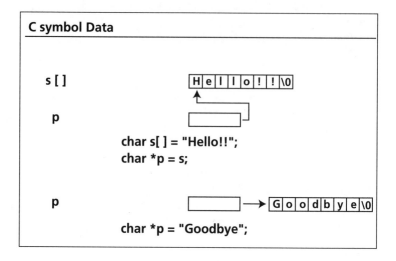

Figure P.2 Effect of pointer definitions on data allocation.

When s[] and p are declared separately, as in the first case, the identifier s is always available as a constant, pointing to the start of the string. In the second case, the only access to the string data is provided through p, the pointer. If p is later assigned a new address, then access to the string data may be permanently lost. (It's still there in memory, but there's no way to refer to it.)

The first approach, it should be noted, does not result in the allocation of any more program data; its only drawback is that it creates more symbols for the compiler to deal with. The choice of which approach to use should be guided by the logic of your particular program.

Definition

Pointers to functions (function pointers) provide an amazing capability: the ability to call another program or function and say "call me back at this address." Your own function—the *callback* function—can then modify some aspect of the other function's or program's behavior. This kind of capability has great usefulness in many advanced applications: object orientation, terminate-and-stay-resident software, and programming for graphical user interfaces such as Microsoft Windows, to name just a few.

The concept may strike you as terribly abstract in the beginning, so in this topic I'll use a simple example—the qsort library function—and take it slowly.

Syntax

A pointer to a function (function pointer) is declared with the following syntax. You also use this syntax to call the function pointed to, in an executable statement:

```
(*function_ptr)(arguments)
```

You can specify a function address with *function* or &*function*. Note the absence of parentheses following the name, which means that the function is not actually being called:

```
function_ptr = function;
function_ptr = &function;
```

Example

One of the many useful functions in the C++ standard library is the qsort function, which sorts any array that you pass it. The function uses the quick-sort algorithm for sorting.

But the qsort function doesn't know how to compare the elements. One person might use qsort to sort an array of integers, whereas someone else might use it to sort an array of strings. How does qsort judge which of two elements is "greater" than the other?

The answer is that you must write a function that actually does the comparison. The qsort function calls your function back every time it needs to compare two elements.

The prototype for the qsort function is:

```
void qsort(void *base, size_t num, size_t width,
    int (*compare)(const void* p1, const void* p2));
```

The first element is a pointer to your array (**void*** means that qsort doesn't assume any particular type of array). The second and third arguments contain the number of elements and the size of each element. The **size_t** type is an alias for **unsigned int**.

The last argument, compare, is not a real function name; it is just a pointer name. You can call your comparison function anything you wish. Then you pass along the address of this function to qsort. This argument is the strangest of declarations—an argument declaration that is actually a function prototype!

```
int (*compare)(const void* p1, const void* p2)
```

This prototype says that your callback function must take two pointers and return an integer. Note that the types in the last set of parentheses qualify arguments *of your callback function*, and not qsort itself. The arguments of the callback are **const** arguments, so your callback function must not use the arguments to modify any values. (See "const Keyword.")

Let's say that you want to sort a simple array of integers:

```
int a[] = {27, 1, 100, 5, 63, -3, 7, 0, -11, 8};
```

You need to write a callback function that returns 1, 0, or –1, depending on whether the first argument is greater than, equal to, or less than the second argument, respectively. This is easy to do with integers:

```
/* cmp: Integer comparison function:
   Return 1 if *p1 > *p2,
          0 if equal,
         -1 if *p1 < *p2
*/

int cmp(const void *p1, const void *p2) {
    int i, j;
    i = *(int*)p1;
    j = *(int*)p2;

    return (i > j ? 1 : (i == j ? 0 : -1));
}
```

The type cast, **(int*)**, is necessary for using the **void*** pointers. See "Explicit Type Conversions" for an explanation of this kind of C++ code.

Now that the callback function has been written, you call qsort to sort the array, passing the address of the callback as the fourth argument   :

```
qsort(a, 10, sizeof(int), &cmp);
```

When you make this function call, qsort uses the first three arguments for information on the array. The last argument gives the address of your callback function.

This procedure creates an interesting flow of control between your program and the qsort library function (see Figure P.3).

Within qsort, the code to execute your callback function might look like the fragmant shown next. This is sample C++ code from a possible implementation of qsort. Here the function is called through compare, the function-pointer argument as it appears in the declaration. Remember that compare is a pointer passed to qsort by qsort's caller, so the actual callback function will be different for every program

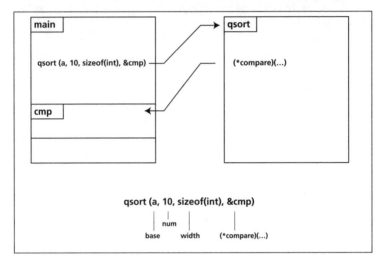

Figure P.3 Use of a callback function.

```
if((*compare)(ptr_elem1, ptr_elem2) > 0)
    swap(ptr_elem1, ptr_elem2, width);
    ...
```

Because you use the function pointer, compare, to call your function, qsort lets your code do the actual comparison between any two elements. Determining which elements to compare is qsort's job.

With any luck, the subject of pointers to functions hasn't yet overwhelmed you. It's simply a way of calling a yet-to-be-determined function or a function supplied by another program or process. An expression such as "(*compare)" is a stand-in, of sorts, for a function supplied elsewhere. In calling qsort, you're saying, "Call me back at this address." This gives C++ a flexibility undreamed of in most programming languages.

456

Polymorphism

Definition

Polymorphism is a big, scary word that means the same thing as "using virtual functions." This is another example of C++ jargon you could profitably eliminate from your vocabulary except that you often run into it in the literature.

Basically, if you understand virtual functions, you understand polymorphism. You can say that virtual functions are the C++ mechanism for enabling polymorphism—which is the ability to respond to the same message (or function call) in many different ways. *Polymorphism*, translated literally, means "many shapes" or "many forms." For example, suppose you have a CShape class with a virtual function, Print:

```
class CShape {
public:
    virtual void Print(void);
    . . .
```

Because the Print function is virtual, each class that is derived from CShape can provide a different implementation of Print.

```
class CSquare : public Cshape {
public:
    void Print(void);  // overrides CShape::Print
    . . .
```

The Print function is polymorphic because it represents a general function description rather than a fixed block of code. The point is not that a single function can respond in a variety of ways (you could do that with a **switch** or **if-else** statement) but rather that, in theory, there is *no limit* to the way Print can be implemented. Classes can be added in the future that provide new implementations of Print. For more information and examples, see "Virtual Functions."

457

Primitive Data Types

Definition

A *primitive data type* is one of the data types provided directly by C++. These types include **char**, **int**, **short**, **long**, **float**, **double**, and the **unsigned** variations of the integer types (all except **float** and **double** are integers). These types are the building blocks upon which you can develop more complex types.

Examples

The subject of primitive data types is important in C++, because certain operations are valid only on primitve-type variables and pointers. For example, you cannot assign an array directly to another array. Instead, you have to operate on the individual elements, which may be of a primitive type. This also extends to strings, a fact that is a stumbling block for people coming from a Basic background:

```
char str1[80];
char str2[] = "Hello, goodbye."

str1 = str2;    // ERROR! Invalid assignment.
```

The individual elements of str1 and str2 have type **char**, which is a primitive type, so you could do the following:

```
str1[0] = str2[0];
```

The strcpy function uses a series of such operations to copy one string to another. You need to include STRING.H to call this and other string functions.

```
strcpy(str1, str2);
```

See "Data Types" for a summary of all the primitive data types.

Definition

There is no built-in PRINT command or keyword in C++, but you can print data by calling the printf function included in the standard C++ library provided with every C++ compiler. You need to include the STDIO.H header file before calling printf so that it's properly declared. This book does not cover most library functions, but I discuss printf because it's so universal.

Syntax

A call to the printf function has the following syntax:

```
#include <stdio.h>
```

```
printf(format_string, arguments);
```

Each of the arguments is a value corresponding to a format specifier in the *format_string* (a null-terminated character string). Each argument is a numeric value or pointer, as appropriate. The **printf** function returns the number of arguments printed.

printf Formats

Table P.1 summarizes the format specifiers that can appear in *format_string*.

Table P.1 Format Specifiers for format_string.

SPECIFIER	DESCRIPTION
%c	Print a single character (on most systems, the ASCII table is used to interpret values).
%d, %i	Print as a decimal integer.
%u	Print as an unsigned decimal integer.

SPECIFIER	DESCRIPTION
%o	Print integer in octal format.
%x, %X	Print integer in hexadecimal format.
%e	Print floating-point in exponential format. Example: 1.273110e+01.
%E	Same as %e, but use capital E: 1.273100E+01.
%f	Print floating-point in standard format. Example: 12.73110.
%g	Print floating-point in %e or %f format, whichever is shorter.
%G	Same as %g, but use capital E.
%s	Print null-terminated character string; argument is interpreted as a pointer to this data.
%p	Print pointer value in hexadecimal format (similar to %x).
%%	Print a literal percent sign (%).

Format Modifiers

When you call printf (especially to print floating-point numbers), you may want to control how many characters are printed. The printf syntax lets you modify the meaning of each format in the following ways, in which c represents a format character:

```
%[-]minc
%[-]min.precisionc
```

Here the brackets indicate that the minus sign (-) is optional. If included, it indicates that the data is to be left justified within the print field.

The *min* modifier is a decimal number indicating size of the print field. For example, the following format specifies a decimal integer printed into a field at least five characters wide:

```
%5d
```

The *precision* modifier is also a decimal integer. Its meaning depends on the format:

- Maximum number of characters printed in a string format (%s).

- Number of digits after the decimal point in a floating-point number (%f, %e, etc.).

- Minimum number of digits in an integer (%d, %i, etc.).

Example

Suppose the following statement appears in a program:

```
printf("The %s temperature is %5.4f.", "Alaskan", 25.7);
```

When the program is run, the output you'll get is:

```
The Alaskan temperature is 25.7000.
```

Definition

The **private** keyword has two uses in C++: member access and base-class access. The first use is the more common of the two: it declares that a class member has private access, meaning that the member can be referred to only within the class's own member functions.

Unless there is a good reason to expose a member to other objects, it's a good idea to make it private. The advantage of private members is that you can change them without breaking code that already uses the class. Only the interfaces between classes need to remain fixed. Because other objects cannot "reach in" and refer to private members, dependencies cannot arise between this hidden part of a class and the rest of the program. This arrangement reduces a source of errors and makes classes easier to maintain.

Example: Member Access

To declare members with private access, place the **private:** keyword in front of the member declarations. All the members that follow, up to the next member-access keyword, have private access. Within a **class** declaration, private access is the default. In the example below, the members a, b, and c have private access.

```
class AClass {
    int a, b;
public:
    AClass(int i, int j, int k);
    double x, y;
private:
    int c;
};
```

Example: Base-Class Access

As a base-class access specifier, the **private** keyword modifies inherited members so that all of them become private in the derived class. In the example below, every member declared in CBase is inherited by CDerived, but it becomes a private member as far as CDerived is concerned. Note that **private** is the default here as well.

```
class CDerived : private CBase {
    // Some declarations
};
```

Definition

The **protected** keyword has two closely related uses in C++: member access and base-class access. The first use is the more common of the two: it declares that a class member has protected access, which is similar to private access in most respects.

The difference between private and protected access is that a protected member is visible not only in the class in which it is declared but also in any class derived from this class. Private members are visible only in the class in which they are declared. The practical effect of protected access is to give other people, deriving classes from your class, the opportunity to refer to the same variables that you do.

In understanding inheritance and member access, keep in mind that members are always inherited (with the exception of constructors). However, private members, unlike protected and public members, are not *visible* in the derived class. This means that the private data members take up space in memory but cannot be referred to in code written specifically for the derived class.

Example: Member Access

To declare that members have protected access, place the **protected:** keyword in front of the member declarations. All the members that follow, up to the next member-access keyword, have protected access.

```
class AClass {
    int a, b;
protected:
    double x, y;
    int c;
public:
    AClass(int i, int j, int k);
};
```

464

In this example, members x, y, and c are protected. The members a and b are private by default, and the constructor, AClass(int, int, int), is public.

In the following derived class, DClass, function definitions can refer to x, y, and c, but they cannot refer to a and b (even though a and b take up space in DClass objects).

```
class DClass : public AClass {
// Function declarations
};
```

Example: Base-Class Access

As a base-class access specifier, the **protected** keyword modifies inherited members so that a member that is public in the base class (CBase in this example) becomes protected within the derived class (CDerived). Note that **private**, and not **protected**, is the default base-class access.

```
class CDerived : protected CBase {
    // Some declarations
};
```

Definition

The **public** keyword has two uses in C++: member access and base-class access. The first use is the more common of the two: it declares that a class member is public and therefore accessible to any user of the class.

Any member with public access becomes part of the interface of the class: the part of the class that is seen by the outside world. By default, the members of a type declared with the **class** keyword have private access, so it's important to use the **public** keyword to make some of the members visible. On the other hand, it's a good idea to carefully choose which members to make public, because one of the principal concepts of C++ is that some members should be kept private to minimize dependencies between objects.

Example: Member Access

To declare members with public access, place the **public:** keyword in front of the member declarations. All the members that follow, up to the next member-access keyword, have public access.

```
class AClass {
    int a, b;
public:
    AClass(int i, int j, int k);
    double x, y;
private:
    int c;
};
```

In this example, members a, b, and c are private. Members AClass (a constructor), x, and y are public.

Example: Base-Class Access

As a base-class access specifier, the **public** keyword enables the derived class to inherit all the base-class members without modification in their status. Note that this is not the default (**private** is the default), so it's important to remember to use **public** here.

```
class CDerived : public CBase {
    // Some declarations
};
```

Definition

The reference operator (&) provides the same functionality that pointers provide, while hiding pointer syntax. For example, if you pass an object by reference, an address is placed on the stack as illustrated in Figure 3.1 (in Chapter 3, "Pointers, Strings, and Things"). The actual behavior is the same as if a pointer were being passed. But the source code hides all the pointer syntax, making it look as if you're passing the object by value.

Declaring a reference parameter is like passing by reference in Basic, Pascal, or FORTRAN. If you're a C programmer, using the reference operator may seem like a step back to the "beginner's way" of doing things. But the reference operator is supported to enable certain kinds of functions: copy constructors and assignment functions. As explained in Chapter 6, copy constructors in particular would be impossible to write without the reference operator. The result would be an infinite regress.

NOTE C++ uses the ampersand (&) in three distinct ways, one of which is the reference operator. The uses are distinguished by context. The reference operator appears only in declarations as part of a type specification. The other two uses—the address operator and bitwise AND—appear in expressions that evaluate to a value.

Syntax

The reference operator (&) is applied in variable, data, and function declarations in the same way that indirection (*) is applied to specify pointer types.

```
type &symbol
```

The declaration creates *symbol* as a reference to an object of the given type. If the declaration occurs as a variable declaration (not an argument or function return type), the reference must be initialized to an l-value (usually a variable):

```
type &symbol = l_value;
```

Usage 1: References as Aliases

The simplest way to use a reference is as an alias for another variable. When you first declare a reference, it must be initialized to an existing variable of the same type. It is illegal to declare a reference variable without initializing it. For example:

```
int a = 0;
int &stand_in = a;

a++;
stand_in++;
printf("stand_in = %d\n", stand_in);
```

This code, if you run it, reports a value of 2 for stand_in. Remember that stand_in is an alias for the variable a, so changes to either variable affect both of them. The previous code behaves the same way as the following version, which uses pointers:

```
int a = 0;
int *p = a;

a++;
(*p)++;
printf("stand_in = %d\n", *p);
```

469

Usage 2: References as Argument Types

Although I've listed it second, this usage is much more important than the first one. Reference arguments implement pass-by-reference in a way that is similar to other high-level languages, such as Basic. For example, you could use references to write a function that swaps two values:

```
void swap1(double &a, double &b) {
    double temp = a;
    a = b;
    b = temp;
}
```

Because a and b are passed by reference, the function can change the value of the arguments passed. The previous function behaves the same way as the following:

```
void swap2(double *a, double *b) {
    double temp = *a;
    *a = *b;
    *b = temp;
}
```

However, there is an important difference between these two functions. When calling swap1, a caller passes arguments directly:

```
double x = 3.0, y = 5.7;

swap1(x, y);
```

The call to swap1 passes two addresses, but that fact is hidden at the source-code level. When you're calling swap2, the use of addresses is made explicit:

```
swap2(&x, &y);
```

Note that here the ampersand (&) represents the address operator and not the reference operator! It's easy to confuse them, because both of them have a connection to pointers.

Usage 3: References as Return Values

You can use the reference operator to declare a return type for a function. Doing so obligates you to return a persistent object—that is, an object whose lifetime exceeds that of the function. If you return a local variable, then the caller, in effect, gets back a pointer to an object that no longer exists after the function returns. For example:

```
long& faulty(void) {
    long new_var;
    ...
    return new_var;  // ERROR! new_var about to
                     //   be destroyed.
}
```

If the return type were not a reference, then returning new_var would not be a problem. In that case, the caller would get its own copy of new_var rather than a pointer to new_var.

Assignment operator functions are good examples of functions that return a reference. These functions return a reference to the left operand, enabling the value to be efficiently reused in larger expressions. Here is an example of an assignment operator from Chapter 7, "Class Operations":

```
CStr& CStr::operator=(const CStr &source) {
    cpy(source.get());
    return *this;
}
```

The following declarations are equivalent:

```
long& i;
long &i;
```

The style of the first declaration is in some ways more convenient, because it calls attention to the fact that long& and CStr& are distinct types: "reference to long" and "reference to CStr." The only drawback to this style is that with multiple definitions, it is misleading. For example, the first declaration in the following code declares only one reference; j and k are ordinary variables of type long.

```
long& i, j, k;   // Only i is a reference!!!
long &i, &j, &k; // i, j, k are all references
```

Definition

The **register** keyword requests that a variable be allocated in one of the processor's registers, if possible. In the early days of C, this was one of the things that most impressed some programmers. Because of optimization technology, this keyword is now considered relatively unimportant.

If you've programmed in assembly language, you know what a register is. If not, suffice it to say that registers are special memory locations residing inside the processor. Values are routinely moved in and out of registers all the time. If an intensive amount of calculation is going to be done with a particular variable, a program can be made significantly faster by reserving a register for the exclusive use of that variable.

Syntax

You can modify a variable declaration by preceding it with the **register** keyword, which is one of the storage class specifiers.

register *declaration*;

The items declared should be of an integer or pointer type.

Example

In the following example, the variable i is used intensively for array manipulations—being accessed in potentially thousands of operations in a row—and is therefore placed in a register:

```
void init_array(int a[], size, data) {
    register int i;

    for (i = 0; i < size; i++)
```

```
        a[i] = data;
}
```

The use of the **register** keyword is not binding on the compiler; it is actually only a suggestion, or hint, about how registers should be allocated. With the advent of improved optimizing technology, many current C and C++ compilers make their own sophisticated judgments about how best to allocate register usage. Therefore, if the program would profit by reserving a register for a variable, a good optimizing compiler is probably doing this anyway, making the keyword a bit superfluous.

Some compilers, in their arrogance, simply ignore this keyword altogether. With older compilers, however, use of **register** can make a difference. In any case, it never hurts to use it.

Remainder Operator (%)

Definition

The remainder operator, also called the modulus operator, returns the remainder when one integer is divided by another integer. For example, 7 divided by 2 is 3 with a remainder of 1, so the expression 7 % 2 evaluates to 1.

Syntax

The remainder operator (%) forms an expression from two integer subexpressions:

quantity % divisor

The syntax is the same as division (/) except that the remainder, not the quotient is the result.

Usage

The remainder operator has any number of uses, but a common use is to determine when an integer is exactly divisible by another integer. For example, the following function determines whether a number is odd or even. It returns 1 if the number is even, and 0 otherwise.

```
int is_even(int n) {
    return (n % 2 == 0);
}
```

In general, if a number n is exactly divisible by a divisor d, then n % d evaluates to 0.

The operator can be used to enhance the binary-expansion program in Chapter 2. In this version, the code prints a space after every fourth digit.

```
for (i = 1; i <= 16; i++, input_field <<=1) {
    putchar((input_field & 0x8000) ? '1' : '0');
    if (i % 4 == 0)
            putchar(' ');
}
```

Definition

The **return** statement causes a function to immediately return control to its caller. Optionally, it can return a value. It's similar to **return** or "exit function" statements in other languages.

Syntax

The **return** statement, which appears in one of the following two forms, is a complete statement in C++:

```
return expression;
return;
```

The first version should be used in any function that does not have a **void** return type. The second version should be used only in functions with **void** return type, in which case its use is optional. The only purpose of **return** in this case is to exit early from a function.

Example

In the following example, the factorial function uses the **return** statement to report the results of its calculation.

```
i = factorial(4);    // i gets the value 24.
...
long factorial(int n) {
    long result = 1;

    while (n)
        result = result * n—;
    return result;
}
```

Definition

Run-time type information (RTTI) is the C++ technique for answering the question, "What type of object was I passed?" As explained in Chapters 8 and 9, you can be passed an object through a pointer. In such a case, the object's exact type is unknown; given a pointer of type T*, the object can be of type T or a class derived from T.

For example, assume that a class CShape is declared and a number of classes are derived from it: CCircle, CSquare, CTriangle, and so on. If you're passed a pointer of type CShape*, does it point to a circle, a square, a triangle, or some other type of object? The answer is important, because not all derived classes support all the same operations and data members. The issue arises when you're interacting with an existing library; in your own code there are usually other ways of resolving the problem.

C++ approaches the question of "What type was I passed?" by providing two operators: **dynamic_cast** and **typeid**. These operators are relatively recent additions to C++, and not all compilers support them.

The dynamic_cast Operator

The **dynamic_cast** operator converts a pointer into a more specific type of pointer, but only if it matches the object's actual type. In other words, it compares an object's type to a specified type and provides a recast pointer if there is a match.

dynamic_cast<*new_type**> *pObject*

If the actual type of *pObject** is the same as *new_type* or a type derived from *new_type*, **dynamic_cast** returns a pointer of type *new_type**. Otherwise, it returns the value 0. For example, the following function gets a pointer to a base class, CShape. The function tests the object pointed to against type CCircle. If there's a match, the function prints a message and uses the resulting pointer value to get the diameter:

```
#include <stdio.h>

void do_shape(CShape* pShape) {
    CCircle *pCircle;

// If pShape points to a circle, the next statement
// places a valid pointer in pCircle. Otherwise,
//  pCircle is assigned 0 (null pointer value).

    pCircle = dynamic_cast<CCircle*> pShape;

    if (pCircle) {
        puts("shape is a circle.");
        printf("diameter = %f\n", pCircle->diameter);
    else
        puts("shape is not a circle.");
}
```

This example assumes that the CCircle class has a member called diameter, which other classes may not have. The function never attempts to access this member unless it first verifies that it was passed a CCircle object.

The typeid Operator

The **typeid** operator returns an identifier (ID) for an object, which can be compared to other type IDs or printed as a diagnostic message. The operator can be applied to classes as well as objects. Note that you must include the file **TYPEINFO.H** to use the results of the operator.

```
#include <typeinfo.h>

typeid(class)                    // - OR -
typeid(object)
```

479

For example, a function can test the condition that an object is of type CSquare:

```
if (typeid(obj) == typeid(CSquare))
    puts("Object is a square.");
```

The type ID can be printed as a diagnostic message during program development and debugging. The **typeid** operator returns an object of class **type_info**, which has a member function called name. This function returns a null-terminated character string.

```
puts(typeid(obj).name());
```

Definition

There's no built-in INPUT command or keyword in C++, but you can input data by calling the scanf function included in the standard C++ library. You need to include the STDIO.H header file before calling scanf so that it's properly declared. This book does not cover most library functions, but I discuss scanf because it's so universal.

The scanf function does not print a prompt message. You need to do that separately, using printf.

Syntax

A call to the scanf function has the following syntax:

```
#include <stdio.h>
scanf(control_string, arguments);
```

Each format specifier in the *control_string* determines how to read and interpret data; the function reads text, converts it, and then copies data to the address indicated by the corresponding argument. For example, if the format calls for integer input (%d or %i), the corresponding address should give the address of an integer (for example, &n).

scanf Formats

Table S.1 summarizes the format specifiers that can appear in *control_string*:

Table S.1 Format Specifiers for scanf.

SPECIFIER	DESCRIPTION
%c	Next character input (even a white space) copied to **char** destination.
%d, %i	Decimal integer input converted to numeric value and sent to integer destination (but %i accepts octal input with 0 prefix and hexadecimal input with 0x prefix).
%u	Same as %d, but destination is an unsigned integer.
%o	Integer input interpreted as octal; destination is integer.
%x, %X	Integer input interpreted as hexadecimal; destination is integer.
%e, %f, %g	Floating-point input, in any format supported by printf. Note that if the destination is of type **double**, format needs to be qualified with "l", as in "lf".
%s	Characters copied to string destination until non-white space encountered.

All the arguments to scanf must be address types. Typically, this means combining a variable with the address operator (&). However, the name of a string is already an address type, so you should not use the address operator in that case. For example:

```
#include <stdio.h>

int  id;
char string[256];

printf("Enter name and id number: ");
scanf("%s %i", string, &id);
```

Format Modifiers

Between the percent sign (%) and the format character, an "l" can appear, indicating that the format is "long." This is necessary in the case of arguments with a destination of type **double**, which will not get correct data unless "l" is used to indicate the type. For example:

```
double   x, y, z;
float    flt_var;

scanf("%lf %lf %lf %f", &x, &y, &z, &flt_var);
```

You can also use "h" (short) and "l" (long) to modify integer formats. It's a good idea to use these modifiers if a variable is specifically declared **short** or **long** rather than **int** (which just uses a default size).

Other Characters in the Control String

Aside from format specifiers, other characters in the control string are usually not important. Blank spaces and tabs are simply ignored. Other text characters (not preceded by %) are expected to match the input verbatim, so that scanf("abc%n") skips past the input "abc" and then reads an integer.

This last feature of scanf—reading past fixed characters—may not sound very useful, but it is helpful sometimes with its sister function, fscanf. The fscanf function is nearly identical to scanf except that it reads input from a file. In a data file, a pattern of fixed text characters may be embedded in the file. You may need to read past the fixed characters to get to the numeric data.

N O T E There are number of common mistakes with scanf. By far the most common is to forget that arguments must be addresses. This can be a nasty error, because it causes data to be sent to a random address. The following statement can cause unpleasant results for your program:

```
scanf("%d", id_num);
```

If id_num is an integer, make sure that you give its address to scanf:

```
scanf("%d", &id_num);
```

Another common mistake is to forget that the proper input format for arguments of type double is "%lf", and not "%f". Forgetting this will cause your program to get values that seem to come from outer space.

Scope

Definition

Scope is an attribute of variables, and it refers to how much the program knows about a particular variable. The variable is said to be *visible* over that section of the program.

Examples

This all sounds abstract and fuzzy without examples. A simple example is a local variable. Because it's defined within a function, a local variable can be used only within that function. A variable defined inside a statement block (compound statement) has even smaller scope. It is visible only within that block.

```
void my_func(int n) {
    int i, j;

    for (i = 0; i < MAX_SIZE; i++) {
        double x_coord, y_coord;
        ...
        }
}
```

Here, the scope of i and j is functionwide. The scope of x_coord and y_coord is restricted to the compound statement within the **for** loop. Outside this block, a reference to x_coord or y_coord would be an error.

Global variables have scope throughout the current module (or possibly farther, if **extern** declarations are used). The syntax for a global variable definition is identical to that of a local variable; the difference is simply that global variable declarations are placed outside of function definitions.

In C++, scope can also be created through class declarations and namespaces.

Definition

The **short** data type is an integer that is two bytes (16 bits) wide. Although the ANSI C standard states only that the size of a **short** be at least two bytes, the vast majority of C++ compiler implementations—especially on personal computers—use exactly two bytes.

Range

–32,768 to 32,767.

Syntax

You can declare any number of short integers by placing **short** at the beginning of the declaration statement:

[*storage*] [*cv*] **short** *items*;

Here the brackets indicate optional prefixes: *storage* is a storage-class specifier (**auto**, **extern**, **register**, **static**), and *cv* is **const**, **volatile**, or both. The *items* are one or more simple or complex variable declarations.

Example

The following statement defines a simple variable (cake), an array (id_nums), and a pointer (ptr_to_short):

```
short   cake, id_nums[10], *ptr_to_short;
```

Usage

Although **short** and **int** are equivalent types on many systems, the **short** type is best reserved for situations when space is at a premium: for example, in a structure written

486

out to a file or repeated many times in an array. The **int** type is defined as the natural size for a given system and may be either two or four bytes, depending on what would be optimal for the system to use in calculations; **int** is generally the better choice for simple variables.

Statement

Definition

A statement is the fundamental unit of execution in C++. Declarations are also statements.

The term *statement* is a concept of grammar in C++, just as it is in ordinary language. You don't really need to know what the parts of speech are called in a language in order to speak the language—although it doesn't hurt, and might conceivably help. The practical knowledge is what's important, even in C++.

Mainly, you need to know is that statements are usually terminated with a semicolon (;) unless they are compound statements (using braces) or function definitions. The relationship between expressions and statements in C++ is very close: append a semicolon to any expression and it becomes a statement.

Syntax

The following list summarizes all the executable statements in C. The most common category is the first: expressions. In C++, an expression can contain assignments and all kinds of function calls. In other languages, assignments and some kinds of function calls (procedures) are considered types of statements.

This syntax is totally recursive. For example, a compound statement contains any number of statements, each of which can itself be a compound statement.

Each executable statement in C++ is one of the following:

- Expression statements, consisting of an expression terminated by a semicolon:

  expression;

- Compound statements, consisting of braces enclosing one of more statements:

  { *statements* }

- Null statements, consisting only of a semicolon. Such statements do nothing but are syntactically valid; one useful example is a labelled null statement at the very end of a function to serve as a target of a **goto**.

  ;

- Jump statements, which transfer control of the program to another location. These include:

  break;
  continue;
  return;
  return *expression*;
  goto *identifier*;

- **if** statements; in this syntax, brackets indicate that the **else** clause is optional:

  if (*expression***)**
      statement
  [else
      statement **]**

- **switch** statements; see "switch Statement" topic.

- Loops, including **while**, **do-while**, and **for** statements; see the individual topics.

- **try-catch** blocks; see "Exception Handling" topic.

Any statement can be given a label, making it a target for a **goto** (or, with **case** and **default** labels, a target within a **switch** statement). The forms of labeled statement are:

identifier: *statement*
case *constant_expression***:** *statement*
default: *statement*

Not all lines of code in a C++ program are executable statements. Many are declarations, which may define a variable, state that it is an **extern** variable, define a new type (**enum**, **struct**, **typedef**, or **union** declaration), or prototype a function. Some program lines may also be taken up by directives and comments.

Function definitions and directives are not terminated by semicolons, but type declarations and definitions are.

Definition

The **static** keyword has four distinct uses in C++. Although some of these uses are related to each other, it's difficult to make a blanket statement about what they all mean. The four uses are:

- Giving local variables longer lifetime than a function (static local variables)

- Changing the scope of functions from external to module-level only (static functions)

- Allocating only one instance of a data member for an entire class (static data members)

- Limiting a member function to accessing static data members only (static member functions)

In general, *static* is an overloaded term. The fact that it is used in so many different contexts reflects the fact that the designers of C and C++ have a great interest in keeping the number of keywords small.

Syntax

Syntactically, all uses of the **static** keyword are consistent with each other. The keyword modifies a declaration by being placed in front of that declaration:

static *declaration*

When the **static** keyword is applied to a function (whether a member function or not), apply it to the prototype or inline declaration. You don't need to repeat **static** in the function definition.

Usage 1: Static Local Variables

The **static** keyword is probably most often applied to local variables. The effect is to give the variable the same lifetime as the program, while retaining local scope. In practical terms, this means that the variable retains its value between function calls.

```
void call_waiting(double x, y) {
    static int number_of_calls = 0;

    number_of_calls++;
    // ...
}
```

In this example, the variable number_of_calls is initialized exactly once: the first time the function is called. Thereafter, it retains its value between calls so that (in this case) it is equal to the number of times the function has been called.

Usage 2: Static Functions

A static function is recognized only within the current module (source-code file). By default, a function has external storage class, meaning that, thanks to the linker, all modules in the program can access the function. But when you apply the **static** keyword to the function's declaration, the function is not given external linkage.

```
static void myfunctiononly(int n);
...
void myfunctiononly(int n) {
    // Declarations
};
```

492

One of the prime uses for static functions in C is to provide a way to give a function limited scope. In C++, such a practice is generally unnecessary, because you can control function scope much more finely with classes and namespaces.

Usage 3: Static Data Members

Throughout this book, I've tended to make blanket statements about data members being stored in individual objects. For example, if a class has a data member called Thing, each object of that class stores a different value for Thing.

Although that's true generally, its not true of static data members. A static data member has one value for the entire class. Any object of the class can access the member, as a general rule, but the objects don't have their own copies of this member.

One use for static data members is to provide a mechanism for communication between objects of the same type. Static data members have class scope just as ordinary data members do—that is, they can be accessed only through reference to the class or an object—but in every other respect they are like global variables. A static data member must not only be declared but also must be defined exactly once, somewhere in the program, just as a function must be defined. For example:

```
class CStudent {
    static long number_of_students;
public:
    CStudent() {++number_of_students;}
    ...
};

long CStudent::number_of_students = 0;
```

Here, the variable number_of_students starts at 0 and is incremented by one each time an object of type CStudent is created. Note the use of the scope operator to define the variable.

One of the interesting quirks of static data members is that they can be referred to through objects (*obj.member*) or through the class itself (*class::member*). In this case, number_of_students can't be accessed outside the class, because it is private.

Usage 4: Static Member Functions

A static member function is a function that can refer *only* to data members that are static. If you declare a member function static and then refer to any nonstatic data member, the compiler catches it as an error. A further limitation is that static member functions can call only other member functions that are also static.

Static member functions have these restrictions without gaining any compensating special abilities. The only advantage of static member functions is a slight gain in efficiency: when a static member function is called, it does not get passed the hidden *this* pointer, because it is needed only to access nonstatic data members.

In the following example, the only purpose of the get_num_students function is to access number_of_students, which is a static data member. So get_num_students can safely be made static as well.

```
class CStudent {
    static long number_of_students;
public:
    CStudent() {++number_of_students;}
    static long get_num_students(void);
    ...
};
```

```
long CStudent::number_of_students = 0;

long get_num_students(void) {
    return number_of_students;
}
```

Definition

The storage class of an item determines how it is stored in memory and whether it is linked to other modules—assuming you are writing a multiple-module program. For example, an **auto** variable (almost any local variable) is allocated on the stack along with function-call information, and the **auto** variable is destroyed as soon as the function terminates. A **static** variable is fixed at a specific place in memory, hence the name "static." Storage class, in theory, is separate from scope (the visibility of an object), although some kinds of storage class specifications do, in practice, limit or alter scope in some way.

Syntax

Storage class in C++ is always specified by placing a storage class keyword (**extern**, for example) at the beginning of a declaration:

```
extern int amount;
```

Table S.2 shows the four kinds of storage class.

Table S.2 Storage Class Specifiers.

STORAGE CLASS	DESCRIPTION
auto	Default for local variables; allocates variables on the stack, for temporary storage.
extern	Default for functions. Object recognized in this and all other modules.
register	Requests that register be reserved for data object.
static	Default for global variables. Object is allocated in program data area and has same lifetime as program.

For more information, see the topic for the particular keyword.

Definition

A string literal consists of text enclosed in quotation marks; you can use it as constant data in your program, just as you can numerals (27, 3, 100, etc.). When a string literal appears in your program code, the compiler allocates space for it and replaces the string expression with the address of this data. Therefore, you can use string literals in contexts (such as the printf function) that expect an address to **char** data.

Syntax

You form a string literal by enclosing text in double quotation marks ("):

"text"

When the compiler reads a quotation mark (except in comments), it interprets the characters that follow the mark to be part of the string literal until the next quotation mark is reached, which ends the string.

Special Characters in Strings

The following characters have special meaning inside a string:

- The backslash (\) is an escape character and is not read as a normal character. To specify a literal backslash, use two consecutive backslashes (\\).

- The character sequence \n represents a newline character.

- The character sequence \t represents a tab.

- The characters \xxx, where xxx is a constant octal number, place the numeric value xxx directly into the string. You can specify hexadecimal numbers by preceding the number with a literal **x**. (To see what equivalent character this produces, consult the appropriate table for your system—this is the ASCII table on most systems.) You can use \0 to embed null (zero) values.

- The characters \" represent an embedded double quotation mark. A single quotation mark (') can be embedded freely.

- The backslash, at the end of a line, is a line-continuation character. The compiler continues to read each character it encounters into the string, except the backslash and the physical end of line (newline) that it is reading past. (See example for clarification.)

Here's an example

```
char *path_name = "C:\\WINDOWS\\SYS";
char *silly_string = "\"Get out the veto pen,\" said \
Bill."
```

The strings path_name and silly_string, when printed on-screen, look like this:

```
C:\WINDOWS\SYS
"Get out the veto pen," said Bill.
```

Definition

Although the use of the **struct** keyword in C++ is compatible with the way it is used in C, it takes on wider capabilities in C++: the **struct** keyword declares a class in which public access is the default (rather than private access, which is the default for classes declared with the **class** keyword). In other respects, a **struct** declaration follows the same rules that a **class** declaration does, including support for member functions.

Because C has no concept of private or protected access, every member of a C structure has, in effect, public access. Therefore, because C++ gives **struct** classes public access by default; you can port C structures. At the same time, you can add features not supported in C: member functions and different member-access levels.

Syntax

Declarations using **struct** use the standard C++ syntax for classes.

```
struct name [base_class_declarations] {
    declarations
} [object_definitions];
```

Here, brackets indicate optional elements, and *declarations* consists of any number of data member or member function declarations. For futher explanation of syntax, see the topic "Class Declarations."

Example

The following declaration creates a class, move_ratings, with a four data members. Because the class is declared using the **struct** keyword, all the members are public.

```
struct movie_ratings {
    char movie_name[20];
    char director_name[30];
    int  Roger;     /* 1 = thumbs up, 0 = thumbs down */
    int  Jane;
};
```

Definition

The **switch** statement (**switch-case**) provides an efficient way to respond to a set of alternatives. The statement tests a particular expression—usually a variable—and jumps to different locations depending on the value.

If you think this sounds like a series of **if-else** statements, you're right, because anything you can implement with **switch** you can implement with **if** and **else**. However, when **switch** can be used it is helpful, because it results in cleaner, more compact, easier-to-read programs.

Syntax

A **switch** statement forms one unified statement in C++:

```
switch (expression) {
case constant_expression_1:
    [statements]
case constant_expression_2:
    [statements]
...
case constant_expression_n:
    [statements]
[ default:
    statements ]
}
```

Here, brackets indicate optional items. You can have any number of **case** statement labels, and there is no minimum number. The action of the **switch** statement is to evaluate the *expression*, and then jump to the **case** label with the value that matches the result (or **default**, if none of the labels has a matching value).

In each block of statements, the last statement executed should usually be a **break** statement; otherwise, execution falls through to the next case. The reason **break** is needed is that the case keyword is just a label and not a statement, and it does not alter the flow of control. The **switch** statement jumps to one of the labeled statements, but from there execution continues normally unless interrupted with **break**.

Examples

Suppose you have a program that prints a number not as "1," "2," or "3," but as "one," "two," "three," etc. One way to do this is with a series of **if else** statements:

```
if (n == 1)
    printf("one\n");
else if (n == 2)
    printf("two\n");
else if (n == 3)
    printf("three\n");
```

You can get the same functionality from a **switch** statement, which is leaner and a little easier to follow:

```
switch (n) {
case 1:
    printf("one\n"); break;
case 2:
    printf("two\n"); break;
case 3:
    printf("three\n"); break;
}
```

In terms of run-time efficiency, the **switch** version will be at least as optimal as the **if else** version and possibly a little faster, depending on the compiler implementation. The **switch** version tests the value of n only once, after which it jumps directly to the appropriate label. The **if** version has to test n repeatedly and keeps jumping to the next **if** after each test fails.

The flow of execution "falls through" when the **break** statements are omitted. To see how this works, first suppose that you have the following test program. (The putchar function is a macro defined in STDIO.H that prints a single character to the standard output device.)

```
#include <stdio.h>

void print_val(int n);

void main() {
    print_val(1);
    putchar('\n');
    print_val(2);
    putchar('\n');
    printf_val(3);
}
```

If the print_val function consists of the **switch** statement introduced earlier, the program prints the following result:

```
one

two

three
```

But suppose that print_val uses **switch** without any **break** statements:

```
void print_val(int n) {
    switch (n) {
    case 1:
        printf("one\n");
    case 2:
        printf("two\n");
    case 3:
        printf("three\n");
    }
}
```

In that case, the program prints this strange result:

```
one
two
three

two
three

three
```

In the case of n equal to one, the control of execution jumps to the statement labeled case 1 but does not stop there. Execution simply continues right past the next **case** labels. This fact may seen annoying, but it makes C++ more flexible. There might be times you want to combine the action of different cases. For example:

```
switch(c) {
    case 'y':
        printf("sometimes ");
    case 'a':
    case 'e':
    case 'i':
    case 'o':
    case 'u':
        printf("is a vowel");
        break;
    default:
        printf("is a consonant");
        break;
}
```

This **switch** statement uses a couple of tricks. First, the 'y' case falls through to the other cases so that it prints the word "sometimes" and keeps on going. Second, the vowel

switch Statement (continued)

cases are all combined. In terms of C++ syntax, the second printf statement is a labeled statement with five labels, which is perfectly valid.

If the test expression is 'y', this **switch** statement prints the following result:

```
sometimes is a vowel
```

Figure S.1 summarizes the flow of control in this statement.

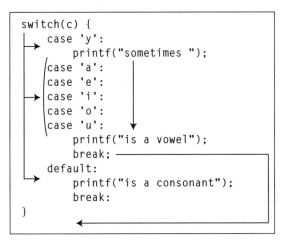

Figure S.1 Flow of control in a switch statement.

505

N O T E The C++ switch statement does not support testing string values, because strings are arrays, not simple variables. If you need to supply a series of alternative actions depending on a string value, the only way to do this is to use a series of if else statements and use the strcmp function to test for equality. For example:

```
if (strcmp(str, "one") == 0)
  n = 1;
else if (strcmp(str, "two") == 0)
  n = 2;
...
```

Definition

Templates are a C++ technique for generating type and function code. The most common use for templates is to create collection classes. For example, you can define a linked-list template and use it to generate a linked list for integers, a linked list for strings, a linked list for type **double**, and so on. The beauty of this approach is that you have to write the linked-list code only once.

Many C++ programmers are enthusiastic fans of templates as a tool for writing reusable code. Writing a linked-list class (for example) can require a great deal of work, but little of this work is type-specific. All the algorithms that work for a linked list of **double** also work for a linked list of **long**. It would be nice to be able to leave the type blank and then specify the type later via a "fill in the blanks" mechanism. This is exactly what templates do.

The type, which is unspecified during the definition of the template, is called a *parameterized type*. This is a unique feature of C++, wherein a type, rather than an object *of* that type, is an argument.

Syntax

There are two kinds of C++ templates: class templates and function templates. Class templates are the more interesting, bu3t function templates are necessary to support class templates. The syntax for templates is deceptively simple. (The trick is in applying the syntax.)

```
template <template_args>    // class template
    class_declaration
template <template_args>    // function template
    function_definition
```

The *template_args* are much like arguments to a function. However, they allow a unique kind of argument declaration:

class *arg_name*

Here, the meaning of the **class** keyword is different from the keyword's usual meaning. The "class" (to be supplied later) can be any valid type, and need not be a user-defined type.

After being defined, templates are used by specifying a template name followed by an argument:

template_name<arguments>

Example 1: A Simple Class Template

Here is the syntax for a simple class template taking a single class name as argument:

```
template <class arg>
class template_name {
    declarations
};
```

The parameterized type, *arg,* is expanded into the declarations. Wherever *arg* appears in declarations, *arg* is replaced by an actual argument (such as **int**, **long**, or **char***) when the template is used.

Figure T.1 shows how template expansion takes place. The expression *template_name<type>* is a type specification formed by expanding the *template_name* with the given *type*.

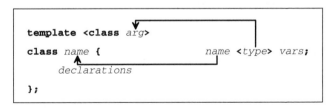

Figure T.1 Simple template expansion.

508

Here's a simple template example. For any given type T, the template called "pair" defines a new type consisting of two members of type T.

```
template <class T>
class pair {
    T   a, b;
};
```

To use this template, specify a type as pair<T>, in which T is an actual type:

```
pair<int>    jeans;   // jeans contains two ints
pair<double> gloves;  // gloves contains two doubles
pair<CStr>   glasses; // glasses contains two strings
```

Figure T.2 illustrates how the **int** type is expanded in the case of pair<int>.

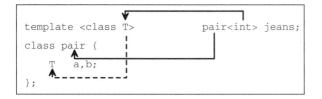

Figure T.2 Template expansion for pair<int>.

The type specification pair<int> is therefore expanded into a class containing two members:

```
class pair<int> {
    int   a, b;
};
```

Similarly, pair<double> and pair<CStr> are expanded as follows. You don't actually *see* this expansion, but you should know that this is how C++ interprets the meaning of the pair<double> and pair<CStr> type specifications.

509

```
class pair<double> {
    double   a, b;
};

class pair<CStr> {
    CStr   a, b;
};
```

Example 2: A Generalized Stack Class

Although it's a minimal implementation, the following example shows a generalized collection class that might be useful. Notice how the parameterized type T appears a total of four times inside the class declaration.

```
template <class T>
class stack {
    T *stackp;
    int size;
    int index;
public:
    T pop(void) {return stackp[--index];}
    void push(T item) {stackp[index++] = item;}
    stack(int sz) {stackp = new T[size = sz];}
                  index = 0;
    ~stack() {delete [] stackp;}
};
```

This template is weak in the area of error checking, a fault I'll correct in the next section. Because only one constructor is defined, you must use this constructor in creating stack variables. For example:

```
stack<int>   things(30);
stack<CStr>  strings(20);
```

Here, things is a stack of integers that holds a maximum of 30 items, and strings is a stack of CStr objects that holds a maximum of 20. You can push and pop items on these stacks as soon as they are defined. For example:

```
strings.push("A string");
strings.push("B string");
cout << strings.pop();   // Prints "B string"
cout << strings.pop();   // Prints "A string"
```

The type specification stack<CStr> generates the following type declaration. I produced this code by replacing each occurrence of "T" with "CStr," which is basically what C++ does when interpreting what stack<CStr> means.

```
class stack<CStr> {
    CStr *stackp;
    int size;
    int index;
public:
    CStr pop(void) {return stackp[--index];}
    void push(CStr item) {stackp[index++] = item;}
    stack(int sz) {stackp = new CStr[size = sz];}
                    index = 0;
    ~stack() {delete [] stackp;}
};
```

If you study the template, you'll see that it uses assignment and copy construction (to return a value). Proper use of the template is therefore dependent on these operations working correctly for the given type.

Example 3: Function Templates

The example in the previous section was limited to inline functions. But it's convenient to be able to write functions that are not inlined but rather are defined outside the class. Doing so creates an interesting problem: how do you clarify the scope of a template member function?

The stack template, when applied to the **int** type, creates a type specified as stack<int>. The scope of the type is therefore stack<int> and not just "stack," as you might think. The same is true for stack<long>, and so on. The pop member function is defined as:

```
template <class T>
T stack<T>::pop(void) { ... }
```

We can now write a class template for stacks in which some of the functions are defined outside the class declaration. In this version, error checking is improved, and the push function returns 0 if it cannot legally carry out the operation.

```
template <class T>
class stack {
    T *stackp;
    int size;
    int index;
public:
    T pop(void);
    int push(T item);
    stack(int sz) {stackp = new T[size = sz];}
                   index = 0;
    ~stack() {delete [] stackp;}
};


// Template to define stack template's pop function.
// Check index: if stack empty, return dummy object.
// Type T must have a default constructor!
//
template <class T>
T stack<T>::pop(void) {
    if (index > 0)
        return stackp[--index];
    else
        {T dummy; return dummy;}
}


// Template to define stack template's push function.
// Check index: if stack full, return 0 (failure).
// Otherwise, return 1.
```

```
//
template <class T>
int stack<T>::push(T item) {
    if (index < size)
        stackp[index++] = item;
    else
        return 0;
    return 1;
}
```

The following variable definition creates a stack, of maximum size 50, called strings:

```
stack<CStr>  strings(50);
```

This statement *instantiates* the stack<CStr> type, causing the compiler to generate the type. As the type is instantiated, the compiler declares two member functions—pop and push—which have stack<CStr> scope.

```
stack<CStr>::pop
stack<CStr>::push
```

These declarations, in turn, instantiate the function-definition templates for pop and push, causing the compiler to generate the appropriate function code.

In our final example, the code demonstrates how a template can take multiple arguments. This approach eliminates the constructor and instead uses a template argument to determine size.

```
template <class T, int sz>
class stack {
    T arr[sz];
    int index;
public:
    T pop(void);
    int push(T item);
    stack () {index = 0;}
```

513

```
};

// Template to define stack template's pop function.
// Check index: if stack empty, return dummy object.
// Type T must have a default constructor!
//
template <class T, int sz>
T stack<T, sz>::pop(void) {
    if (index > 0)
        return arr[--index];
    else
        {T dummy; return dummy;}
}

// Template to define stack template's push function.
// Check index: if stack full, return 0 (failure).
// Otherwise, return 1.
//
template <class T, int sz>
int stack<T, sz>::push(T item) {
    if (index < sz)
        arr[index++] = item;
    else
        return 0;
    return 1;
}
```

To use these templates, specify both type and size in the declaration. Here are some examples:

```
stack<int, 10>     ten_little_integers;
stack<float, 20>   floating_islands;
stack<CStr, 50>    tons_o_strings;
```

The first declaration here creates a stack, ten_little_integers, which has a maximum size of 10. Upon instantiating this type, two functions are declared:

```
stack<int, 10>::push
stack<int, 10>::pop
```

These declarations, in turn, cause the compiler to instantiate the appropriate function definitions.

Definition

The **this** keyword, which can appear in a member function
definition, means "a pointer to myself"—that is, **this** points
to the object through which the member function is called.
As weird as it sounds, there are cases in which this is useful.

Although member functions are defined at the class
level, they are called through a particular object. A member
function typically modifies, or at least refers to, the data
members of that object. To make this possible, C++ passes a
hidden argument during a member function call. The hidden argument is a pointer to the object. When you want to
refer to the pointer explicitly, use the **this** keyword.

To better understand this mechanism, consider how
you'd implement member functions in C. You'd have to do a
certain amount of extra work that is unnecessary in C++. For
example, a C++ member-function call might look like this:

```
CPoint pt;
pt.set(x, y);
```

In C, you'd need to declare member functions as functions
associated with the class Point. (Here I use the naming convention *class_function* to avoid conflicts with other classes.) Then you'd pass a pointer to the particular Point structure to be acted upon, along with the other arguments.

```
struct Point pt;
point_set(&pt, x, y);
```

Notice the extra argument at the front of the argument list.
In fact, this is exactly what C++ does, but you don't see it.
C++ hides this detail from you.

When you want to use the hidden pointer in member-function code, use the **this** keyword. Most of the time, using **this** is unnecessary, because C++ assumes the use of **this** whenever you refer to data members. For example:

```
CPoint::set(double newx, double newy) {
    x = newx;  // x means the same as this->x
    y = newy;  // y means the same as this->y
}
```

The C version, which does the same thing, requires explicit use of **this**:

```
set_point(struct Point *this, double newx, double
    newy) {
    this->x = newx;
    this->y = newy;
}
```

Examples

A common use of **this** is to return a pointer to the current object. An assignment-operator function is required to return the object itself. This may sound strange, but consider what happens in the following statement:

```
a = b = 1;
```

The expression b = 1 is evaluated first. The expression places 1 into the variable b and then evaluates to a result—namely, a reference to b itself. Similarly, functions that implement assignment must return a reference to the left operand—and it so happens that the left operand is the object through which the function is called.

The assignment operator for the CStr class (taken from Chapter 7, "Class Operations") uses the **this** pointer to return a value:

```
// Assignment function for CStr class:
// This is implemented as a member function of the
//  left operand (in the expression a = b). Therefore,
//  to return the left operand, return the object through
//  which the function is called.
//
CStr& CStr::operator=(const CStr &source) {
    cpy(source.get());
    return *this;                // Return myself!
}
```

The indirection operator (*) is applied to **this** because the function returns a reference (CStr&) and therefore uses *value semantics*. Even though the function returns a pointer to the object, it must pretend that it returns the object itself and not a pointer. The indirection operator means "the thing pointed to": in this case, the object itself.

The **this** keyword might also be used when you call a function that takes the object itself as an argument. If this function is not within the same scope (is not another member function of the same class), then you may need to use **this**. For example:

```
CPoint::set(double newx, double newy) {
    x = newx;  // x means the same as this->x
    y = newy;  // y means the same as this->y

    verify_point_values(this);
}
```

Even here, the use of **this** would be unnecessary if verify_point_values were another CPoint member function. But if for some reason it was a global function, the use of **this** would be necessary.

517

Definition

The **typedef** keyword is one of those keywords that C++ could theoretically do without, but it can be a nice convenience when you know how to use it.

A **typedef** declaration takes a complex type declaration and represents the type with a single name. This name can then be used to define new variables, exactly as keywords such as **int**, **char**, **short**, **long**, etc. Use of **typedef** can reduce the amount of program text to enter; moreover, as long as you are clear about what your types are, using **typedef** can be an aid in making complex declarations simpler and easier to understand.

 Unlike C, C++ code does not require the use of typedef to create structure names. The section "typedef and Classes (Structures)," in this topic, elaborates this point.

Syntax

A **typedef** declaration looks almost like a variable declaration, except that it is preceded by the word **typedef**:

typedef *declaration*;

When preceded by **typedef**, a *declaration* does not define variables but new types. Each identifier not previously defined becomes a type name.

Example

A description of **typedef** syntax will almost certainly seem too abstract without examples. Remember this basic rule: to define a type, write a declaration as if you were defining a variable of that type, then precede everything with **typedef**.

For example, you could define a character string holding 80 characters this way:

```
char big_string[80];
```

This statement creates a character string named big_string, allocating 80 bytes in the program data area. To declare the character string as a type, precede the declaration with the **typedef** keyword:

```
typdef char big_string[80];
```

Now big_string is not a variable but a type name; it defines exactly the same type that big_string would have (as a variable) if **typedef** were not present. Therefore, this declaration defines a string stype having 80 characters.

Here, big_string is used to create four strings, each 80 characters in size:

```
big_string   s1, s2, s3, s4
```

Here, big_string is used just like **char** or **int**, so that this statement is a valid variable definition. This declaration is equivalent to the following:

```
char s1[80], s2[80], s3[80], s4[80];
```

Not only is big_string useful in variable declarations, but it becomes a valid type name in all contexts, including function return values and explicit type casts. (Of course, in the latter case, the compiler has to know how to convert data to the indicated type.)

An interesting and useful technique is to use the name big_string within even more complex declarations. For example:

```
big_string       s1, *p, array_of_string[10];
```

This declaration defines the following variables:

- sl is a character string holding 80 characters.

- p is a pointer to a character string (note that its type is **char****, not **char***).

- array_of_strings is an array of 10 elements—each of *those* elements is a character string holding 80 characters. This definition therefore allocates 800 bytes of program data.

You can even reuse a name declared with **typedef** inside another **typedef** declaration. For example, here the new type is named array_of_string_type:

```
typedef      big_string array_of_string_type[10];
```

typedef and Classes (Structures)

In C, you cannot declare a **struct** data type and then immediately use the name of the structure to define variables. C programmers frequently use **typedef** to create true type names from structure names.

C++ avoids this problem—all class names are automatically type names (including **struct** classes). Consequently, there's no need to use **typedef** to create a type name synonymous with a class or structure. However, the C approach to defining types is fully supported for the sake of compatibility.

Here is an example of the C approach to defining a new type:

```
typedef struct Point {
        double x;
        double y;
} Ptype;

typedef Ptype *ptr_to_Point;
```

520

In C++, the first use of **typedef** above is unnecessary, though legal. Given this code in C++, you could use either Point or Ptype to define variables:

```
Point a, b, c;
Ptype d, e, f;
```

typedef and #define Directives

There are some situations where the use of **#define** will ultimately produce the same results as **typedef**, but many situations where it will not. For example, support you define an integer pointer type:

```
typedef int *p_int;
p_int    p1, p2, p3;
```

This second statement here creates three pointers: p1, p2, and p3. Suppose you attempted to use **#define** the same way:

```
#define p_int int*
p_int p1, p2, p3;
```

This only creates one integer, p1, because after the pre-processor replaces p_int, the statement becomes:

```
int*    p1, p2, p3;
```

which is equivalent to:

```
int    *p1, p2, p3;
```

And this statement does not make pointers out of p2 and p3. Therefore, using **typedef** is the most reliable way of defining a new type. Remember that **#define** does not really define a type anyway; it is imply a tool for text replacement.

Definition

Unions are often difficult for people to understand when they're first learning C++, in part because unions have nearly the same syntax as structures but serve a different purpose.

Simply stated, a union allocates several different data members *at the same address.* You may object that if several variables occupy the same address, writing to any one of them overwrites all the others. This is true. But this is no problem when you want to use the same area of memory for different data formats at different times.

The example in this topic presents a relatively simple situation, illustrating how a union might be useful in an advanced program.

Syntax

The syntax for a union declaration is:

union [*struct_type_name*] {
    declarations
} [*union_variables*];

Here, brackets are used to indicate optional items. Note that a union declaration is always terminated by a semicolon, unlike a function definition. Each of the *declarations* is a variable declaration, following the standard rules of syntax.

Although the union syntax is nearly identical to that of structures, union declarations rarely appear alone. Instead, union declarations are usually nested inside a larger type— usually a structure (as shown in the "Example" section that follows).

The rest of the union syntax echoes that for structures. In particular, you refer to members the same way:

union_variable . member

Example

Suppose you want to create a "variant" data type similar to the one supported in most versions of Visual Basic. A variant data type can hold data in different formats—integer, string, floating point, and so on.

The variant data type needs to store data in a variety of formats; but at any given time, it only needs to use one of these formats. It can hold either integer or floating-point data, for example, but it doesn't need to hold both an integer and a floating-point at the same time. Logically, then, the same data area could be reused for both.

You could use a simple structure, allocating one member of each kind of data and not worrying about reusing memory space. This would work, but it would be wasteful of memory.

Here is an efficient structure to implement a variant data type. It contains a nested union as its second member:

```
struct variant {
    short type;
    union {
        short c;
        long  i;
        char  *s;
        double  f;
    } data;
};
```

The two members of the structure are type and data. The second member (a union) has four members: c, i, s, and f.

All the union members overlap in memory, starting at the same address. Figure U.1 shows illustrates the memory layout for a variable of type variant, whose address (for the sake of example) starts at 0x1000. The example also assumes that pointer size is four bytes, although on some systems it is two.

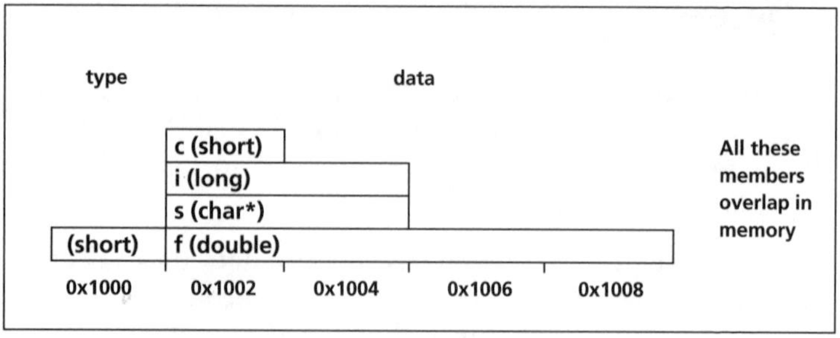

Figure U.1 Memory layout of the variant type.

Clearly, writing to any of the union members corrupts the data residing in all the other members. But the variant structure is not designed to use more than one of these members at a time.

Given this structure/union declaration, you could assign values to a variant by writing out both the data type and the data itself. For example:

```
enum { CHAR, INT, STR, FLOAT};

struct variant v1, v2;

v1.type = FLOAT;
v1.data.f = 27.5;

v2.type = STR;
strcpy(v2.data.s, "Hello");
```

Here, the **enum** keyword is used to provide a set of constants (CHAR is 0, INT is 1, STR is 2, and FLOAT is 3). Their only significance is that they indicate different formats. CHAR, INT, STR, and FLOAT could be fixed at any values as long as they were different from each other.

The example shows that the data path to a member must be fully qualified (see Table U.1).

Table U.1 Referring to Member of a Union within a Structure

REFERENCE	DESCRIPTION
v1	A structure.
v1.data	A union within that structure.
v1.data.f	A member of the union within the structure. This is a reference to primitive data of type **double**.

You can write a generic function that prints the value of a variant structure depending on the current format:

```
void print_var(struct variant v) {
    switch(v.type) {
        case CHAR:  printf("%c", v.data.c); break;
        case INT:   printf("%i", v.data.i); break;
        case STR:   printf("%s", v.data.s); break;
        case FLOAT: printf("%f", v.data.f); break;
    }
}
```

Definition

The **unsigned** keyword is a modifier that helps to create a series of types in C++. You can place **unsigned** in front of any integer type (**char**, **int**, **short**, or **long**) to create a type containing unsigned data. When **unsigned** is used alone, it means the same as **unsigned int**.

An **unsigned** data type has no plus or minus sign; it therefore can't contain negative numbers—it contains only positive numbers and zero. In exchange for giving up negative numbers, you can represent twice as many positive numbers. For example, the range of **short** is –32,768 to 32,767, whereas the range of **unsigned short** is 0 to 65,535.

Types and Ranges

Table U.2 summarizes the ranges of different integers, including **unsigned** types. Note that except in the case of **char**, an integer type is signed unless preceded by **unsigned**.

Table U.2 Signed and Unsigned Integer Ranges

TYPE	RANGE
signed char	–128 to 127
unsigned char	0 to 255
short	–32,768 to 32,767
unsigned short	0 to 65,535
long	–2,147,483,648 to 2,147,483,647
unsigned long	0 to 4,294,967,295
int	Same as **short** or **long**, depending on the system
unsigned int	Same as **unsigned short** or **unsigned long**, depending on the system
unsigned	Same as **unsigned int**

Conversions and Unsigned Data

Although C++ lets you intermix signed and unsigned data freely, you should be careful about the effects of conversion and type casts when unsigned types are involved. Surprisingly, the following small program prints two different results:

```
#include <stdio.h>

void main() {
    int i1, i2;

    i1 = (signed char) -2;
    i2 = (unsigned char) -2;
    printf("The value of i1 is %d.\n", i1);
    printf("The value of i2 is %d.\n", i2);
}
```

The output of this program is:

```
The value of i1 is -2.
The value of i2 is 254.
```

In a nutshell, program produces this result because the same data is interpreted differently, depending on whether the type that holds it is signed or unsigned. In the case of a one-byte type (**char**), the bit pattern 1111 1110 represents either –2 (signed) or 254 (unsigned). Through a process known as sign extension, this bit pattern becomes 1111 1111 1111 1110 when –2 is assigned to an integer variable (i1). The bit pattern becomes 0000 0000 1111 1110 when 254 is assigned to an integer variable (i2).

Unsigned data is by far the easier of the two cases to understand. With an unsigned data type, the largest number possible is all ones: 1111 1111 when stored in one byte. This quantity is 255, and it is *zero-extended* when convert-

527

ed to a larger type. For example, 255 becomes 0000 0000 1111 1111 when stored in two bytes.

Signed types use *two's complement* arithmetic to represent negative numbers. Under this scheme, the leftmost bit determines the sign: a one in the leftmost position means that the number is negative. Consequently, the upper half of an unsigned range becomes negative in a corresponding signed range. (In other words, the values 128 to 255 in an **unsigned char** type become the negative range, –128 to –1, in a **signed char**.)

In the two's complement scheme, you represent a negative number as follows:

1. Perform bitwise negation on the corresponding positive number.

2. Add one.

For example, to get –1, you first take the bitwise negation of 1 (0000 0001) to produce 1111 1110. Adding one produces 1111 1111. So 1111 1111 represents –1.

Similarly, –2 can be produced by taking the bitwise negation of 2 (0000 0010) to produce 1111 1101. Then add one. So 1111 1110 represents –2.

What's tricky about signed numbers is that you can't simply tack on leading zeros as you can with unsigned numbers and expect to get the same quantity. For example, –1 is represented as all ones no matter what the width of an integer, so (strange as it seems) 1111 1111 and 1111 1111 1111 1111 represent the same number. Signed data is converted to larger sizes through sign extension, which works as follows:

1. Examine the leftmost bit.

2. If the leftmost bit is 0, add leading zeros to convert to the larger type.

3. If the leftmost bit is 1, add leading ones to convert to the larger type.

Figure U.2 shows how -2 and 254 are sign-extended and zero-extended.

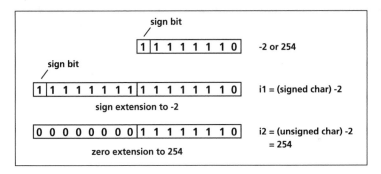

Figure U.2 Conversion of signed and unsigned data.

With typical processors, signed operations are performed at virtually the same speed as unsigned operations. In particular, most processors have built-in support for operations such as sign extension. The choice between signed and unsigned types, then, should rest entirely on what kind of data you need to store, because the processor can handle both types with equal efficiency.

Signed and unsigned types are often interchangeable, but the difference is significant in the following situations: in a printf or scanf format character (%u always prints an unsigned value); in assigning to a larger integer type, as done here; and in multiplication and division.

Definitions

One of C++'s unique features is that you can write functions taking any number of arguments—so that the function might be called with one argument during one function call and ten arguments in the next. To write these functions, you need to use a series of macro functions declared in STDARG.H.

Declaration Syntax

Functions with variable argument lists are declared and defined as others are, except that ellipses follow the last argument:

[type] function_name(arguments, ...)

Here the ellipses (...) are intended literally. The *arguments* are any number of standard C++ argument declarations, separately by commas if there are more than one.

Writing the Function Definition

To write a function that takes multiple arguments, first include the STDARG.H header file:

#include <stdarg.h>

You can then use the following definitions and macros to access the variable argument list. These are the arguments passed to the function after the last of the standard arguments.

Macro or Definition	Description
va_list *arg_ptr*;	Defines argument pointer (*arg_ptr*), which is used to read the variable argument list.
va_start(*arg_ptr*, *last_arg***)**;	Initializes argument pointer to start of the variable argument list; *last_arg* is the last argument in the standard argument list.
value = va_arg(*arg_ptr*, *type***)**;	Gets the current argument (which must have specified *type*) and advances to the next argument.
va_end(*arg_ptr***)**;	Terminates reading of the argument list.

Example

The following function prints out all the integers passed to it, and then prints the total. The first argument (which is a standard argument) specifies how many integers follow it.

```
#include <stdio.h>
#include <stdarg.h>

void print_ints(int num_of_args, ...)
{
    int total = 0, i;
    va_list  ap;

    va_start(ap, num_of_args);
    while(num_of_args--) {
        i = va_arg(ap, int);
        printf("%d\n", i);
        total += i;
```

```
    }
    printf("Total is %d.\n", total);
    va_end(ap);
}
```

If you call this function with the following statement

```
print_ints(3, 20, 35, 15);
```

you get this output:

```
20
35
15
Total is 70.
```

Definition

In almost every respect, a virtual base class is like any other base class, but under certain special circumstances, it can save space. Through multiple inheritance, it's possible to inherit the same ancestor class through more than one parent. (This is similar to what happens when two cousins marry.) A virtual base class contributes only one set of members, no matter how many times it is inherited.

As with virtual functions, the name *virtual* is a bit misleading. A virtual base class is no less real than any other base class. The "virtual" in virtual base classes refers to the fact that beneath the surface, an extra calculation is made to access a virtual base class member; the member's offset is not fixed. But none of this is visible to a C++ programmer, except for the use of the **virtual** keyword.

If you don't use multiple inheritance, virtual base classes have no effect on program behavior, so don't bother with them. There is a slight performance penalty for the use of virtual base classes.

Examples

Consider the case of a class, CChild, that inherits from classes A and B. A and B, in turn, both inherit from the class CPnt:

```
class CChild : public A, public B {
    // Declarations
};


class A : public CPnt {
    // Declarations
};


class B : public CPnt {
    // Declarations
};
```

The CPnt class has two members: x and y.

```
class CPnt {
public:
    double x, y;
};
```

Figure V.1 illustrates the inheritance tree for these four classes. The interesting question is, how many copies of x and y are present in an object of type CChild? As the figure indicates, a single CChild object has two sets of x, y pairs: one inherited through A and the other inherited through B.

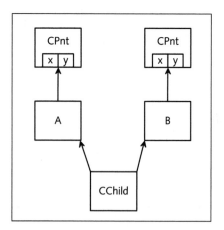

Figure V.1 Multiple inheritance without virtual base classes.

And in fact there two sets of pairs; you can differentiate them in code through the use of the scope operator. One set belongs to the A side of the family, and the other set belongs to the B side.

```
CChild kid;
kid.A::x = 100;
kid.B::x = 333;      // Does not access the same variable
cout << kid.A::x;    // Prints the value 100
```

In such a situation (rare though it may be), you might consider it desirable to inherit only one copy of CPnt members,
thus saving space. To do so, qualify derivation from CPnt
with the **virtual** keyword:

```
class A : virtual public CPnt {
    // Declarations
};

class B : virtual public CPnt {
    // Declarations
};
```

Now, the grandchild class, CChild, inherits from CPnt only
once. The inheritance tree converges at the top, as shown in
Figure V.2.

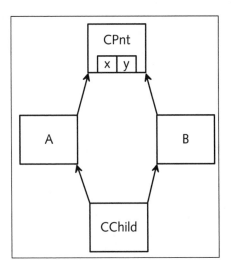

Figure V.2 Multiple inheritance with virtual base classes.

535

Virtual Functions

Definition

Virtual is one of the more interesting words in computer science. It refers to something that is not altogether real but behaves as well as (and in some cases better than) the real thing. The term *virtual functions* is in some ways misleading. A call to a virtual function is in every respect a real function call. The only thing unusual about virtual functions is that the same function call may result in jumping to different blocks of code at different times.

 For a general introduction to virtual functions, as well as syntax and examples, see Chapter 9, "Virtual Functions and Why They're Good." This section discusses some fine points of the subject.

Technically speaking, a virtual function is a member function in which the address of the function is not fixed until run time. (This technique is also known as *late binding*.) Unlike other functions, a virtual function call is always guaranteed to bind to an object's implementation of that function, even if the object is accessed through a base-class pointer. In C++, virtual functions have a strong connection to inheritance. All derived classes can override the definition of a function in a base class (unless it is private, of course), but only virtual functions can be safely overridden in all cases.

The problem with overriding a non–virtual function is that you create multiple implementations of the same function. This is not a problem if an object's type can be fully determined at compile time. But what if you are referring to an object through a pointer? For example, in the following code, assume that the CTriangle, CSquare, and CPenta classes are all derived from CShape and that each overrides the Print member function.

```
CShape *arr[3]; // array of three ptrs to CShape

arr[0] = new CTriangle;
arr[1] = new CSquare;
arr[2] = new CPenta;

for (int i = 0; i < 3; i++)
    arr[i]->Print();
```

If the Print function is virtual, then each call to Print calls the appropriate version of Print for the particular object: for example, CTriangle::Print is called for the triangle object. Otherwise, each call to Print calls the same function, CShape::Print.

Another case in which virtual functions can matter is when one member function calls another. In the following example, assume that the Init function is inherited without change by each derived class but that each class provides its own version of Print:

```
void CShape::Init(double x, double y) {
    ...
    Print(); // Call Print for appropriate class...
             // This always calls CShape::Print if
             //  function is NOT virtual.
}
```

Clearly, virtual functions provide extra flexibility needed in some situations. But do these situations happen very often?

In sophisticated programming environments such as Microsoft Windows, such situations happen all the time. For example, the message-handling code for a window must be implemented with virtual functions. There is no way for the Window Manager to know about all the possible responses an application might have to a message, so the decision of what function code to execute must be handed to the application. This delegating of responsiblity to an application or object is what virtual functions are all about.

The same functionality can be provided in C, incidentally, by using callback functions. What distinguishes virtual functions from callbacks is that the former are a much more structured approach, with better support from the language. Callback functions have to be declared with function-pointer syntax. Virtual functions hide the pointer syntax completely and require only the introduction of a single keyword, **virtual**.

In any case, it's useful to understand the trade-offs involved: virtual functions impose a slight performance penalty, so it's inefficient to make *all* your member functions virtual. But if there is a reasonable chance that a function will be overridden by a derived class, it is good policy to make the function virtual. For the slight loss in performance, virtual functions provide greater flexibility. The practical benefit for programs is that program control can be more decentralized. Fewer decisions about what code to call need be placed in the main loop or program.

The decision of what code to execute is deferred by making a virtual function call, much as if you sent a general message such as "Print yourself." An object responds in the appropriate way for its specific class, regardless of how you gained access to that object. In a way, it's almost as though the knowledge of how to respond is built into the object. This flexibility, in turn, helps realize the general goal of object orientation... to create a set of autonomous units that communicate by sending each other messages.

Definition

What all the uses of **void** have in common is that they suggest the condition of emptiness or nothingness. C and C++
are possibly the only languages to have *nothing* as a type.
Yet **void** is a practical keyword, and ultimately it's no
stranger than the number zero is in arithmetic.

Usage

The best way to understand **void** is to understand the three
contexts in which it is used:

- In function prototypes and definitions, **void** can
  appear by itself in the argument list to indicate that
  the function takes no arguments. This is helpful
  information and less ambiguous than simply leaving
  the argument list blank. In a prototype, a blank
  argument list would mean that there might be arguments but they aren't specified yet:

```
int update_global_vars(void);
```

- In function prototypes and definitions, a **void** return
  type indicates that the function does not return a
  value. This makes the function like a procedure or
  subroutine in another language. Again, **void** is useful, because if the return type were omitted it would
  be assumed to have **int** (and not **void**) return type.

```
void print_results(int count, double area, x, y);
```

- In pointer declarations and type casts, **void*** is the
  generic pointer type. A pointer of type **void*** can
  hold an address but cannot be dereferenced until it
  is first cast to another type. The reason **void*** is use-

ful is that certain functions (such as malloc) accept or return an address without a specific type. Having a **void*** type indicates a generic address, whose use will vary depending on the function's caller.

```
void *pv;    /* generic pointer */
```

If you want to be fanciful, you can think of **void** as being the most existential or Zen-like of C++ keywords. But don't let void intimidate you. It's there to serve useful, miscellaneous purposes. The designers of C++ reused the same word, **void**, for each of these situations rather than let additional keywords proliferate. This is in keeping with the philosophy of C++: its compact and concise quality, from which stems much of its elegance.

Definition

In a beginning-to-intermediate program, you'll probably never use **volatile**. Its use is confined mainly to systems programming and to programs that interact with the hardware.

The word *volatile* suggests something unstable and uncontrollable. In computer terms, a volatile object is one that can be changed without warning by an outside agent: the system clock, for example, or a memory-mapped video buffer, or a semaphore used for inter-process communication. Such objects, if not handled in a special way by the program, are likely to cause errors.

Example

The compiler normally assumes that data never changes except as a result of a statement in your own program. The compiler can therefore place a value in a register and leave it there, not having to go out and access memory. For example, consider the following statements:

```
x = object;
y = object;
z = object;
f(object);
```

Under normal circumstances, the compiler can produce optimal code by placing object in a register, generating assembly-language code like this:

```
MOV   reg, object
MOV   x, reg
MOV   y, reg
MOV   z, reg
PUSH  reg
CALL  f
```

The problem is that if object is volatile, its value may have changed between the first instruction and the last. In that case, each time object is referred to, the program should go out to memory and retrieve its value again:

```
MOV  reg, object
MOV  x, reg
MOV  reg, object
MOV  y, reg
MOV  reg, object
MOV  z, reg
MOV  reg, object
PUSH reg
CALL f
```

This less optimal code is necessary for something that interacts with the rest of the system (for example, a semaphore used to communicate with other processes). By declaring an object **volatile**, you tell the compiler it has to handle the object with added care. It can't assume that the value of the object hasn't changed between instructions.

The following example declaration declares two **volatile** data items—x and y—and one volatile pointer, *p_sys_object. The pointer itself doesn't require special handling, but each access of data through the pointer (using *p_sys_object in an executable statement) requires a new memory access.

```
volatile int  x, y, *p_sys_object;
```

Syntax

The syntax of the **volatile** keyword mirrors in every respect that of the const keyword, so see the "const Keyword" topic for details. For example, you can't assign the address of **volatile** object to a pointer unless that pointer also has a **volatile** base type (echoing the rules for **const**).

Paradoxically, a variable may be both **const** and **volatile**:

```
extern const volatile int  *p_to_sys_clock;
```

This declaration states that an outside agency (the hardware in this case) may alter what this pointer points to without warning but that the program code must not change this value. The hardware can change the value, but the program can't.

As a consequence of syntax rules, such a pointer value cannot be assigned to another pointer unless that pointer is also declared **const volatile**.

Definition

A **while** loop is the fundamental loop structure in C++; you can write any other control structure by using a **while** loop (although in some cases the result would be cumbersome). Simply stated, a **while** loop executes a statement or statements as long as a specified condition is true.

Syntax

A **while** statement forms one unified statement in C++:

while (*expression*);
   loop_body_statement

The *loop_body_statement* is frequently a compound statement (see "Example"). Because the entire **while** loop forms one statement, it can be nested inside other control structures. The loop repeats execution as long as *expression* evaluates to a nonzero (true) value.

Example

The following statements output characters from a string until the end of the string is reached. The end of a string is indicated with a null (zero) value so that the test expression, *p, is equal to zero when the end of the string is reached. The **while** statement considers zero a false condition and so stops.

```
#include <stdio.h>
...
p = string;
while (*p) {
    putchar(*p);
    p++;
}
```

The **while** statement is not terminated with a semicolon in this case because it ends with a compound statement. This code is a good candidate for a **for** loop; it also could have been written more concisely as:

```
#include <stdio.h>
...
p = string;
while (*p)
    putchar(*p++);
```

Index

Index